Sticks and Stones, Feathers, Charms and Bones

An Original Oracle of the Elfin Peoples of the Ancient Future

By The Silver Elves

Dedication

We dedicate this book to our dear mothers who taught us the spell "Stickes and stones will break our bones but words will never hurt them."

The young magician asked the old elf,
"What do I do if I drop my wand
in the middle of a ritual?"
The wise old elf replied,
"You pick it up and go on with the ritual.
Or you leave it lying there and go on with the ritual.
Either way, you complete the ritual."

"Nearly all elves are diviners,
but the oracles we read most often
are the sigils of karma, fate and destiny
writ plain in the lines on people's faces."

Table of Contents

... Note: You may wish to use this Table of Contents as a quick reference to find the page corresponding to your oracle outcome. See Introduction for instructions.

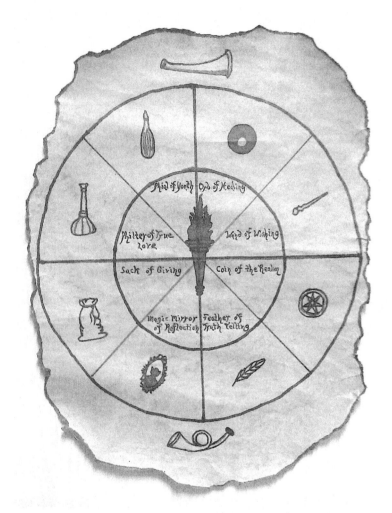

This is the original oracle board for the system of divination that uses the ten Sacred Magical Treasures of The Silver Elves: beginning with The Orb of Healing (top right wedge going clockwise by eights), The Wand of Wishing, The Coin of the Realm, The Feather of Truth Telling, The Magic Mirror of Reflection, The Sack of Giving, The Philtre of True Love, and The Phial of Eternal Youth, with The Elf Horns of Calling outside the Outer Circle and The Torch in the center of the Inner Circle.

Introduction

There are two potential systems of divination that use the ten Sacred Magical Treasures of The Silver Elves as a base. One of these is the system we have created and introduced in this book, *Sticks and Stones, Feathers, Charms and Bones*, using the original oracle board seen on the cover (and also there is a black and white version on page 12), with an Inner and Outer Circle, each circle containing the Sacred Magical Treasures of The Silver Elves. There are ten of these treasures in all: The Orb of Healing, The Wand of Wishing, The Coin of the Realm, The Feather of Truth Telling, The Magic Mirror of Reflection, The Sack of Giving, The Philtre of True Love, The Phial of Eternal Youth, The Elf Horns of Calling and the The Torch of the Eternal Silver Flame. In this system, to cast the oracle, one may simply throw the Sticks, Stones, Feathers, Charms and Bones upon the board and read the outcome according to the position in which they land. The oracle interpretations for this method are found within this book.

There is a second way to use this oracle, which is to have the Sacred Magical Treasures of the Silver Elves as icons instead of Sticks, Stones, Feathers, Charms and Bones and lay them upon the same board as used in the first method. This second method we hope to illuminate in a future book.

THE SACRED MAGICAL TREASURES OF THE SILVER ELVES

Both forms of using this oracle involve the ten Sacred Magical Treasures of the Silver Elves. In the form we are introducing in this book, they are the places on the 'board' where the sticks, stones, charms, etc. may fall when thrown and then be consulted for interpretation as to the meaning of the oracle.

The Sacred Magical Treasures are as follows:

THE ORB OF HEALING

The Orb of Healing has the power to heal anyone of anything: disease: mental, emotional, physical; accident or birth defects.

THE WAND OF WISHING

The Wand of Wishing gives one the power to fulfill and grant wishes.

THE COIN OF THE REALM

The Coin brings success and prosperity.

THE FEATHER OF TRUTH TELLING

One cannot help but tell the truth when holding this feather and pointing it at someone compels them to tell the truth.

THE MAGIC MIRROR OF REFLECTION

This mirror shows one as one is and as one can be and merges the two so the path between them becomes evident.

THE SACK OF GIVING

This is Santa's sack. It represents gifting, regifting, and generosity.

THE PHILTRE OF TRUE LOVE

One who drinks from this Philtre will find true love.

THE PHIAL OF ETERNAL YOUTH

The waters of the Phial grant Youth Eternal.

THE ELF HORNS OF CALLING

These horns call the elfin together and if an elf or fae hears this call sHe longs to find hir kindred. These horns have powerful effects particularly upon the outer circle, and lay just outside of it.

THE TORCH OF THE ETERNAL SILVER FLAME

This is the torch of the Eternal Silver Flame that burns ever in Elfin. Even if Elfin seems to be totally gone from the world, to have never existed, this torch still burns and awakens the fire of spirit in all those of an elfin nature. This torch burns in the inner realms of Elfin.

MAKING THE BOARD

We selected to make our board out of a heavy brown paper, primarily because that is what we had on hand and also because we thought it would be useful to be able to roll up the board like a scroll, tie a ribbon around it, and be able to carry it with us easily out in Nature to do the oracles. Of course, you may elect to draw your board on paper as we have done or paint it on a more permanent wooden board or table top. And if you would like to draw a board on pavement or directly on a concrete floor, of course you may use colored chalk. We leave this up to your creativity.

To make the board (make a replication of the board on the cover of this book), first draw the inner and outer circles. Then divide the circles in four equal parts, then into eight equal parts all together (like a pie). Next write within the Inner Circle in the sectioned parts the names of the first eight Sacred Magical Treasures of The Silver Elves, that is: The Orb of Healing, The Wand of Wishing, The Coin of the Realm, The Feather of Truth Telling, The Magic Mirror of Reflection, The Sack of Giving, The Philtre of True Love, and The Phial of Eternal Youth. Then you need to draw symbols of these eight magical treasures in the Outer Circle in the corresponding sectioned parts. Hopefully your drawing will be more beautiful than ours, but remember that the Shining Ones who guide this oracle will understand and be supportive of all creative efforts no matter how humble. Then draw The Elf Horns of Calling outside the Outer Circle (top and bottom) and the The Torch of the Eternal Silver Flame in the very center of the Inner Circle.

GATHERING AND USING THE TOKENS FOR THE ORACLE

Essentially, for this oracle you will need ten tokens in all to represent sticks (two: big stick and short stick), stones (two: large stone and small stone), feathers (two: light feather and dark feather), charms (two: personal charm and otherworldly charm) and bones (two: long bone and short bone).

In gathering the tokens, you need to consider how you will be using them for the oracle. There are two ways you may use them. The first way is the way we generally do this oracle. You can take all the tokens and toss them together on the board for a general reading or for a particular question and see how they fall. (You also may throw only one or two tokens at a time for a specific question, but we advise using all of them for a thorough reading.) You will be noting which circle they fall in, Inner Circle or Outer Circle (or outside the

Outer Circle), and also within which of the ten Sacred Magical Treasures of the Silver Elves they fall, and then read the interpretations in this book accordingly. We will be explaining more on this as you read along further.

But you may also try the second way to use the tokens if you wish, and just reach into a bag and choose just one or a few tokens with symbols representing sticks, stones, charms, etc. upon them. If you do it this way, it helps if they are all the same size so you can't tell whether you are pulling out the Dark Feather or the Long Bone, and so forth. In this case, we find it easier to get some small tiles that are often used in bathrooms and kitchens, and we paint the symbols upon them. You could also find a fallen branch and cut it crosswise to create little tokens. Really, whatever idea you think of that would work would be great.

You may wish to experiment. That's what we do. However, you probably don't wish the tokens to be too big and if you are using actual objects, real feathers, sticks, charms, bones and stones rather than tokens, you need to consider whether they will break if you throw them together. This is particularly true of the stones.

When we were gathering the tokens for this oracle, we just looked around our elven home and found what was available. But then our elf home is filled with miscellaneous magics that we have collected over the years or that have been given to us. If we hadn't found it in our home, we would have gone for walks and found what we needed out in the world. Sticks and stones and feathers are easily available, even in Waikiki where we live.

We also came across some 'Elf coins,' available on the internet from a company called *Norse Foundry*. They come as two sets of five coins, that is, two each of the different sizes and shapes. We marked one set to distinguish it from the other (with a red dot in our case), and assigned different tokens to each coin. One represents the Big Stick, another the Short Bone and so on. But this same company also has 'Norse coins' available, so you could potentially use them in combination with the Elf coins. Be creative and do what works for you. Or you could just use a bunch of pennies or quarters or whatever you have and paint symbols upon them. You're a clever elf so we're sure you will figure something out that works for you.

INTERPRETING THE ORACLE

When consulting the oracle, you will be reading the interpretations in this book according to where your sticks, stones, feathers, charms and bones land upon the board. First you will note the landing position of each token. Did it land on the Inner or Outer Circle? Or did it land on the center of the Inner Circle on The Torch or outside the Outer Circle on the Horns of Calling? And then if it landed in one of the circles, note what is the corresponding Sacred Magical Treasure that it landed upon? With this information, you may then turn to the chapter on each token and read the interpretations according to their landing positions.

The book is divided into five parts relating to the five types of tokens — Sticks, Stones, Feathers, Charms and Bones, with two chapters in each part for each token, one for the large and one for the small size. So for instance, Part One . . . Sticks contains two chapters, one for the Big Stick and another for the Short Stick; Part Two . . . Stones contains two chapters, one for the Large Stone and another for the Small Stone; etc. So there are ten chapters in all containing interpretations for the ten tokens. Also each chapter is divided into two parts and contains the interpretations of the meaning for both the Inner Circle and Outer Circle and the

Sacred Magical Treasures of The Silver Elves within each as they specifically relate to that token and position. There are eight magical treasures within the Outer Circle and nine within the Inner Circle (that is, eight plus the Torch in the Center).

Now for consulting the oracle, the first paragraph in the Inner Circle section of each chapter will give you an oracle interpretation for your token if it falls in the center of the Inner Circle on the inner Torch of the Eternal Silver Flame of Elfin. And the first descriptive paragraph in the Outer Circle section of each chapter will give you an oracle interpretation if your token lands outside (top or bottom) of the Outer Circle in the Elf Horns of Calling. So when doing the oracle, read the interpretation for whichever your token lands upon. Read the first paragraph of the Outer Circle if it lands outside the Outer Circle and the first paragraph of the Inner Circle if it lands in the center on the Torch. And if it lands within the Inner Circle or Outer Circle and on a Sacred Magical Treasure other than The Torch, then only read that particular magical treasure corresponding to that circle and token. We explain this again in Chapter One using The Big Stick as an example. You may wish to use the Table of Contents as a quick reference for finding the page numbers of the oracle outcome.

No oracle can tell you exactly what is happening or going to happen. The ancient oracles of Delphi and other places were usually rather vague and ambiguous in their pronouncements. It is our assumption that nearly everyone who gets a book like this either is already a diviner or wishes to be one and thus has a certain talent for interpretation already. The responses you get in this book are meant to help you consider how to think about a situation and to prompt your own intuition in interpreting it, which, in our experience, occurs anyway even among those who are not diviners. They will simply take whatever we tell them and hear what they wish to hear, in that way interpreting the oracle for their own s'elves. And that is the way it is meant to be. So let the answers you get stir your mind, your instincts and your intuition and see what occurs to you. This is ultimately about tapping into your own prophetic ability.

WHAT DOES IT MEAN IF THE TOKEN FALLS IN THE VERY CENTER?

If it happens that your stick, stone, charm or some other token falls in the very center of the board, without favoring any one direction, then you are a very lucky person and the response says that Elfin and the magic of the elves, in particular the magic of the Shining Ones, will send you a vision, dream or sign that will guide you on your way and help you achieve what you desire.

Of course, when you are actually using sticks and feathers and bones, they tend to be directional and even if they fall precisely to the center you may wish to look at where the stick is pointing and where it is coming from and read that influence as well.

DO I THROW ALL THE OBJECTS?

It may be that your question is very specific. Like, what is my power in this situation? In which case, you may wish to only use the Personal Charm. Or you may ask, in what fashion will the spirits help me and then the Otherworldly Charm might be best. Or if you want to know what is behind the situation, what karma or fate has brought you to this circumstance, then the Small Stone might be the wisest choice.

However, for a balanced reading it is perhaps best to throw all the magical objects, either together or one at a time to see the various aspects of the situation and get a full view of what is going on. But that is up to you.

ASKING QUESTIONS

You don't have to ask a question of the oracle; you can just get a general reading. However, if you do make an inquiry, try to be as specific as possible. This is to your benefit. You, after all, will be the one who ultimately has to interpret the oracle's response in terms of your own life. The more general your question is, the more likely it is to put you in a quandary. Be as clear as you can. This will help to decrease confusion. Of course, if you ask a general question and you are unsure of what the oracle means, debating whether it means this or that, you can always ask another, more specific question or ask a question for each direction or possibility and weigh the different answers.

If it so happens that you get more or less the same response in each case, then it may not matter which you choose to do, although you are still left with choosing and it may be most effective if you use your instincts to do so.

"The Elves say:
Life is a puzzle in which we only have some of the
pieces. To see the whole picture, we must find
our kindred and unite our pieces with theirs.
Thus do we create a vision of Elfin."

Part One

. . . Sticks

Unless your sticks are very small or you use tokens instead of sticks, when thrown onto the board they will likely extend over more than one area. It is helpful in this case to establish in your mind which end is the pointing end of the stick, most likely the narrow point of the stick, and which is the wider, fatter end or the handle of the stick. When reading the oracle, you might consider that the wider end of the stick indicates the background of the question and the pointing end of the stick is where things are likely heading, or the direction you are going in.

Chapter 1:
The Big Stick

The Big Stick denotes one's motives in the situation you are in and asking about in your oracle. So one uses the Big Stick to ask questions about what one wishes to achieve and about ones drives, motivations, desires and inner spiritual path.

When thrown on the oracle board (see cover of book), The Big Stick may land on either the Inner or Outer Circle and in one of the Sacred Magical Treasures of The Silver Elves contained therein. This chapter (as are all the chapters in this book) is therefore divided into two parts and contains the interpretations of the meaning for both of these positions, the Inner and Outer Circles, and the magical treasures within each as they specifically relate to that position. So for instance, if your threw the tokens and The Big Stick landed in the Outer Circle and in The Orb of Healing area, then you would go to the section in this chapter called The Outer Circle: The Elf Horns of Calling and find the sub-section titled The Orb of Healing and that is what you would read as your oracle interpretation. If The Big Stick had instead landed in the Inner Circle, but also in The Orb of Healing area, then you would go to the section in this chapter called The Inner Circle: Torch of the Eternal Silver Flame of Elfin and read the sub-section there titled The Orb of Healing.

Furthermore, the first paragraph in The Inner Circle: Torch of the Eternal Silver Flame of Elfin will give you an interpretation for your token if it falls in the center of the Inner Circle on the Torch. And the first paragraph in the The Outer Circle: The Elf Horns of Calling will give you an interpretation if your token lands outside the Outer Circle on the Elf Horns of Calling. So when doing the oracle, read only the section for whichever your Big Stick lands upon.

The Inner Circle:
The Torch of the Eternal
Silver Flame of Elfin

If the Big Stick falls upon or significantly touches the inner Torch, it indicates that there are deeper, greater spiritual powers at work here than you realize. Double check your motivations and be sure there isn't any doubt or unclarity about what you are doing and why you are doing it. Choose what is right and fair for everyone and you can't go wrong.

And instead if the Big Stick lands on any of the other Sacred Magical Treasures within the Inner Circle besides the Torch, then you read the corresponding treasure below:

THE ORB OF HEALING

The Orb of Healing brings healing to a situation or points to the need for healing but even then, it radiates healing into what is going on. Being the inner realm, it indicates this healing is coming directly from the spirit realms, the realms of Elfin and Faerie. When the Big Stick lands here one is called to make healing one's primary motivation in this situation. Do whatever you can to make things better for everyone involved. This will bring you success and luck not only in the material world, but more importantly in the world of spirit and magic, which are the true and lasting dimensions.

In reference to questions about love, romance, relationship and friendship, this energy promotes healing in the situation, healing for yours'elf but also an improvement for everyone. If you strive to be the best you can be as a person, this will bring you great luck. Be your highest s'elf in dealing with others here. Examine your motives and make them as pure and as enlightened as you possibly can. Others will be affected by your example and this will bring blessings for everyone.

Inquiries about business, job, money and so on as also favored by an improving influence. This is a time of blessings, but it will not endure, so make the most of this favorable cycle while it lasts. As the old saying goes, make hay while the sun shines. If you are intent on success, then put all your energy into it at this juncture and that will yield great rewards in time.

Obviously, an inquiry about health and healing gets a very positive response when the magical object falls here. The Big Stick does indicate a need to put lots of energy into the situation. To be thoroughly dedicated to healing. Do you really wish to heal? Does the person you are attempting to help sincerely desire healing? Or is there something they are getting out of the situation, pity, compassion, sympathy, attention or something else that makes the illness worthwhile to them? Examine yours'elf and the situation carefully.

As to questions about your spiritual life and path, your life in the magical realms, this is also a very positive response, although one that indicates that healing is coming to you and that you need to get yours'elf into situations, circumstances, environments, and with people who will foster your spiritual and magical growth, even if these relationships are only on the internet. Hang out with those who can help you improve and for your own part help others do the same and this will prove rewarding.

THE COIN OF THE REALM

When the Big Stick falls in the inner world of the Coin of the Realm, one is blest in terms of money and financial success. Clarify your goals for yours'elf and others if necessary. Know what it is you really want, and ask yours'elf, having achieved this, what shall I do next? Where do I go from here? Each movement is a step toward success. Since this is in the inner world, the results will be more magical than necessarily strictly monetary. The Coin of the Realm in this case may be the power to get what you want, or a sign indicating the way. The spirits are with you and aiding you from their plane of being. Continue on.

If you were asking about love, relationship, romance and friendship and got this for your answer, then you have or will get everything you need, particularly of an energetic nature, to fulfill your wishes and desires. Clearly, this is a good sign, and surely an indication that something will come to you as a gift from the spirit world or as a gift from another person, that will aid you in your progress toward your relationship goals. The mere fact that you are getting gifts, whatever they may be, is a good sign, so receive them with an open heart. It may only be a compliment, but embrace it.

As we said, questions about money, business, jobs and so forth, are highly favored here. The Coin of the Realm is a good response to money questions, no matter the magical symbol that falls here. Being that it is the Big Stick, one may consider sharing one's luck. It is said by the elves that if one doesn't share one's good fortune, one will lose it. Ask yours'elf how you can spread the good luck around and thus sustain it.

If it is health and healing you are inquiring about, then this response asks you to consider how your attitudes toward finances and your relationship with money and financial success is affecting your health or the health of others. Are you so driven that you don't even take a break to revive yours'elf? Are you caught in a situation where you have no choice but work all hours of the day and night trying to support yours'elf or your family? If so, this place offers some relief. There is some financial magic coming your way and this should help you to heal.

As to spiritual questions, questions relative to your path, your magic, the development of your elfin s'elf, your true s'elf, then again you are blest. This oracle provides you with the energy you need to evolve even further. If you are asking, which way should I go, or what is the right direction to go in, or should I do this or that, or get involved with this one or the other, a sign will be provided. Trust your instincts but also, keep an open mind, the spirits will show you the way and the way, in this case, will offer you some sort of real benefit. Look for the door to opportunity to open and move forward as soon as it does.

THE WAND OF WISHING

In the inner circle of the Wand of Wishing, receiving the Big Stick asks one to meditate upon one's true wishes. What do you want as a soulful spirit? And how will getting what you desire in the situation you have inquired about lead to you developing as a spirit? How does this fit into your Destiny to be a Shining One, a radiant example of Elfin and elven magic? Or if you are faerie, becoming a radiant example of faerie magic, and so on. Who will you be when you have perfected yours'elf? And how does this situation get you there, closer to being who you truly desire to be?

Relative to questions about love, romance, relationship and friendship, this response indicates that the possibilities of success are very strong and even likely. However, again, the question for you is, does this relationship further you on your spiritual path? Does it promote what is best in you? Does it challenge you to be your best? And if not, how do you find those that will do so? It is one thing to get what you want, quite another to get what is really good for you.

Regarding inquiries about business and finances, this reply

gives you magic for getting what you want or achieving what you wish to achieve. But what is your spiritual responsibility in this situation? What will you do with the money and influence that comes to you? Will you share it? Will you help others? How can you make it work for you in the realms of magic? What magic can you do to promote continued prosperity? And why do you want or need this in the first place? Does it increase your power as a spirit? As a magician/enchanter? Or does it keep you chained to the material world and its illusionary concerns?

Health and healing are especially favored here. Everyone, deep with thems'elves, wishes to heal for to heal means to survive. It is part of our quest for immortality. Those who don't wish to survive are under a dark spell of suffering that makes them wish they were dead so they can end it all and return to the oblivion of the Nether-Nether. But, unless one is a Shining One, karma will just bring one back again, so let's get on with it, shall we? Heal, be healing, let this be your true and manifest motivation.

As to one's spiritual life and path, this answer says that one is doing well. What you wish is coming true and you simply need to continue on the path, do continual practices of purification, which is to say meditate upon and contemplate your motives on a daily or regular basis. You don't have to go insane and be anal retentive about this but keeping an eye on one's motives is a good thing. The progress into Elfin is step by dance step and we ascend a foot at a time. Continue on and the magic will guide you, aid you and reward you.

THE FEATHER OF TRUTH TELLING

Getting the Big Stick in the inner realm of the Feather of Truth Telling urges one to consider what one wants in terms of one's immortal s'elf and being. What are your spiritual goals? What are the long term goals of your spirit? Who are you becoming? Who do you wish to be? And are you doing those things that will make that possible?

When the question has to do with relationship, love, romance and friendship, there is an indication that the truth, particularly those deeper truths that have been hidden are about to come out. Is there something you need to disclose? It might be better to do so than to wait until others find out some other way or from someone else. Or it could be that you will discover what they are really like, what they really want as individuals. Is this compatible with your own spiritual progress? If not, move on and do so happily. And don't worry, you will find the person or persons that are right for you but not until you've gotten rid of or departed from those who are not beneficial to your evolution.

As to inquiries about business, money, jobs and so on, this response directs one to look at one's long term goals and also, more importantly, ask if this job or business is in tune with your long term goals? Is it a moral situation for you? Are you compromising yours'elf by being involved with this business? The truth of the matter will become clear very soon and you will need to make a decision about your spiritual future.

On inquiries about health and healing, this reply directs you to consider the truth of the situation. What spiritual or karmic force, or what inner or unconscious motive is fueling this illness or disorder? Here, there is a need for a bit of sorcery. You need to get to the root of what is going on in order to heal. It is not just a matter of treating the symptoms but of eliminating the causes of the dis-ease.

As to questions about your spiritual life and path, this response is all about the Truth and the Truth will lead you where you need to go. Even if it makes you uncomfortable at first, even if you seem at a disadvantage compared to others in the short term, you will profit and benefit from the revelations that will come. This is all to the good for you. It may not seem like a stroke of good luck but it is.

THE MAGIC MIRROR OF REFLECTION

Getting the Big Stick in the inner dimension of the Magic Mirror of Reflection calls one to reflect upon the situation as it is and contemplate its potential. Ask yours'elf, are you really motivated to get what you desire in this situation? Is it even worth the effort? Does it bring you closer to the fulfillment of your true and perfected being? And where are you now, how did you get here and how do you get where you wish to go? Sometimes it is said that you can't get there from here, but you can always get there from here, it just may not be directly, instantly and it may require you to do a bit of shifting and transformation. You can always get there, but do you know the way?

Questions that are about love, romance, relationship and friendship require one to consider one's ideals, one's dreams, and one's illusions. How much of this situation is affected by your desire to see it and have it turn out a particular way? That is not entirely a bad thing. Our imagination and our wishes, and therefore our positive attitude and thinking, can definitely be a bonus to moving a situation toward what we desire, but it is a determent when it comes to actually examining the relationship and seeing it for what it truly is at the moment. Still, it is not easy to give up one's illusions and it is even harder to use them in an effective fashion to obtain what we wish.

Inquiries about business, finances, job success and so forth also suggest that one examine one's situation truthfully and accurately. This may make some folks depressed, but it need not, we are only looking at what is, in a forthright and honest fashion, without bias or lying to ours'elves. Then, you can look at what can be, for getting the Big Stick in this inner realm means that you have the magical power to alter this situation and move things toward your desired outcome. Look at what is, honestly, then do the magic to move it toward what you feel it should be.

If health and healing are your concern, then a clear examination of your life habits, or the habits of those you wish to help heal, are in order. Doing magic, doing Reiki, doing hypnosis, or Mesmerism, doing this or that energetic healing is one thing; living one's life in such a manner as to promote and keep good health is something else. We can't go back to the way things were if we wish them to remain in the new healthier modality. Preserving one's health, maintaining one's health, and thus using preventive medicine through a good life style is key here. Can you heal? Yes. Will you stay healthy? That is the question.

As to your spiritual life, your life of magic, this response asks you to examine why you are involved with Elfin, Faerie or some other spiritual realm. Is it because you wish to escape from the world? Perfectly understandable, most of us do. Is it because you love the magical realms of spirit? Because you wish to be a better, perhaps more powerful spirit? What it is that drives you to explore the world of the spiritual? Not guilt, we hope, as some religious types are motivated out of a fear of going to hell, but what positive motivation draws you to these realms? And how close do you think they are? How close do you think you are to them? Whatever your response, this oracle urges you to persevere on the path.

33

THE SACK OF GIVING

The inner circle of the Sack of Giving refers to the generosity of the Shining Ones and the higher elven spirits who seek to help and uplift us. When one gets the Big Stick in this position, one is called to consider one's relationship to the spirits, what one may have done to deserve this blessing and gift on their part, and most importantly what one is motivated to do with this increased energy and power. How will you use the magic you've been given? And why are you using it that way? Will this further you and others? Will this keep the cycle of prosperity going and flourishing?

When asking about love, romance, relationship, marriage and friendship, this response is like Christmas/Yule season. Time to give presents, but also one is likely to receive energy and appreciation from others. Most significantly it is important to nurture the good, the spiritual and the positive in everyone one encounters. What do you wish for these others? What do you want from them, but also what do you want for them? As always with the Sack of Giving, tokens of appreciation are in order but it is the feeling, the genuine

caring that is the true energy one is gifting. That is a real gift of magic.

As to inquiries about business, jobs and money issues, the Sack of Giving ever urges one to give, but especially in the inner realm to give value. Back up your product with guarantees. If your product is service, serve well, happily and truly. If your only interest is in making money as quickly as possible without giving quality in return, you have gone astray. When you make your motive quality, everything will turn out as it should and to your and everyone else's benefit.

If you are inquiring about health and healing, then a blessing of healing is coming to you from the Shining Ones and the realms of Elfin. Use this gift of healing as best you may. Heal yours'elf, heal your others, spread healing in the world. Let this be your motive in the world, to make it a better place and it will become ever better for you in the realms of spirit and magic, at least, even if it is not so in the material world around you, although that possibility is not excluded.

This is a gift from the spirit world, thus whatever question you may have asked about your path, you should know that the answer is coming shortly. Look around you, it may already be here. It will probably arrive with some token, so listen careful to the next person to gives you something, or to the person who just gave you something. Your response is contained in their words or in the gift its'elf, although it may be in some symbolic form and you might need to interpret it, to puzzle it out, just as you would a dream.

THE PHILTRE OF TRUE LOVE

When you get the Big Stick in the inner circle of the Philtre of True Love, you may wish to ask yours'elf, what is true love? How do you know it when it comes? How do you recognize when you have it? And while this place is very favorable for relationships in general, you may wish to ask yours'elf, how do you get it? How do you bring about true love? What in you will attract those who are right for you? Are you as you need to be in order for your true love(s) to come?

If your question concerns love, romance, relationship, partnership and friendship then this, of course, is a good sign. The Philtre of True Love uplifts every situation concerning love and romance. It always works to make things better between people. It is soulful in nature and ever seeks to reach out and connect to others in a positive way. However, you still may wish to examine yours'elf and be sure that you are ready for true love. That there isn't something going on within you that is going to obstruct the relationship, move you to pick the wrong person, or otherwise destroy the good that this placement does. Are you ready for true love? Can you make it last? It may come but you have to do the work to keep it.

Questions about business, jobs, finances and career when falling in this place indicate that one must be careful of one's motives in these areas, but particularly careful concerning other people's motives. This is not a good position for financial dealings, per se, however it is a very good place for making connections that can lead to financial success, a better job, a promotion, etc. It is good for harmonious work relations and for improving relations in the work place. The door to opportunity may not be opening for you at the moment, however, you could very well make a connection to someone who will open it for you in the future.

If your inquiry had to do with health and healing, then this is surely a good sign but especially for healing that comes from one's interaction and relationship with Nature and with the spirit world. If you are on good terms in the realms of magic, if you are in harmony with Nature, then you will surely heal or have the power to help others do so. Are you in harmony with your environment? Not necessarily the world around you, but the etheric realms of spirit and magic? Attune yours'elf to Elfin and Faerie and healing will come your way.

And if you are asking about your spiritual and magical life, then know that you are loved by the Shining Ones, that all that you need will come to you. You may feel alone in the world, but you are not. The elfin spirits are with you and they will help you on your path. You may feel that you are at a disadvantage in the world compared to others who may seem to have it easier or be more successful, but you are on the path, are they? The love the spirits have for you is true love and they will help guide you from life to life as you will, in time, surely aid them as well.

THE PHIAL OF EVERLASTING YOUTH

If you receive the Big Stick in the inner realm of the Phial of Everlasting Youth, it is suggested that you view yours'elf as an eternal being. If you were immortal (which your spirit is) what would you be attempting to accomplish? What is it you wish for yours'elf? What is it you wish for others? What sort of world do you wish to live in? And what may you do for your part to move the world in that direction?

When asking about love, romance, relationship and friendship, this response says that one might consider meeting new people and making new friends. Since this is the inner realm, the indication is stronger for making new friends on the path or new connections in the world of spirit. Evoke a spirit you haven't called previously. Extend your influence. In doing this, circumstances and people will be moved toward the fulfillment of your wishes. Somehow, children are involved here. Or young people. It is possible that you will receive a sign from them or when they are around.

In terms of an inquiry about business, career or finances, this reply says that you need to consider approaching the situation in a new way, with new and revived energy. Naturally, you wish success, but it is possible you have become a bit exhausted in attempting to achieve it. How can you approach this situation so you are not being drained by your efforts? How can you make this fun for yours'elf? How can you approach this situation so that you are renewed rather than sapped of energy? That is your true motivation, isn't it? To have enduring success that fulfills you?

In regards to health and healing, this is surely a good sign.

Youthfulness is usually a sign of quick healing and a symbol of vibrant life, so in terms of questions about healing, you are blest. But also, do the things the young do, which is to say, run around, be busy, follow your interests, and have a good time as best you are able. This will bring you health and healing. It is said that you are only as old as you think, but we elves would add you are only as young as you act. Fill yours'elf with life and express it fully. And since this is the inner realm, see yours'elf as being youthful. Enter your body of light and live in it for a while. Be young, be immortal, be elven. Live in your imagination and your imaginal world. This can be quite healing. And remember that ultimately will be the real world anyway.

As to the life of spirit, of magic and the path, continue on. Do your magic. Not as rote routine. Don't just go through the motions. Fill it with life and energy? Whatever the question about your path, this is the answer. Feel it. Put feeling into it. Energize your magic in a youthful, rather than ponderous, way. Be like a child doing magic in hir imagination, playacting the magician. But make it real.

The Outer Circle:
The Elf Horns of Calling

If the Big Stick lands beyond the outer circle, it indicates that there are people in the world that are doing things that will affect the situation but it is impossible to see exactly what they are doing and how this will alter things. It is quite possible, however, that when you do discover what they have been up to it will change your own motivation in the situation.

And instead if the Big Stick lands within the Outer Circle,

then you read the corresponding treasure below:

THE ORB OF HEALING

When you get the Big Stick in the outer realm of the Orb of Healing, you are called to purify and clarify your motives in this situation. It is quite possible that you may have some inner conflicts that are blocking your progress, or that you have hidden motives and desires that, even if you get what you wish, will make you wish you didn't get it. So, examine yours'elf, examine what you want, why you want it and clear away all that is irrelevant, unimportant, illusionary and unworthy of you and your higher s'elf, everything that can get in the way of achieving what you desire or make you wish you'd wished more carefully. Heal your motives, heal your inner s'elf and all will go well.

As a response to questions about love, romance, relationship and friendship, this would indicate that you need to do what you can to heal everyone in this situation. Truly strive to make things better for everyone, including yours'elf, but don't just consider your own needs and desires but attempt to understand what everyone in the relationship wishes to get from it. If you act from the perspective of healing, all will turn out as it should. Not necessarily as your lower self desires it to turn out, but as your true and destined s'elf wishes, which is always progress upon the path. Be healing and you will meet those that are right for you.

If the inquiry is about business or money then examine the situation dispassionately. If you do so you will see what is best and you will get a clear view of other people's motives. Also, because this is the Orb of Healing, the situation should gradually improve on its own. You can help it to do so by working on yours'elf, your motives and your instincts and impulses. Look at the situation as clearly as you can, but don't become so detached that you no longer take other people's feelings into consideration.

Obviously, this an excellent sign if the question concerns healing or health. However, you may wish to look to your inner s'elf, try to understand your own unconscious, which often reveals itself through our urges and instincts and harmonize them as much as possible with your desire to heal and to bring healing to others, or even healing to a situation. It is quite possible that being in this situation will, of its own, promote healing. The Orb of Healing is very powerful and affects all that come within its realm.

As to spiritual concerns, questions regarding your path and spiritual life, this response moves one toward one's higher, truer, destined s'elf. The spiritual path is about clarifying and purifying our natures, so the answer here is to keep on the path. Keep up your magic and your regular spiritual practice. Let the Shining Ones illuminate your life with their love and guidance and continue on trusting that they will do so. As long as you are sincere and put in the effort, they will take care of the rest.

THE WAND OF WISHING

Getting the Big Stick in the outer circle of the Wand of Wishing indicates that you need to look not only at what you wish to happen in this situation, the outcome you desire, the best case scenario as you imagine it to be, but also to examine why you want what you desire. What is really motivating you? What deep inner need is this intended to fulfill? And will it do so? Will this satisfy what you really hunger for or is this just another illusion?

Is your question about love, relationship, romance and friendship? Then, the answer here again is to examine your motives in the situation. It is not wrong to wish for love and relationship, and it is certainly right to strive for friendship in all instances, that surely is the Elven Way. Romance is entirely to be desired. But why do you wish a relationship with this individual or individuals? What hunger do you wish to satisfy? What need to fulfill? On the other hand, since this is the Wand of Wishing, the chances of getting what you want are very good.

When it comes to inquiries about business and finances, the issues remain the same. You may very well achieve your desires, get the money you want, the job you desire, the promotion you have been hoping for, the success you have strived to achieve but why do you want this thing? If your motives aren't clear, the outcome, even when successful may be skewed by one's inner hunger. Every spirit seeks its destiny, and if what you wish for isn't in keeping with that destiny, your spirit will make you unconsciously undo yours'elf and trip yours'elf up. Be sure this is what you really want.

If you desire to know about health and healing, then this is especially a good sign. Whatever your motivation, healing is always a good thing for yours'elf and for others. However, once you are healed, will you still want the same things in life?

Concerning spiritual questions, this response says whatever your reasons for treading the Path, continue on. Your motives may not be entirely pure but if you continue to sincerely follow your spiritual path, to tread, or skip, hop or dance on the Elven Way, your motives will be purified in time and you will become more and more attuned to your true nature and your true s'elf. Venture onward.

THE COIN OF THE REALM

When one receives the Big Stick in outer circle the Coin of

the Realm, one needs to consider what one really wants in this situation. Reflect on what your conscious reasons are for what you desire, but also looking deeper, what are your inner motivations? And, perhaps, more importantly in this situation, what is it going to cost you? How much of an investment are you willing to make to achieve your goals? Are you committed all the way? Do you actually have the wherewithal to get what you want? And, if not, how do you get it?

On inquiries regarding love, romance, friendship and relationship, you need to ask yours'elf, do you want a relationship with this person because you really like them? Because you enjoy being around them? Or do you seek relationship in this situation because of what you think you can get from this person, or what you assume they might be able to do for you? Are your motives pure? Are theirs? What is it that they want from you? Are they seeking to use you? Will money bring you closer to others, or divide you?

Regarding questions about business and finances, then this is a fairly good reply. The Coin of the Realm is lucky in terms of money matters, so you have that going for you. And being that it is in the outer realm, that is a plus for material matters as well. Still, you might wish to ask yours'elf, once you get what you want, once you get the money, job or whatever material thing that you desire, what will you do with it? Will getting it really make you happy? What will you do next? Where do you go from here? And once you're old and grey, will it really make any difference?

Questions of health and healing when they fall in this area ask one to consider what is the most healing thing one can do with one's money and financial resources. Are you using it to fulfill temporary desires that harm your spirit, soul and particularly here in the outer circle, your body? Do you really want to heal? Are you willing to invest the energy and resources to heal yours'elf or others? Do you really care about others, or is money and a luxurious life more important to you?

When asking about your spiritual path, this reply directs you to consider your motives in the world. Are you motivated to achieve in the world? Or are you motivated to uplift and enlighten yours'elf and others? Which is greater for you, worldly success or spiritual success? Is it possible to harmonize these drives? And how do you succeed in the world without violating your spiritual beliefs and principles? If you can answer these questions, you have the answer to the question you posed to the oracle.

THE FEATHER OF TRUTH TELLING

The Feather of Truth Telling reveals the truth, the Big Stick has to do with one's inner, true motives, and here in the outer circle especially one's motives concerning one's interaction with the world. If you have been lying to yours'elf or you have hidden agendas, beware, they will probably come out. And if others have hidden motives, it is likely they will be revealed as well. The truth about the situation will out eventually, and eventually is now.

If your question concerned love, romance, relationship, marriage or friendship, then this response directs you to look at the situation carefully. There is probably something you haven't seen, haven't considered about what is happening. Look more carefully and thoroughly. Especially, try to understand other people's motives. What is it that they really want? Is this something you can give them? Is it good for you and for them? This is not a bad sign, but not necessarily a good omen, either. It depends upon what the truth of the situation and you need to endeavor to do your best to discover what that is.

This reply to questions about business, jobs, money and financial dealings, also urges one to investigate what is going on. Particularly to find out what is behind what is happening. Why is it occurring? Who is behind this? What can you do to clarify things? To make your own goals and motives clear? To remove or soothe misunderstandings? Is there someone who is deliberately muddying the waters? Little backstabbers, tattletales and gossips doing their dirty work? If so, you will likely discover who they are. That, in its way, is a sort of progress. They probably won't stop but you will know not to trust them anymore.

If the issue is health and healing, then this is a good response because the depth of the problem will be revealed and more than likely its solution. In genuinely seeking healing for yours'elf or others, you are surely moving in the right direction and that, in and of itself, is very healing. Being on the right path is always beneficial, at least to our souls, and it is mostly from our souls that we heal, although spirit is important as well. Pursue healing with a good deal of spirit and healing will flower like blossoms in spring.

For questions regarding one's path, one is directed to examine one's place in the world. We can't help living in the world to a certain extent, that is our fate, our karma, our particular level of evolutionary development at this time in our ascension toward becoming Shining Ones. But, what is your place as a spirit in the world? What is your responsibility? And especially in this place, how much can you reveal to others about your path? Who can you trust with your inner s'elf in the outer world? How secret need you keep your own inner secrets, for your safety as well as theirs? Who will understand your path? Who will, at least, have an open mind about it? Tread carefully, this is a time of revelation, guard your magical secrets well.

THE MAGIC MIRROR OF REFLECTION

The Big Stick in the outer realm of the Magic Mirror of Reflection denotes that one needs to consider the past, particularly the past as it concerns the question you have asked, or if you have just thrown the oracle without a specific question, then your own past, your past lives, and how you came to be where you are today. How did you get here? And from whence did you come? It is not about questioning your own motives, exactly, but questioning why you have those motives in the first place and, just as importantly, what is it that really motivates you in this situation?

When asking about love, romance, relationship, partnership and friendship, this response tells you to examine the past carefully. This is the Magic Mirror of Reflection so this is not just about your motives but what it is that the other person wants. Do they want the relationship and if so why? Are they cold toward you and if so, why? Don't look at it from your point of view. Don't reflect their rejection back upon yours'elf. Try to understand what it is that they really want. What motivates them? Listen to what they say about you and understand this is about them really. They are revealing thems'elves with every word and deed. Observe carefully. Where is this coming from? What unfilled needs do they have? And if you really want a relationship with them, how do you go about helping them fulfill those needs? But then, will they want you for who you are or what you can do for them? And is that okay with you?

Inquiries about business and finances suggest that you reflect carefully on the circumstances involved with this situation. Not only what is going on now, what has led up to it, but what has been other people's experiences when involved in or striving to achieve the same things. It's not that things are exactly the same for you or the situation is absolutely identical but there may things you can learn from

45

other people's experience that will be helpful to you.

If the inquiry concerns health and healing, the question is: what led up to this need for healing? Are we dealing with something genetic? Something that has arisen from one's life habits? An accident? A twist of fate? Which usually means either destiny or karma/fate, or both. This is sort of the magical diagnostic phase. Having done this, you can set about healing. And being the Big Stick, if your motive to heal is strong enough, healing will take place.

Inquiries concerning one's spiritual path and life of magic suggest that one needs to go through the process of recapitulation, of thoroughly examining one's entire life, past lives, motivations, everything. (See Carlos Castaneda's book *The Eagle's Gift*.) While the sorcerers suggest one does this on one's own in isolation, these elves have found that this is a less effective method and one should only do it that way if one doesn't have anyone to give one assistance. Like transformation and Step Programs, it works much better when one has a group and a sponsor to aid one. (See Martha Char Love's and Robert W. Sterling's book *What's Behind Your Belly Button?*) And while you're at it, ask yours'elf: Why are you here? What is your soulful and spiritual mission in this world? What is the magical gift you bring to the world?

THE SACK OF GIVING

Getting the Big Stick in the outer dimensions of the Sack of Giving urges one to give of ones'elf generously and most particularly to share one's feelings, desires, motivations and to express ones'elf as fully as one is comfortable in doing or perhaps to extend the boundaries of comfort by a little bit. Let people know who you are. Let them see your true s'elf. Come out of hiding, at least for a bit, and reveal your true elfin, magical s'elf.

Inquiries about love, romance, relationship and friendship get a positive response if you have been kind and generous to others. You could give now, if you haven't given previously, but don't expect a quick return. If you have already given, given of yours'elf sincerely, given gifts and tokens of appreciation with no expectation of return, then the time has come when the cycle will swing back the other way and you will find the Universe and the Magic reciprocating, even if the individuals you gave to don't do so directly. The route may be circuitous but it will be certain. All you have given out will return multifold.

When it is a question about business, job, finances, etc., this is a good response, however, it advises you to take part of what you get and use it to benefit others. This is the principle of tithing. Pay your taxes happily. All you give out will return. If you have a business, free samples are in order. Let people get to know you and your business. Draw them in. There is nothing like something free to attract people.

If you are asking about health or healing, then give healing abundantly. Spread healing everywhere. Create healing amulets and talismans and give them away to those you love, those who may need healing, or anyone who is open to it that you may encounter. Energize small sums of money with healing vibrations and give them to the homeless. Nudge the world toward the better. All will return to you.

As to questions about your spiritual life, let the abundance of your spirit flow into the world. Smile, be happy, show a vibrant spirit, let the world see the magic that has transformed your life, even if they are only seeing it in a disguise. Camouflage to the elves is like speaking another language to people who don't understand elven. It is a way of communicating to them in the only words they understand. Yet, if you can fully be yours'elf, if it is safe to do so, if you dare, then do.

THE PHILTRE OF TRUE LOVE

Upon getting the Big Stick in the outer circle of the Philtre of True Love, one is asked to consider what one truly loves. Not only what do you desire, and surely you can contemplate that as well, but what is it you truly, deeply love in your life, in the world, in the Universe? Are you going after what you really like and love or are you just making do? What really attracts you? What arouses your interest? Sparks your imagination? Awakens your spirit and your soul? What revives and enthuses you?

If you are asking about love, romance, relationship, friendship, then who do you love? Who do you wish to love you and why? What is it about that person or persons that attracts you so? Is it just one thing? Their body, for instance? Is it their soul? Their spirit? Their clever mind? The way they make you feel? And if you were around them for years, would you still feel the same? This is a good sign for love and romance, without question. The Philtre of True Love obviously favors success in relationship. But what is your part in this relationship? What are you contributing to it? And while it will all work out in your imagination, what do you think the reality may be? How do you bring the two into harmony with each other, which is to say how do you make your dreams reality?

Business, finances and questions about one's job or work are less well favored here, unless the question concerns business relationships. Then, this response favors finding those one can do business with on a long term basis, on finding and making friends at work or through one's job. Connections are the key anyway, so make the most of the time and endeavor to improve your financial relations. This will prove beneficial for you.

As to inquiries about health and healing, then good relationships, sincere relationships, genuine relationships are clearly favorable for healing. Ask yours'elf, are you sincere in your reasons for the various relationships you have? Are you honest in your dealings with others? Find the right people and you will find healing.

As to one's spiritual path, one's magic, one needs to be attuned to one's own soul. Our soul connects us to everything and everyone in the Universe. Through it we can learn, know and ultimately achieve all things. It is about connection. Are you loving the path? Is your path bringing you love and right contacts? It should. Love your path and let your path be one of love and everything will come to you in time.

THE PHIAL OF EVERLASTING YOUTH

If one gets the Big Stick in the outer circle of the Phial of Everlasting Youth, one is asked to consider what the long term consequences are of getting what it is you desire. What does this mean for you and others in the future? Everything that happens has a history. What history will this create? And is it really something you wish to remember years from now? And what consequences will you be dealing with further down the way? Is this what you truly desire?

In a response to questions about love, relationship, romance and friendship, this oracle bids you to seek what endures in the situation. Act as though your actions will affect you and others for the rest of your life and theirs, even for lifetimes to come. And yet, at the same time, the oracle suggests that you approach things from an innocent, childlike way. If your intentions are pure and good, all will turn out well. Rid the past from your heart. Don't be compelled by past experiences, driven by your traumas and expectations from your earlier life, look, see and feel things afresh. Let this be a new experience for you.

On questions concerning business or finances, one is called to consider that one may be inexperienced in this situation. That someone else may be wiser in dealing with these issues and to seek the advice of those who have already been successful. But also ask yours'elf, why this is important to you in the first place. Is this something you really want, or something others expect of you, or that karma or the world and thus fate have thrust upon you? And if this is not what you really desire, then how may you find and fulfill your destiny in this situation, because, even when things turn out differently than we expected or desired, our destiny is still at work. How can we assist it? Where can you apply your magic to affect this situation?

In regards to health and healing, this reply suggests that being youthful is a key to healing. Are you feeling your age? Exercise, a good diet and most importantly a good attitude are crucial to staying youthful and resilient. Stiffness and rigidity are signs of death. Be open minded, open hearted, and don't forget to stretch. Hatha Yoga is greatly advised here. Still, being the Phial of Everlasting Youth, it is quite possible that you will experience a period of renewal. You will feel, at least temporarily, revived and rejuvenated. Take advantage of this opportunity.

As to your spiritual life, try to remember your first awakening. What made you aware of the spiritual path in the first place? What or who awakened in you the significance of the path. Is this something your parents drummed into you? Or is this something someone guilt tripped you into following? Are you just doing it because others are doing it? Because it's a fad and it's the 'in' place to be at the moment? Doing it because it's a good place to meet potential lovers? (Always a good motivation on the spiritual path according to elves.) What did you feel about life and the world before someone articulated it into some doctrine or dogma? Renew your life on the path and follow it because that's what you want to do. Because it feels right to you and good fortune will come from this.

Chapter 2:
The Short Stick

The Short Stick indicates what compels one, what outer force, circumstance and energy is influencing ones life and driving one on their spiritual path.

The Inner Circle: The Torch of the Eternal Silver Flame of Elfin

You are probably feeling it, although you are not entirely sure why, but if the Short Stick lands upon or significantly touches the inner Torch, then the Shining Ones have an important part in what is going on and while you may feel like a bit of a pawn in the game they are playing, they have your interests in mind as well and you will surely benefit from the situation as long as you strive to do what you feel is truly right and fair for everyone.

And instead if the Short Stick lands on any of the other Sacred Magical Treasures within the Inner Circle besides the Torch, then you read the corresponding treasure below:

THE ORB OF HEALING

When the Short Stick falls into the inner circle of the Orb of

51

Healing it is a good indication that while things are limited in this situation, and while outside forces or people may be interfering with you in some way, demanding your attention or dragging you away from your intention or just getting in the way, the propensity for things to improve and get better, particularly with your concerted effort and will, is quite good. The Orb of Healing influences the situation for the better, so this is a good sign whatever your question.

If your inquiry is directed toward issues about love, romance, marriage, relationship or friendship, this response indicates that while the situation may be difficult, while others may be imposing themselves in the situation when they have no right to do so or that circumstances make the relationship more difficult than it needs to be, that, in fact, the cycle is in the midst of change and that things are moving toward getting better. This development may not be instantaneous. Things are unlikely to get better all at once, but they are moving in a more positive direction, so take your time. Pushing things won't help, but be aware and make small moves when the time is right.

If you were asking about business, finances, or job or career success and development, then this position denotes that a time of gradual improvement is beginning. This is not a time for large scale investments. It is not a good idea to ask your boss for a raise, as yet. There are still things in motion, but the movement is toward a more favorable financial situation for you and you can feel good about that. Things will be getting better, just very slowly. Don't give up just because progress is slow.

Issues concerning health and healing are very positively favored here. Because this is the Orb of Healing, improvement in health and one's ability to heal will develop a bit faster than if one is asking about relationship or money. Still, there are limits, so don't expect things to happen instantly. Progress will still be slower than you might like it to be, but there should be definite and marked signs that you are heading in the right direction.

Spiritual concerns, questions about one's magic and one's path are also well favored here. However, the signs you get of progress, the communications you get from the Universe, from the spirits, from your ally, from the Shining Ones or from your oracles, may take some effort to interpret. This will not be a direct and obvious sign. Let your unconscious play upon the matter. Leave your imagination free to roam. See what comes to your mind and don't doubt it. Trust your instincts and ask your dreams for more information.

THE WAND OF WISHING

Getting the Short Stick in the inner dimensions of the Wand of Wishing points to the fact that while your wishes may come true, probably will come true, that their fulfillment may be delayed and/or that they will undergo transformation in the process of materialization. This is okay, because it is you really who is the primary reason for the change. You are changing the way you feel, or altering what you desire, and thus your wishes are being transmuted as well. The time it is taking for fulfillment is a good thing. You are in the inner circle, the place of formation, the source of energetic being and your wishes haven't, as yet, fully reached the planes of materialization. This is an amorphous realm, like unshaped clay, you can still adjust things as you wish, and form it as you will.

If your inquiry presents concerns about love, marriage, romance, relationship and friendship, then this place is good for moving things toward the way you wish them to be, but go slowly. You are pushing air here. You are shaping water. Trying to force things will create resistance or things will simply elude you. This realm responds to the imaginal, the clear mind, the will backed by feeling and intent. This realm shapes its'elf around enchantment. It goes to what interests and delights it. Become clear about what you want and let the magic come to you.

When asking about business, money, job concerns, or prosperity the Short Stick in this place denotes a chance to overcome limitations that are upon you. Here is a gray area. Don't cheat, but loopholes are fair game. Shift the world from above and wait. Waiting is very important. This energy will not manifest immediately. And if you push and push and push you will merely exhaust yours'elf without actually accomplishing anything of value or substance. Do your magic and wait. Watch carefully. Things are about to change.

On questions about health and healing, the indications are very positive for healing but, it may take some time to recover. Take that time. Don't rush things. Don't jump out of bed as soon as you feel a bit better. Advise those you help heal to fully recover as well. Sickness is often our psychés and bodies telling us to take a break. If we don't follow that advice we *will* break in time. So, relax. Enjoy the pause. We know the world is probably urging you to just get back to work, but really, in the long run you will get more done if you are fully healed.

And concerning questions about one's spiritual life and development, one's path, one's magic and enchantment, this response urges you to do more magic. Do more meditation. Put more energy into your relationship with the spirit realms and the spirits. This is the time. The results may not come till later, but the time to do is now. Feed you spirit. Nurture your magic. See your body of light and imagine yours'elf as you truly are in the realms of spirit, as you truly will be in time manifest in the world.

54

THE COIN OF THE REALM

While the Short Stick can compel one, motivate one, often in ways that one doesn't wish to be compelled, compelled by circumstance rather than desire, it can also, in that sense, point to a limitation or a lack of some sort. One is attempting to fulfill an unfulfilled need or necessity. Being that it is the inner region of the Coin of the Realm, the indication can be that one doesn't have the resources to do what one desires and feels compelled to get what one needs somehow. One is driven to achieve, for being in the inner circle this is really more about one's spirit than the material world. One wishes to have the recognition and respect that one feels one has a right to and which may seem withheld by others or by the world at large.

If you were asking about love, romance, relationship or friendship, then you need to ask yours'elf: are you getting what you need in terms of appreciation and respect from your friends and social circle? Do they help you feel good about yours'elf or are they always tearing you down? Maybe, jokingly teasing you, thinking it's funny, but it still hurts, and although you don't show it, it makes you feel doubts about yours'elf. How do you find those who are supportive of you? Start with being supportive of those around you. Don't engage in petty cut downs. Preserve your dignity and that of others. Treat them with respect and they will begin to respect thems'elves and you as well.

When asking about business, finances and job success, this response indicates that you need to work on your reputation. Your success, in great part, depends on this. If you are driven to succeed in the material world, the world of business, then your reputation is extremely important. If you get a good reputation, money will flow to you like wealth to the rich. It is a curious fact of the world that people give much more to those who already have than to those who are in need and whom they tend to look down upon. Get people looking up to you and the success you desire will come.

If your inquiry had to do with health or healing, then the indication here is that one has plenty of energy for healing but one may lack the confidence to do so, may feel uncertain about one's ability to heal or help others heal. But you need not feel uncertain. Do the healing. If you need to, do the healing again, and again and again. Let the need for healing drive you. Let it be a call from the spirit world summoning you to heal and to create healing environments in the world. Invest your time, energy and your money into things that support healing. This is the right thing to do.

On questions about one's spiritual life and path, this reply says that one may not have everything one would like for pursuing one's path, one may not have the very best magical tools or the fancy vestments or other accouterments that others have, but what is important is the sincerity and genuineness of one's approach. Men and others in the material world may judge you by how you dress or how rich you may be, but the spirits only look at your energy. If your interaction with the magic is real, if it comes from your heart and soul, it will be far more powerful than those who use form as a substitute for content. Carry on, elfin, you are on the right path.

THE FEATHER OF TRUTH TELLING

Getting the Short Stick in the inner dimensions of the Feather of Truth Telling can make it a bit difficult to see the truth, particularly, in most cases, because one just doesn't wish to face the truth. It is very much like getting an answer to an oracle that one doesn't want to hear. In fact, that is exactly what it is. If you are asking about relationship, business or whatever the question is: you're unlikely to like

56

the answer. It is not what you were hoping to hear but it is the truth and while some people prefer to live a lie, to embrace the illusion and avoid the truth as much as possible, that will never do for a magician, particularly for an elven mage.

If your inquiry has to do with relationship, romance, love, marriage or friendship, then unfortunately, things are unlikely to turn out as you wish. This is not to say that they will be entirely bad, but basically not nearly as good as you'd like. The situation is limited and the success you were probably hoping for is unlikely to happen anytime soon, if at all. If you are asking about developing a relationship with someone, this response indicates that it will be very difficult to do so. If you are asking, will so and so ever leave me alone? Then, the reply is: not any time soon.

Questions about business, finances, job and career success are similarly obstructed. The truth is, this is just not a good time for you, it is unlikely to change quickly, the energy and the circumstances that you were counting on are just not there. Still, that doesn't mean that things won't change in time, or that the situation is utterly hopeless, just that there is no use wasting your time and energy when the time for success isn't right. Hang on. Wait. We know, you are sick of being told you have to wait, but there it is.

When asking about health and healing, this response denotes an unfavorable time for healing. The spiritual energy is just not there. Perhaps it is a planetary alignment or something in the environment, but quick healing is very unlikely. It may be that you will have to put up with this condition for a while, but don't despair, things will eventually change and in the meantime, do what small things you can do to make things better. This is a somewhat hard truth, a bitter pill to swallow, so to speak, but it is only by acknowledging the truth that we become prepared to deal with it adequately.

As to questions about one's spiritual and magical path and life, this reply says that the energy is most likely flat at the moment. Nothing stirs on the astral planes, at least nothing that bodes well. This may be the calm before the storm. There is danger afoot, but little you can do about it but be true to your s'elf, your soul, your path and to your kindred, to prepare yours'elf as best you may and be ever vigilant while being as relaxed as you can be under the circumstances. Something is impending, but what it is, is unclear and unformulated as yet. Don't waste your energy fretting about it but be cautiously alert.

THE MAGIC MIRROR OF REFLECTION

Upon getting the Short Stick in the inner realm of the Magic Mirror of Reflection, one is advised to look at ones'elf closely, particularly to examine one's ego and one's ego involvement in the situation. How much of what you wish to happen in this circumstance involves your ego, your sense of s'elf and your sense of importance in the world and your need for recognition? You should to know this about yours'elf, for it is a weak point, and you have to be honest with yours'elf about your weaknesses lest they be used against you.

Concerning questions about love, romance, relationship and friendship, this position for the Short Stick indicates that this is probably not a perfect situation. This is not the response you want to get if you are asking: is this person my soul mate, because it indicates that the relationship has a long way to go in order to develop into what you desire. It is possible it is you who are not quite ready for such profound involvement, it may be the other person; it could be both of you, or it could even be the situation itself. You may live on opposite sides of the country or the world. But things are just not where you wish them to be and it would help a great deal if you were completely honest with yours'elf about this. If you go on casting a glamor on your own mind, you will regret it in time.

Business concerns, financial questions, issues about your job or career, require you to examine the situation carefully. Are you genuinely up to this? And really, is this truly what you want? Don't compromise yours'elf if it isn't going to turn out to be worth it in the long run, and it's not. It is not that there won't be benefits in this situation, but they will not be quite what you were hoping for and your dignity is more important than financial success. Money will come and go but your dignity is something that will follow you through the lifetimes. Don't cast it away, particularly not for trinkets.

If your inquiry is about health or healing, then this position indicates that you need to examine the source of the illness. What is really causing it? You need to get to the root of the problem to deal with it on a permanent basis. Otherwise, you will just be encountering it again and again and again. Since this is the inner circle, the difficulty may originate from the spiritual planes, and it is probably best if they are dealt with on the astral/shamanic planes as well. But be totally honest with yours'elf, why is this happening? Is there karma involved? And how can you clear it once and for all?

Spiritual questions, questions about your path and your magic are always favored in the inner realms of being. It is true there are limitations upon you. Perhaps they are limitations of karma. It is possible you can only go so far in this lifetime or at this time, however, you *can* make progress and though it may be slow, if you don't give up, if you persevere, things will eventually evolve in the direction you wish them to go. And you should know that you always have the support of the Shining Ones, of your kindred in Elfin and Faerie. Don't bother to judge how far along you are or may be. Don't compare yours'elf to others. Just do the magic, do the spiritual work on yours'elf and keep coming. In the end, we will all wind up in Elfin or Faerie together, equals in our hearts and souls.

THE SACK OF GIVING

Having the Short Stick fall in the inner circle of the Sack of Giving obligates one to give gifts in some way. However, since this is the inner circle the gift may be of energy, magic or some other energetic form. But the fact that you are in a situation where a gift is required is not in doubt. Perhaps the spirits expect something from you. Ask yours'elf, have I fulfilled all my promises to the spirits and the spirit world? Have I given everything that I promised to give? Fulfilled all my obligations? This is very important. And even if you don't owe the spirits, this would be a good time to get ahead of the game so they may owe you. Do some favors. This may prove very useful for the future.

If you are inquiring about love, marriage, romance, relationship or friendship, this indicates that a spirit of generosity will produce the results you desire. It may be that you have to give to someone you don't wish to give to, who, to your mind, doesn't really deserve a gift, but none-the-less, giving is in order. In fact, giving to those who don't deserve it, those who have proven themselves to be a pest and a hindrance is the very thing to do. It will confound them and this is a good thing.

Questions about money, business, job success and prosperity, find a good response here and are positively aspected if you remember to bring gifts of some sort, tokens of appreciation for all whom you deal with. Take them out to lunch or bring them donuts or give them some other gift but give. This may cost you, but it will also prove to your benefit in time. You may feel you have no choice in the matter, that your time and energy is being consumed without any return but all magic comes back to us. Have faith, the magic will fulfill itself.

If your concerns are about health and healing, then while you may have to take time to heal or be sidetracked into taking care of others, at least healing will take place and this is to all your benefit. Again, in the inner circle, this is primarily a matter of energetic investment not necessarily material gifts. It is your energy that is required here. It is your time, your magic that will make the difference. And you do wish things to be different, don't you?

As to your spiritual life, your path of magic and s'elf realization, this reply tells you to continue with your practice. It may be that meditation, or some other technique you have been doing takes a lot of energy and doesn't seem to produce much in the way of results, but continue on. You may not seem to be making progress but you are. You may be evoking spirits and it doesn't seem like they are able to fulfill your desires, but the magic is in process and it will help if you have faith and continue to evoke. Evoke often. Call to the spirits. Call to the Shining Ones. Tell them of your life, your will and your circumstances and await an answer. They will respond when they can. But respond they will and you will find that it will be perfectly suited to your needs and your destiny.

THE PHILTRE OF TRUE LOVE

Getting the Short Stick in the inner dimension of the Philtre of True Love suggests that you consider who your true family is, who you are connected to at present, who are the ones who nurture you and further you and why they are doing so. It is true sometimes people may praise you, bring you gifts, or hang around you for the wrong reasons. Still, those who help

61

should be rewarded, but remember, you may not be able to trust them with the inner secrets of your soul and your spirit's aspirations. And while it is possible that there are those who are attracted to you, or to whom you are attracted, who are not really right for you or you them, they, too, should be furthered on their way. Still, it is best if you don't put too much energy toward a relationship with them for that will only delay the arrival of those you are truly meant to be with, who will help fulfill your destiny and you theirs.

If you are inquiring about love, romance, marriage, relationship or friendship then this response indicates that there are magical concerns involved here. What is your true will? Do the people around you further this? Would getting involved with a particular person really help or hinder your progress as a magician? Are they part of your destiny? Really? Think carefully about this? At the same time, don't ignore your natural attractions. If you are getting involved with someone just because they say they are on the same path, or interested in the same things, but you are not attracted to them, or you have reservations, heed those feelings. It is quite possible that things aren't quite as they should be. That doesn't mean you should stop associating with them entirely, but you may wish to limit that association.

Questions that have to do with business, finances, career and job issues falling in this place call one to realize that such relationships are mostly temporary. Unless they have personal meaning to you, proceed with caution. Are these the people you really want in your life? Yes, you may need them for your business or job advancement, but remember this is business, not personal, and you need to keep it that way in most cases. While the Short Stick tends to limit success, it is good for making preliminary contacts. Take the first step and introduce yours'elf if you have the opportunity, or make the opportunity, but don't push it. Leave it be for a while after that.

Health and healing are favored in terms of being around those who are healing to you, or for you being a healing influence in other's lives, but the Short Stick limits that connection. Makes it somewhat hard to link up or have the time to be together. Other things are always pressing in on one, demanding one's time. Distractions abound. Still, do the healing and the healing will take effect. It just may take a little while to do so.

As to questions regarding your spiritual life, your path, your magic, this place denotes that while you may wish for a relationship with the higher spirits, that you have evoked the Shining Ones, or have called for their attention, they are unlikely to be responding at this time. It is not that they haven't noticed you, or heard your call, but their reply will come in its own time and that is unlikely to be soon. Still, continue with your magic, assured that all magic returns to us in time and if you are truly following a spiritual path, you shall be uplifted by the spirits when the time is right and you will find those who are truly meant for you, who can further you on the path as well as awaken your spirit and your soul.

THE PHIAL OF EVERLASTING YOUTH

Receiving the Short Stick in the inner circle of the Phial of Everlasting Youth may indicate that whatever you are asking about, the result will be limited and not last as long as you wish it would. These are two opposing tendencies. One seeks to prolong things and make them last forever, the other, of circumstance, restricts by its nature. Try to find a balance in the situation. Endeavor to find what will endure in the situation and focus on that. When time has passed, what will remain? What will turn out to have been worthwhile? What will you remember?

When your question concerns love, romance, relationship,

friendship or marriage, the emphasis is on keeping the relationship young, fresh and doing what you can to revive it. The world impinges on these relationships, drawing people away, either physically through time and distance spent apart or merely through continual or periodic stress. What can you do to relieve the tension? What can you do to make the relationship more like children being easily and happily together? You may not be able to totally stop the pressure the world is putting on you, but you can learn to deal with it more effectively.

The same is true of business, money or career. There will be a lot of pressure on the situation, making it hard to endure and keep things going. Is the extra effort required worth it? Are you committed to making this situation last? Do you have a choice? And if you are looking elsewhere, the same condition applies, making it hard to find an alternative that is truly viable. However, while this state will go on for a while, it will not last forever. All things in the world are subject to change, and the cycles of manifestation, wax and wane. Bide your time and await your opportunity.

Of health and healing, this reply favors slow sure progress. This is healing done drop by drop. Keep up your regimen. Progress may be slow but it is progress and that is what is really important. Fast results are extremely unlikely, and if they do happen unlikely to endure. Steady, regular practice and healing efforts are favored here. Don't give up. You are heading in the right direction. It is just that it will be at a snail's pace.

As to your spiritual life and path, your progress into Elfin and the evolutionary development of your spirit and your soul, this position of the Short Stick advises you to take the world with a grain of salt. It will seek to draw you away in other directions, to interfere with your focus, to disturb your meditation, to get you all riled up about this, that or the other thing, which are of little significance in the long run and while you may have to deal with these things, they are no more important in their way than having to urinate. Get it done, wipe yours'elf and get back to making progress on what is really significant, which is your spiritual and magical destiny.

The Outer Circle:
The Elf Horns of Calling

If the Short Stick goes beyond the outer circle, it tends to denote that you are not the main player in this scenario. There are a lot of egos involved, each striving to move things in the direction they wish and most likely coming into conflict with each other. Strive for harmony and you will get the best possible result from the situation as well as meeting with those most like you and most likely to further you.

And instead, if the Short Stick lands within the Outer Circle, then you read the corresponding treasure below:

THE ORB OF HEALING

Getting the Short Stick in the outer circle of the Orb of Healing may slow things down, since outer forces and people will tend to block, interfere with and delay your progress, but the Orb still moves things toward healing and progress, particularly toward success in the world and in your physical body. Its effects may be slowed down but they will work, none-the-less, moving you toward success in your life and your endeavors.

Love, romance, relationship, marriage and friendship are also favored for improvement. However, that doesn't mean that there are not or will not be outside interference, it is just that these intrusions into your world can only delay what is happening, they cannot prevent progress altogether. They are like pests that bother you but cannot do any real harm. Ignore them if you can. Shoo them away if possible, but mostly get on with what you are doing. Make progress toward your relationship goals, even if the progress is slow and leave these pests behind. Don't get entangled with them for that will just draw attention and energy away from where it needs to go. Concentrate on your goals.

Business, finances, career and job success are also slated for improvement despite the fact that the situation is difficult and the envious and your competition oppose you and seek to put themselves forward even though, or particularly though, they don't deserve it. Don't let this worry you. And don't vie with them for attention. Do a good job and let time take care of things. The emptiness of their boasts will be revealed soon enough.

Naturally, health and healing are highly favored in this position. And questions that have to do with healing are answered by slow but sure healing and recuperation. Yes, it will take a bit of time but take that time and let yours'elf heal and advise others to do the same. Apply your healing powers consistently and regularly and you will see real results in the course of time and that is what is really important, after all.

When asking about your path, your spiritual and magical life and development, this response denotes real advancement in the material world. This is not inner spiritual transformation so much as a sign or response that happens in the world through material manifestation. Again, the fact that there are those who are seeking to interfere with you, or deride your efforts, is unimportant in the long run. What counts is that you are receiving response from the world and the voice of the naysayers will be drowned out by the Horns of Elfin calling you to gather with your kindred. If you can, hold a gathering or go to one. There is someone who will provide you with something you need there.

THE WAND OF WISHING

If you get the Short Stick in the outer realms of the Wand of Wishing, it may mean that your imagination is too limited in this situation, or that others, and this is even more likely, simply don't believe in you and don't give you the help and support or encouragement that would make achieving your goals easier. Don't let that stop you. But at the same time, don't pursue this course merely as a way to get back at them, to "show them;" for that, while giving you some power, may bind you to proceeding on this course long after you'd naturally abandon it for something better and it ties you to those that are simply not adequate as friends. You can do much better.

Relative to questions about love, romance, relationship, marriage and friendship, this response indicates that things are moving somewhat slowly, and not without obstructions, toward the achievement of your desires. Don't give up and most importantly don't get entangled in the obstacles nor spend more time on them than you need to. They are just bumps in the road. Go over them carefully and keep on going. If you keep going back to them or try to remove them you are just delaying getting to the result that you desire.

Inquiries about business, job, career, or finances are also favored but again this is despite the interference and obstructive activity of others about you or difficulties in the situation itself. Still, the Wand of Wishing moves things toward fulfillment and you need but continue on making steady progress toward your goals. The result may not be quick but success is coming and there should be some small sign relative to this in the near future. Stay alert for some communication from the spirit world, although it will most likely manifest in the form of an event or communication from someone.

If you were inquiring concerning health or healing, then visualize yours'elf or the person you wish to heal as being fully well and healthy and keep that vision going. It is quite likely that there will be people in your life who will keep offering you drugs, alcohol, or foods that violate your diet and which are unhealthy for you. It may be tempting to accept their offer, but if you wish to remain healthy and continue healing you need to turn them down. Stay on the healing path and all will go well.

As to your spiritual life, your life in magic and your path into Elfin and Faerie, keep wishing. Your wishes are a magic in themselves and even though the world may oppose or interfere with your spiritual progress, those of the world are lost, while you are on your way to the magical realms where love rules, magic reigns, and every true wish is fulfilled.

THE COIN OF THE REALM

The Coin of the Realm is a potent energy for luck and financial success and in the outer circle it has a great deal to do with the material world, the world where money really counts, and money "talks" and so on. However, the Short Stick indicates compulsion. Getting the Short Stick here means obligations, responsibilities, things one must do with one's money and energy, pay taxes, pay the rent, pay, pay, pay. This is not mad money. Not *spend it as you will* money, but it is good for reducing your debt and relieving some of the burdens that are upon you. It may not seem like a good thing, but it is.

When asking about love, relationship, romance, marriage, or friendship, there is an indication of a need to spend some money. One may not wish to do so, probably doesn't wish to do so, but there it is. It's going to cost you. However, in spending you are gaining something. You are moving closer to the fulfillment of your goals and that is what you really want, isn't it? The money isn't really that important, is it?

Questions about finances, business and jobs are always favored when a symbol falls into the realm of the Coin, but again, there is money due, investment required, or some other financial obligation attached for you getting what you desire. On the other hand, at least, you have the money or will get it, for the Coin of the Realm provides. So, go ahead and spend the money. Don't complain about this, good fortune will come. Although, it may not seem like it, this is an investment in your future and your financial success.

Inquiries about health and healing also demand an investment of money, energy or something else. There is no way around it. This is going to take a lot out of you but it will be worth it. Healing is always worth it. Investing in your healing abilities and powers, learning new techniques, going to workshops, buying tools, crystals or other things that aid your healing or healing abilities, are all favored here.

As to your spiritual life, your life as a magician, enchanter, as an elf, fae or other, the world is just going to make demands on you. There is no way around it. But you also need to put money into your path. As much as you can to further you. As much as you can afford, while taking care of the necessities of the world. Put your money where your mouth is, as the saying goes, and buy what you need to advance in your magic. Now, we understand, that magic and the world of spirit are not primarily about money. It's about your spirit, your personal energy, your sincerity, your enthusiasm, your passion and drive and about your imaginal facility. However, sometimes there are books that help, tools that can aid us, they are not primary things, but still this is the time to buy them.

THE FEATHER OF TRUTH TELLING

When the Short Stick falls in the outer circle of the Feather of Truth Telling, one may feel one is in a situation where one is obliged to speak but the whole and unadulterated truth may not be the wisest thing to say. Here is where diplomacy comes in. How can you tell the truth, more or less, without getting into trouble and particularly without offending others? Your powers of enchantment are called for here, your charms and your discretion. There are ways to tell the truth that are a little easier to take than others. This is the world of spin, but not one that is used to deceive but a spin that puts the truth in a positive and healing light which will be accepted, even embraced, by those who hear it.

On questions about relationship, romance, love and friendship, we are cautioned to tread carefully. Be aware of other people's feelings. Not everyone is prepared to take the hard, cold truth. You may wish to warm it up a little bit. Tiptoe through that flower bed of love. The truth must and will come out, but if it ruins what you are trying to achieve in relationship or causes hostility that will endure even after the relationship is supposedly over, then there will be continuing problems and you certainly don't want that.

If business, finances or job success is the main concern, then look at the situation carefully. The truth is being revealed but probably not directly. You need to read between the lines. If you are looking for an apartment and it says it is a nice old place in a fairly quiet neighborhood, that means that it's probably a dilapidated wreck in a slum and the gunfire will only be heard sporadically. Check the fine print. Don't be fooled by the spin. Discover the true facts and then act. There is more to this situation than is immediate apparent.

Someone is probably trying to hide the truth, but that, in itself, should tell you most of what you need to know.

Issues that have to do with health and healing will probably come out. Don't worry, you have the power to heal, use it. But you may also consider the healing power of words. Use your words to heal yours'elf and others. Use positive thinking, positive visualization, empower, nurture and promote those around you and use positive s'elf referencing. Feel good about yours'elf and present yours'elf in a positive but accurate and genuine light. You don't have to fake it. You don't have to make up what isn't true. The truth is powerful enough when seen in the right light. View yours'elf in the healing light of the Shining Ones and all will be well.

As to concerns about your spiritual and magical life, be honest about where you are at the moment. At the very least, be honest with yours'elf. It is only by seeing where you truly are on the path that you can find the way to where you wish to be. If you pretend you are already there, but don't put in the effort it takes to get there, you will live in illusion for ages and never make progress until you give up the pretense and accept yours'elf for the elf or fae or other you are, as you are. You are quite adequate as a spirit without all the hoopla. What does your naked spirit look like without all the fancy dress of desire and pretense?

THE MAGIC MIRROR OF REFLECTION

When the Short Stick falls in the outer circle of the Magic Mirror of Reflection one may wish to contemplate the forces currently at play in the world, particularly as they affect the question you have asked of the oracle. Why are things the way they are? And are you satisfied with the situation? Unlikely, since you are asking about it. When these elves were professional diviners, doing, in the course of time, over

75,000 readings, we found that some folks only came to us when things had gone bad, particularly in their love situation. They would be gone for ages when in love and then when things went wrong, they'd be back again. Questions to oracles, seldom arise from satisfaction with one's situation.

If your inquiry concerned love, romance, relationship or friendship, then reflection upon what drives the situation is in order. Not primarily what drives you to wish for this relationship in the first place, not your psychological motivations, but what will you get out of this in the world and how will this affect your life and situation in the world. How will your other friends respond to a new person? Will this person fit in? Will they change your life? What will they demand of you and what responsibilities will you bear by being involved with this person? What are their expectations? And most important, what do their friends, family and those connected to them think of you? With this place, the truth cannot be hidden, you just need to be willing to look clearly and honestly and without the preconceptions at your desire.

When you want to know about business, finances or job success, this response indicates that there are forces in the world either working for you or against you, or both. Examine the situation carefully. What is obstructing you? Who is on your side? Are you sure? There are those who pretend to be our friends while secretly undermining us for their own benefit or just plain joy in destruction and manipulation. Why do you need this in the first place? What are the circumstances behind this question? What is the real need here? If you examine the situation, the truth become clear and so will your path. Success in this particularly situation is not guaranteed, but we do guarantee that if you are true to your path, you will be guided in the right direction.

On questions of health and healing, one is urged to

examine the environment. Getting this reply is generally an indication that there are environmental factors involved here. Perhaps social factors of stress and strain. Something from the outside is contributing to this illness. What can you do to relieve this situation? How can you change the situation? You may have to consider moving elsewhere. Is that possible? Or getting new friends, joining a new social circle of those who are more harmonious.

As to your spiritual life and path, getting this response indicates that you need to pay careful attention to the way others perceive your spiritual life and magical path. Look around you. Do you need to be more circumspect? Or is your caution overdone? Can you come out more and to whom? Or do you need to hide for your own safety. Do you dare let people know how different you really are? The Magic Mirror of Reflection tends to reveal the truth and even if people don't know the truth, they will sense it. How can you allay their uncertainties and paranoias about anything and anyone that is different?

THE SACK OF GIVING

When one receives the Short Stick in the outer circle of the Sack of Giving, it indicates that whatever one is involved in, whatever one's question concerns, that giving, donating, even if it is re-gifting, is very important. Because it is the Short Stick, the chances are either that you are in a situation where you are obligated to give but may not really or entirely wish to do so, or that you don't actually have that much to give, or both. Still, give what you can. Give what you can afford. Don't give until it hurts. Give so that it helps, however little that may be, and it will rebound to your own benefit in time, multiplied. Realize that you are not really losing anything, although it may seem that way, you are actually investing, even though it may not feel like it is the case at the time.

If your inquiry had to do with love, romance, relationship or friendship, you are in a situation where you need to offer gifts of some sort, but you may feel that what you have to offer is inadequate, not enough, and perhaps will not be received well. And that may very well be the case. However, give anyway but instill your item with magic. Make it a talisman. Let it radiate what you desire in the situation and subtly move things in the direction that is best for you. If things don't turn out quite as you wish, don't worry, they are moving you toward your destiny and that is what is really important.

When your question concerns business, finances, or your work situation, then getting the Short Stick here denotes a situation where you are probably forced to work, or feel compelled to do things you don't entirely care for, but are not receiving adequate recompense in return. Still, you need to give a little anyway. Create a magic rock or other talisman and hide it in your work place. Let it radiate healing for the situation to draw to you what you want, need and deserve. It may take a little time, the Short Stick compels but seldom as we wish it to, but in time the magic will move it in the right direction.

Inquiries about health and healing may arise from the very fact that while one feels a need for healing or to help others heal, one doesn't really have enough energy at the moment to perform a healing ceremony or ritual. One may feel a bit depressed and unable to do much about it, but, every little thing counts. Even if it is just putting out a wish to heal, that will arouse healing energy and with this increased energy you can do more healing. Wish to heal.

If you are asking about your spiritual and magical life, then it is likely that there are forces in the world trying to draw you away from your path. You may feel that you don't have time to dedicate to your spiritual practices. You need to find a way to integrate your spiritual life into your mundane life. Meditate on the fly. Attempt to stay serene as you navigate the world. And, even though you may not be able to do much, at this point, do little bits of magic. Bits of elfin starlight left here and there in the world. It may not seem like much, but it helps.

THE PHILTRE OF TRUE LOVE

When one gets the Short Stick in the outer realm of the Philtre of True Love one is often faced with circumstances that limit one's ability to connect with others. There may be a person or persons with whom you'd like to have a relationship, but the situation prevents it or makes communication very hard, makes it difficult to be together or even meet up. Perhaps you are from different social circles. This is the typical nice girl attracted to the guy from the wrong side of the tracks sort of deal and vice versa. Maybe they are from a different culture, ethnic group, or religion. Whatever the details of the situation, the problem remains the same, it will be tough to develop a relationship to this person due to outside influences.

If your question involves love, romance, marriage, relationship or friendship, then the above very much applies. Circumstances interfere with progress in this relationship. And the circumstances may very well be interfering or disapproving parents, friends or associates, as well as distance, time factors and other things that can make getting together awkward or inconvenient. However, while this is true and while you may consider carefully if there is karma involved here, or merely the Universe, the Magic, telling you this is not the right person for you, you should also note that all conditions are a matter of time. Wait awhile, at least a few weeks to a month, and if this question still concerns you, then do the oracle again and see if you get a better result once the planets have shifted and the moon cycles have changed. If you get the same response, then you can pretty much forget things changing soon. But, it is quite possible the atmosphere will have altered and better influences may prevail.

If your inquiry involves business, finances, job advancement, etc., then this placement makes it difficult, but not impossible, to connect with the right people. Since this is the Philtre of True Love, it favors contact between those who are meant to be together; so, the right connections are probably in your environment. It is not that you don't know who they are, or are waiting for them to come but that you are simply kept from making that connection at this time. Perhaps, you are being led elsewhere, forced to involve yours'elf with those you are not really interested in (as though your parents were fixing you up with blind dates). But whatever the reason, this situation will be difficult. Bide your time and it is possible things will change.

When you have asked about health and healing and get this reply, you may have an awful time finding those who would be healing in this situation, or those who have the information you need on the herbs, techniques or other things that would aid in healing. Keep pursuing the information. Keep researching. It may not be coming immediately. You may feel stalemated and stymied, but that is only temporary. Healing may be slow and your ability to harmonize with the individual who needs your help in healing may not be as good as you'd like it to be, but keep up the healing work and let it take effect. It just may take longer than you'd like.

As to questions regarding your spiritual and magical life and path, this placement also makes it exasperating to get in touch with those who can help you on the path. If you were a yogic type it might mean that your guru/teacher lives far away and you are unable to get there at this time to receive the blessing or initiation that you need and have earned. For the elfae, it may mean that one is having a hard time finding one's kindred. But the admonition and the solution is to keep on the path. Keep up your magical practice. Make progress on your own and in due time the Universe, the Divine Magic, and the Shining Ones, will see your need as well as your devotion and will surely send you the ones who are right for you.

THE PHIAL OF EVERLASTING YOUTH

Having the Short Stick fall into the outer circle of the Phial of Everlasting Youth suggests one should relax and let things develop as they will. There is no sense pushing the issue. That would only delay things even longer. Find peace with the current rate of development and others around you may ease up a bit as well, and if not, they will spin off in other directions to meddle in other people's lives. You just need to be patient and continue onward, undeterred by those who think they can live your life better than you can.

If your inquiry is relative to love, romance, marriage, relationship or friendship, then this response is very good for developing lasting relationships, however, this may clearly take some time and it may not be an easy road to travel. There will surely be other things drawing you away, numerous temptations diverting your attention, a good deal of interference from those who have no business being involved in the first place and a whole lot to learn about this relationship and the individuals you are involved with or wish to be involved with. Still, the long-term prospects are good, and that is what you want, isn't it?

Of questions concerning business, career, job or money, this place is favorable for starting something new, although it won't be easy at first and in fact, is likely to be rather difficult. However, if you hang in there, success will come and its effects will be quite enduring. So, while a good deal of effort will be required in the 'planting', so to speak, the harvest will eventually be quite substantial. The payoff may not be quick, is unlikely to be so, but it should be quite satisfactory when it does come.

If your issues involve health or healing, then while things might be slow at first, this is a very good place for healing because the youthful aspect of this position promotes quick healing, although in this case it is going to need a bit of a jumpstart to really get things going. None-the-less, the healing influence is very powerful here, so do your healing work and let the healing work. However, since this is in the outer circle, energetic healing may not be enough. Various herbal remedies may be in order. Diet could be important and/or exercise. Check out the possibilities but don't overdo it.

Spiritual and magical inquiries, questions about one's magic or one's path, indicate that one should start afresh. Approach things like a beginner. Open your mind and your heart. Put aside your desirous ego. Let the magic be renewed and fill it with youthful enthusiasm. Be like a child without being childish. Give it the energy, intensity, and seriousness that the young believer gives to their interests and wondrous things will occur. And ignore what outsiders say about your path; they don't know what they are talking about anyway.

Part Two
. . . Stones

I t is quite possible that your stone could be two-sided. You may wish to put a dot or symbol on one side of the stone and leave the other blank and let it represent things that are hidden. Or you could put a different symbol on each side. It is up to you. Individualize this oracle. Make it your own.

Chapter 3:

The Large Stone

The Large Stone indicates what stablizes one in the situation, what keeps one grounded and thus able to endure.

Again, when you throw the Large Stone, it may fall either in the Inner Circle or the Outer Circle and also within one of the Sacred Magical Treasures of The Silver Elves, for which the interpretations for the meaning of the oracle in these positions follows in this chapter. Remember that if the Large Stone falls in the center of the Inner Circle on the Torch, you read only the first paragraph of The Inner Circle: The Torch of the Eternal Silver Flame of Elfin. And if the Large Stone falls outside the Outer Circle directly in the Elf Horn of Calling, then you read the first paragraph of that section.

The Inner Circle: The Torch of the Eternal Silver Flame of Elfin

If the Large Stone lands touching the inner torch, then there are spiritual powers that will help keep you grounded in this situation. If it looks like you will stray from the path they will remind you of it and send you signs of warning. Heed these omens and all will be well.

And instead, if the Large Stone lands on any of the other Sacred Magical Treasures within the Inner Circle besides the Torch, then you read the corresponding treasure below:

THE ORB OF HEALING

Getting the Large Stone in the inner realm of the Orb of Healing emphasizes healing in its various forms as a primary stabilizing force in one's life. A good diet, exercise, or whatever it takes to bring you into balance in an energetic way is very important for you. Being the inner circle, this is mostly about your psychic health, your psychological wellbeing; however, it is hard to be psychologically healthy if your body isn't doing well. Your body is the radio, television, tablet or phone that the energetic wavelengths come in upon. You can listen to the very best shows, but if your device isn't working or is going a bit haywire, that is going to be a problem. So, stabilize your body and your life and you can concentrate on your magic.

When you get this in response to a question about love, romance, relationship, marriage or friendship, it is very good for having or developing a stable relationship. If you are just looking for passing affairs and one-night stands, this is not such a good reply, for it indicates that the other individuals you are encountering are probably seeking a more stable and long-term association. Whatever you do, seek healing in the situation. Act to make things better for everyone concerned and all will turn out well. Don't be desperate, be secure in yours'elf and be confident.

If you are inquiring about job, business, career or finances, this placement is excellent for having or obtaining a stable situation, or stabilizing a situation that already exists. It is not very good for large investment, for big or radical changes or major career shifts unless they truly make your situation more enduring, lasting and secure. Do whatever you can to make the situation better, to improve the circumstances you encounter and this will prove to your advantage in the long run. Again, because this is in the inner circle it is more about attitude than anything. Develop good feelings about what is going on in your life and if you find you cannot do this in this particular situation, then you do need to move on.

Questions about health and healing are always positive for the most part when a talisman lands in the realm of the Orb of Healing. Healing is the key here. And particularly a healthy and healing approach to life. Make healing your lifestyle. Radiate healing wherever you go. Be healing in motion and make this constant and consistent, not just a passing phenomenon. But remember, as a healer you are healing yours'elf. Healing others is about helping them to heal their own s'elves. You can't heal for them but your healing presence will be most beneficial to their own healing. And that's what we want, right? For them to heal? To be healers?

Spiritual inquiries, magical queries, issues concerning your path are also highly favored here, for this energy stabilizes your efforts along the path, improves what you are doing, and keeps your energy constant and consistent. This moves you toward being a force in the astral planes and shamanic realms of being, a presence there, not merely a ghostly thing that wavers in and out but a regular being of light manifesting in the realms of wonder. This is a very good sign, and will increase your power substantially.

THE WAND OF WISHING

Receiving the Large Stone in the inner realms of the Wand of Wishing suggests that you may wish to make your wishes somewhat realistic, practical, and in harmony with your life as it currently exists so that the fulfillment of your desires will not create disruption and disharmony in your world and in the world around you. Getting the Large Stone here indicates that bringing your dreams and visions into balance with what is immediately achievable is the first step toward your more expansive goals. Think of this as a stepping stone.

When you have asked about love, romance, relationship, friendship or marriage in this position, the prospects are very good, for the Wand of Wishing grants wishes. However, it doesn't necessarily grant them quickly. Again, the advice here with the Large Stone is to formulate what you wish in harmony with what already exists and what is therefore realizable in a relatively easy fashion. Don't make the spirits strain on this one. Don't aspire toward love with those who are too far out of your league. On the other hand, if you are wishing for a stable relationship, this will surely help.

Questions concerning business, finances, job and career are also highly favored for security and stability. Large changes are not recommended at this time, although preparatory steps are possible. Aim for what you wish to achieve but make whatever moves you do in a conservative fashion. At the same time, visualize your future, your long-term goals for financial or career success. Where do you wish to be in ten, twenty or thirty years? What do you wish to have achieved by then? This is just the beginning. Baby steps are advised.

As to inquiries about health and healing, the prospects are also positive in a balanced and gradual fashion. Healing will take place, but slowly and surely. Don't try to push things. Focus on recuperating and revitalizing yours'elf or some other person that you would heal, not upon the goals that you will undertake after you are healed or have helped someone heal. Don't get ahead of yours'elf. The key here is stabilization of health and bringing the entire being, mind, body, soul and spirit, into balance.

In reference to issues involving one's spiritual and magical path, this energy increases your power and ability to achieve what you wish in a practical way. Your magic has increased surely; your potency is greater; you've taken a step up in initiation; but not so far as to make a radical change in your circumstances as yet. This is a new realm of manifestation for you, a new and higher year in your spiritual and magical education. Take time to orient yours'elf and get settled into the new surroundings. Learn the ropes before you get too ambitious. There will be time to exercise these new-found powers to their fullest extent, later. For now, get to know the territory as it is before you try to extend the boundaries.

THE COIN OF THE REALM

If you receive the Large Stone in the inner circle of the Coin of the Realm, it is a very good sign for having or developing a stable situation, particularly a stable financial situation. The Coin of the Realm, besides being an indicator of money, also is a symbol of the magic circle, the realm of your being and your sovereignty over your own s'elf, and of the magic circle that is Elfin and Faerie. Thus, this placement of the Large Stone helps to establish, protect and stabilize your magic realm in an enduring and lasting fashion.

If you had a question about love, romance, friendship, relationship or marriage, the Large Stone falling here is very good for having a stable financial situation relative to one's relationships. It is a rather sad fact that many divorces occur because of the pressure of financial difficulties. On the other hand, it may be an even sadder fact that many relationships are initiated because of someone who wishes to be better situated or to profit materially. History is filled with arranged marriages that took place to secure someone's fortune. So, consider this as well, what is the motive of the person you are getting involved with? Is it your financial success they are attract to? What will happen if hard times occur? Still, with this placement, money problems are far less likely, at least for a while.

Inquiries about business, finances, job and career are, as

indicated above, very favorable here. One should be careful when investing, however. This is not a good place for gambling necessarily, but for secure and stable situations. Large windfalls are unlikely, but steady progress and success are highly favored and this is true for your career as well. Keep things on an even keel and carry on into the future.

As to health and healing, when the Large Stone falls here, the situation bodes well for a stable and relatively healthy situation. It doesn't necessarily favor great healing, but it does very much favor things staying more or less the same in a fairly positive fashion. It is unlikely that health difficulties will get worse, rather one's situation will stabilize and that is a good thing. Swift healing, however, is not favored here, rather this is the influence of slow progress. Plus, a calm and steady disposition and a good attitude, since this is the inner circle, is productive of slow but sure healing. It may take some time, but it is progress.

In regards to one's spiritual path and life in the magic, this position of the Large Stone secures one's power on a certain level of development and magical initiation. One has a sort of dependable bank account of magical energy that one can draw upon when needed, as long as one doesn't do frequent overdrafts, one should be able to proceed steadily toward success. You have achieved something, something that has uplifted your spirit and your magical being; something that you cannot lose.

THE FEATHER OF TRUTH TELLING

When you get the Large Stone in the inner realms of the Feather of Truth Telling, one is called to examine one's life of magic, one's progress on the Elven Way or whatever one's spiritual path may be and see that it is balanced, grounded and stable. Be honest with yours'elf. Are you consistent in your practice or are you all over the place? Is your practice regular or off and on? Do you pursue the path and then abandon it, only to return again later? Look at the truth of your life and don't judge, just see what the truth is, then you may wish to act to change things, but that is up to you.

In reference to questions concerning love, romance, relationship, marriage or friendship, this place suggests that you examine the relationships you have or that you desire and ask yours'elf if this person will contribute to greater stability in your life or not. Does this relationship always stir up the ... dust? And, honestly, do you need that in your life? Need someone who brings a bit of chaos into things, so things are not so dull, or is this person just a pain in the donkey? But be honest about it all.

In regards to inquiries about business, finances, one's career or one's job, this position suggests that you need to contemplate the current situation not as an isolated event, but as part of the continuing process of development. When it gets down to it, what is it in you that you can count on. You may not be able to depend on the outer world or even the people you deal with, but there is surely something within yours'elf that establishes your psyche in a secure fashion, and if not, there needs to be. What skill or talents do you have that you can always rely upon? What can you do in the world? This involves first initiation and the establishment of ones'elf as a viable entity in the world. Do you feel secure within yours'elf? Can you be counted on?

As to questions about health or healing, having the Large Stone fall here is very good for having a good foundation to heal and to be healing, but where is that foundation within you? And where does your energy come from? What is the source of your healing that you can go to when you need to energize and revitalize? Where or who are the sacred healing waters of Elfin in your life?

And if you are asking about your spiritual path, your magic and your advancement as a spirit on the path of magic and enlightenment, then center yours'elf. Meditate. Contemplate. No need to ask questions. In fact, that would just get in the way. Bring your mind to stillness, or if it is still chattering eagerly, center on something else and let it chatter away until lack of attention stills it as well. Find your center within and focus on pure feeling being. Feel Elfin, feel your magic, reflect truly without thought or preconception. Let the spirits speak. Just listen. The Shining Ones may be waiting for a pause in the conversation you are holding with yours'elf before they speak.

THE MAGIC MIRROR OF REFLECTION

If the Large Stone falls in the inner realms of the Magic Mirror of Reflection, one is called upon to consider the situation overall and how stable it is and how much movement and flexibility exists in the situation. Will getting what you desire be easy? Or is this situation so structured and unmoving as to make changes nearly impossible? Stability can be a good thing but there is a point where it just becomes stagnate, rigid and unbending. What is the situation here with the question you have asked?

When the question concerns love, romance, relationship, marriage or friendship, one may do well to also inquire how stable this relationship is or will be. Or how established this person is within their old social circle. Are they open to someone new coming into their lives? Are their friends also open, or will they resent you as an intrusion upon their safe, familiar and secure world? In fact, you may wonder, are these people stable human beings? This relationship may seem ideal from a distance, but what will it be like after a month or two? Does it need stability or does it need change? What is the basic ambience of this relationship? If you were going to imagine it as a fictional tale, what would that tale be?

If the issue involves business, finances, job or career, this position indicates that it would be well worth one's time to examine the situation carefully. There is more going on than meets the eye. If the situation is secure, you may ask yours'elf, how you can get it to move toward what you wish. If it is unstable, consider what you can do to bring about greater balance. The important thing is to be as honest and as accurate as you can about what is happening for that will lead you to the answer you are seeking and the path toward the realization of what you desire.

Health and healing similarly require a thorough examination of what is going on. Is one's health stable, or does it seem that one has an illness that just won't go away? Remember, this is the inner circle so one's psyche is an important factor here. One's attitude must be considered. But this is also the realm closer to Elfin and to the magic so your spells should work more quickly and effectively in this dimension. Do your healing. Be honest about the results and do your healing some more.

This being the spiritual realm makes questions about one's spiritual path and one's magic even more significant. Here the question is: How stable and enduring is your practice? Have you fallen into a rut and seem to be doing the same thing over and over with little or no result? Is your practice all topsy-turvy, up in the air, or airy fairy in such a way that you have no real connection between the spiritual and the mundane world and thus your magic is fairly flat? Is it powerful in your imagination but having no effect in the world at all? And most importantly, what do you think you can do about it? First and foremost is to be honest with yours'elf and then, if you view a glimmer of a path, proceed carefully. If not, more contemplation may be in order. But at same time, you will need to act. That is to say if you are a magician (tarot major arcana #1) you will need to take action, to do your magic. If you are a practitioner of Zen (tarot major arcana #0) then you need do nothing except to continue to meditate and go with the flow.

THE SACK OF GIVING

When the Large Stone falls in the inner circle of the Sack of Giving, one is called to give alms in order to secure one's position. There is a line in the *I Ching* that speaks of giving generously to those beneath one in order to establish one's security and this is certainly on the same order of advice. Give gifts to those you wish to have as allies. Since this is the inner realm, this doesn't need to be in the form of money. One can burn candles for the spirits, burn incense, put out offerings of milk and honey for the wee folk, or whatever. But give and thus create an atmosphere of thankfulness in those around you, particularly those who are on the astral and spiritual realms of being.

When you are making inquiries about love, romance, marriage, relationship and friendship, this reply suggests that you make offerings. Certainly, giving gifts to the individuals you admire and desire a relationship with is a good thing, but more importantly, make offerings to the spirits that deal with relationship, to Cupid, or Brid, or whatever spirit or demigod that you know and have association with that has power in these matters. Do a little romance or friendship magic. Give energy to the spirit world and set the wheels in motion to achieve the connections for which you have wished.

Questions about business, finances, job and career are favored in this position because it has to do with money and the distribution of money. Especially, since this is the inner realm, it is good to make offerings and gifts to the needy, to charitable foundations, to spiritual or religious institutions or groups. While the result will not necessarily be direct or immediate, this giving will serve to stabilize your financial and career situation and set you on the path to greater success. So, give, give in the spirit of giving, as though every day were Christmas or Yule. The spirits will see this and respond. As the Olde Tooke used to say to these elves, you have to have something to give something. Giving is a sign of success. Be successful.

If you're interested in concerns about health and healing, then heal. Give healing. Do healings. Do more healings. Keep doing your healing work on a regular and steady basis. Establish a healing ritual, a little daily healing exercise that you do over and over and over again. Spread healing into your life and into the lives of those around you and through them into the world at large. This will return to you in the form of greater health.

Of questions concerning your spiritual and magical life, the Large Stone in this place advises you to evoke often, make frequent and regular offerings to the spirits. Rather like tithing in religious groups, but instead of money, give energy and magic. Make this a habit, at least for a while, a week, or month or whatever time frame you set in order to evoke the magic you desire. You wish to advance upon the spiritual and magical paths? The Shining Ones want that for you as well. Share communion with them regularly and establish a continuing relationship with them in your life.

THE PHILTRE OF TRUE LOVE

Getting the Large Stone in the inner dimensions of the Philtre of True Love is a wonderful sign for balanced and enduring relationships in every area of your life. This position is a blessing for having stable situations develop in your life, for dealing with people, and more than that for improving the relationships that you have. You have been smiled upon by the Shining Ones and their blessings will come to you through someone in your life.

When you are asking about love, romance, relationship, marriage or friendship you are very lucky to have the Large Stone fall here. This is a great indication of the development of true and lasting relationships. If you have already found your true love then this response moves the energy toward making it continue and improve. If you haven't found your soul mate as yet, this energy moves you closer to doing so. Whatever the situation or circumstances concerning dealing with others, this will increase your luck in love and make associations much more favorable for you.

This is clearly favorable for relationships involved with business, finances, job or career as well. This energy moves you toward making contacts and connections with those who can really help you in your career and further your business and financial interests. While this energy also tends to stabilize such relationships, this positive energy doesn't last forever on its own. Work to make the most of the beneficial circumstances while they do last and keep an eye to what endures. Still, though the cycles of life change, they ebb and flow in all things, the overall benefit from this placement is surely a boon for your life.

Certainly, this is also a very healing position as well, but the healing comes from relationships with the right people and is also favorable for healing occurring in relationships that have been difficult or rocky. However, if the relationship you are interested in doesn't seem to get better, that is most likely because it is being moved out of the way so the person or persons who are right for you may come into your life. Don't cling to a relationship, nor attempt to force a relationship, those that are truly meant for you will come and most likely if you get this position, they will come very shortly, if they haven't arrived already.

If yours was a question about your spiritual and magical life and path, then it is quite likely that someone who is going to be very important in your spiritual life will arrive shortly or has just appeared in your life. This is someone who will have a deep and lasting impact and impression upon your life, revealing secrets of magic and spiritual development that will illuminate and enlighten you and increase your potency and power in the various realms of being but particularly in the astral and shamanic realms of light and magic. You have been blest. Congratulations!

THE PHIAL OF EVERLASTING YOUTH

Receiving the Large Stone in the inner circle of the Phial of Everlasting Youth is a very good sign for one's health in general. It is also beneficial for everything that is new, new beginnings or new start-ups, but also for things that are renewed, that are beginning again, being refreshed, revived and revitalized. If at first you don't succeed, this position is favorable for doing it again with better results.

When one is making inquiries about love, romance, marriage, relationship and friendship, this placement favors a new approach, a new attitude, a renewed spirit, a spring in your step the way you feel when Spring first appears after a long, hard Winter. Be confident, but not erratic. If you don't meet with response at first, don't let that get you down. Maintain your confident attitude, for things will work out for you. The spirits are eagerly working on your behalf. The Shining Ones are guiding you to those who are right for you. Keep that fresh approach going. Let your innocence shine. Release your expectations and adapt to whatever comes and then surely what comes will be what you desire. Start again, but don't give up. Remain positive and hopeful and let the magic do the rest.

If your question has to do with business, job, career or finances, the fall of the Large Stone in this position is very favorable for new beginnings or new avenues of endeavor. If you are interested in expanding, in trying out new product lines, in finding a new job, or starting your own business doing what you love to do as a sideline and then hopefully in a full-time fashion, this is a positive response. But you need to endure. That is the most important thing. You can't give up just because things are slow at first. Particularly concerning doing what you love and making money off your art, talents, skills and creativity. It may not be your main avenue of income for a long while but if you endure success will come to you and in the meantime, while it may not support you entirely, it will bring in some extra money as well as a great joy and a deep sense of satisfaction.

As we said at the top, health and healing are highly favored here because of the youthful connotation of this placement. The Large Stone stabilizes one's health, while the Phial of Everlasting Youth keeps one looking young and renews one's health so one looks younger. Being that these are the inner realms, attitude and spirit are very important in regards to this. Thus, this position favors a positive attitude and helps relieve depression. In fact, healing work on someone's depression is greatly favored here. The inner dimensions are energetic in nature, therefore, one's energy, one's vibration is of upmost importance in terms of one's health and one's power to help others heal when the stone lands here.

If the issue has to do with your spiritual path and magical development, the Shining Ones are smiling on you. The tendency for elves and elfae to experience longevity is highlighted in this position. No matter how your body may appear on the outside, your inner nature will shine through, giving you a youthful aspect if you are old and if you are very young you will seem wise beyond your years. This is surely a blessing. The question is, how do you make this energy endure? How do you keep it going? What magics can you do on a regular basis that will attune you ever more closely with the realms of Elfin and thus extend your life and your energy way beyond that of normal folk?

The Outer Circle:
The Elf Horns of Calling

When the Large Stone falls beyond the outer circle, then it is possible that the whole situation is going to go off the rails. There are surely people working, either intentionally or unintentionally to have everything go wrong and fail. Remain calm, stay grounded and you will be able to endure and overcome their interference.

And instead, if the Large Stone lands within the Outer Circle, then you read the corresponding treasure below:

THE ORB OF HEALING

The Large Stone falling in the outer realms of the Orb of Healing is a potent indication of improving health, healing and a general cycle of good fortune coming into your life in the material world. While this may lift your spirits, since it comes in the outer circle, this is more about actual improvement in a material way in your life and not simply a matter of attitude, perspective and point of view. Not that a positive outlook would be remiss here, but it is more of the fact that such an attitude tends, in this case, to be a response to an improving situation than it is a magic designed and exercised to improve one's circumstances.

If your interest is in love, romance, marriage, relationship and friendship, this position is a powerful indication that whatever is going on with you and others in your life should be getting better in a steady and enduring way. It is not as good for forming new relationships, although that is not entirely out of the question, but the possibility of people from the past coming back into your life is accented here. Thus, a new start to an old relationship is favored. This energy won't last forever, however. There are cycles to everything. But it will endure for a time and so do your upmost to secure things while you can.

Questions regarding business, finances, job and career are well favored here as well, particularly since this is the outer dimension where materiality rules. Therefore, an improvement in one's financial situation is expected, although not in a huge fashion but rather in slow incremental developments. This should serve to make you more secure financially overall and more secure in your job or career position. This is not a good time for investment but rather for setting things right that haven't been quite up to par.

As we said at the top, health and healing are particularly favored here, and one should experience an improvement in one's health, but one may also experience an increased power to help others heal. Pursue your healing work steadily. Make your healing practice regular and dependable. Do a bit of healing magic each day or night and send it into the world (it surely needs it) and know that it will inevitably return to you multiplied. In fact, this energy may very well be a response from healings you have performed in the past.

When you are asking about your spiritual path and magical life, this response from the oracle indicates slow and steady progress on one's path. Keep up the good work. You and your magic are evolving to higher and more potent states of being and your magic is beginning to take effect in the world around you, particularly within your realm, which is to say your immediate environment and social circle. This is surely a blessing for you and for all those that are connected to you.

THE WAND OF WISHING

Having the Large Stone land in the outer realm of the Wand of Wishing is a good sign for manifesting what you desire in a material way, although in a balanced and steady fashion. The Large Stone resists the quick and the sudden and influences all things toward stable and dependable progression toward one's goals. However, the Wand of Wishing waves itself about casting spells of fulfillment of all your true desires so you need not worry that you won't get what you wish, but you may need to put in some effort to making it last.

When asking about love, romance, friendship, marriage and relationship, this fall of the Large Stone moves things toward real development in those areas in your life. Your social life should pick up. You will probably run into people that you know that you haven't encountered in a while. But don't overdo things. If you don't burn yours'elf out running about and partying as though there'll never be another party again, you may be able to make some associations that will last and be of enduring benefit. The energy here is for strengthening relationships that already exist, not forming new ones.

Questions regarding business, finances, career or job advancement are similarly well aspected, but again the movement will tend to be slow and steady. Sudden developments and changes are unlikely with the Large Stone. Yet, things are moving toward the fulfillment of your desires, and so while it is unlikely to happen quickly, this placement gives you a very positive response to your question. Things will be stabilizing in a beneficial way. Advancement is coming but coming slowly. Be sure that what you wish for is what you really want.

This is also a very healing position for the stone. If you truly wish to heal yours'elf or others, health shall be yours. But since this is the outer realm, it is important to support this movement toward healing with real and constant effort. Be sure you have a good diet. Do regular exercise. Eliminate those habits that are counter to a healthy life and future. Secure your health on the material plane and you will experience physical wellbeing and longevity.

And in regards to your spiritual and magical life, when the Large Stone falls here the prospects are good for advancing along the path, particularly in a material way, which is to say receiving the tools you need to pursue your magic, or meeting the people that will make your path better and more stable, or even getting more time or making more time for pursuing your magical goals. It is here that the material and spiritual worlds touch and intertwine. Magic, in many ways, is like a string. On one end is the material world, on the other the more etheric and spiritual planes and it doesn't really matter what end you tug, or if you pull on the middle, everything will be moved when you do so.

THE COIN OF THE REALM

Getting the Large Stone in the outer dimensions of the Coin of the Realm is a wonderful sign for a secure financial situation, either having one or developing one. The Coin of the Realm always favors prosperity and here in the outer world it tends to manifests as money or other material objects of value. The Large Stone secures and stabilizes your situation, helps it to endure so that one is prosperous in a somewhat conservative way, for the Large Stone also favors conservation, and thus also is favorable for having savings, money put aside for the future, and establishing a foundation of financial success, for real estate dealings and establishing basic material security.

Questions about love, romance, marriage, relationship and friendship are also favored if they involve securing and stabilizing relationships. It is not as favorable if one is seeking new relationships because one is likely to encounter a situation where the person or persons one wishes to be involved with are already in a social circle that is not entirely open to new people. Often those in long time friendships are wary of anyone new entering the scene. It is not impossible to gradually insert ones'elf in such situations but the word gradual is very germane here and should be remembered even as time goes on. It will take a while before one is accepted in a fuller sense. One will be seen as an outsider for a good while, but don't let that bother you. Don't resent those that doubt you. Be true to the frasority (combining fraternity and sorority and used by the elves as a term denoting fellowship in a non-gender biased way).

Naturally, this is a good response for anything that has to do with business, finances, job or career. However, taking risks with one's money or career is not favored. One may seek to change one's job and that is perfectly okay if one does so in a balanced and stable fashion and one is going to a better and more secure position. The idea here is to really improve things for yours'elf without taking risks. Risky endeavors are to be avoided for this influence favors the established order. Large changes that challenge the system are likely to fail or will surely be resisted and thus take a long time to come about. If you are determined to create substantial changes don't expect anything to happen quickly.

If you are inquiring about health or healing, this is favorable for its steadying effect. Stabilize the situation first, bring things into balance and then healing will occur. The good thing is that this position is very favorable for having or obtaining the resources one needs to heal or carry on one's healing work. It is also very favorable for steady, continued healing work without any loss of personal energy, so one may do one's healing without being drained. One becomes, in a sense, a font of the sacred healing wells of Elfin.

As to one's spiritual life and magical life and path, perseverance is productive of real progress. Keep doing what you are doing. Keep on the path. Continue with what has worked for you so far. If you wish to try new things, integrate them with what you are already doing. Don't overthrow all you have done so far and make a totally fresh start. That would be unlikely to succeed in the long run, at least with this influence. If you wish to do that, wait awhile and throw the oracle again and see what you get. This position is about making your magic steadfast. If you need to obtain certain magical tools to continue on your path, choose the best quality you can find and afford. Purchase those things that will last and that will continue on this path with you for years to come. Quality is highly valued here.

THE FEATHER OF TRUTH TELLING

Receiving the Large Stone in the outer dimensions of the Feather of Truth Telling is meant to move one to establishing the facts and truth of any and every situation. The truth is likely to come out about what is going on, and it is important that the individual who gets this response doesn't resist nor hide from this reality but takes this revelation and uses it to secure thems'elves in the world and to attach thems'elves to evident reality. It is only by facing the facts that one can do anything about changing them.

If you were asking about love, romance, relationship,

marriage or friendship, this fall of the Large Stone indicates that whatever the situation, the truth will be revealed to you soon. This placement is neither positive nor negative in and of itself. It merely points out that the answer you have been seeking will be revealed in a short time but whether you will like this answer or not is in many ways up to you. Since this truth reflects reality it is in your best interest to accept and make the most of whatever comes out.

When the inquiry has to do with business, finances, job or career success and the Large Stone lands in this position, one will find out the facts and if one is able to remain in balance, to remain steadfast in the face of the facts, everything will turn out well in the long run. Remember, this is about the long run. The elves are playing the 'long game' and the illusionary flux of the world is but the tides of the ocean coming and going. They will ever ebb and flow and it is good to know about their movement if one is to sail the seas of life and the world successfully. Whatever is discovered, use it to secure your future. If the news is bad, realize this is only a temporary setback. If the news is good, be mindful that good fortune must be secured if it is to last. Make it last.

Questions concerning health and healing also have a somewhat uncertain response. It all depends upon what you find out; what is revealed to you. However, whatever the facts are, whatever news you receive, do your healing. That part is not in debate. You may be presented with more of a challenge than you were hoping to encounter but you are up to the challenge. Let your healing flow forth and it will return in time in your life and in the lives of those who are connected to you as healing energy.

As to your spiritual life and magical path, this placement of the Large Stone is beneficial to you. It will surely reveal something about your life in the material world, in the world of the normal folk, in the society you live within, but its real importance is that you live beyond that world, within it but also above and beyond it. Take the truth that is revealed to you and lift it up to the higher reaches of manifestation. Respond to it with your best attitude and your finest magic and shape the future by doing so. Your actions are your magic and everything you do molds the world that you will live in, within and without.

THE MAGIC MIRROR OF REFLECTION

If you find the Large Stone falling in the outer circle of the Magic Mirror of Reflection, you are called upon to examine what supports you in life, what keeps you steady, sane and on the right track. If your life is feeling out of balance and things are uncertain, ask yours'elf what you can to do bring things back into balance, to steady and stabilize your life, to get things and keep things going in the direction you desire.

If you posed a question about love, romance, relationship, marriage or friendship, then this reply indicates that you need to look at who contributes to keeping you and your life on an even keel. Who helps you keep going? Who helps you emotionally? And most particularly, who keeps you moving toward your goals and just plain getting up and facing the world every day. Who can you really count on? Who will be there when times are difficult and bad? Who are those who will desert you as soon as the going gets rough? If you asked, will this person love me, you are asked to consider what elements, if any, in this relationship would lead to it lasting. Unless you are just looking for a quick fling, that is a vital question.

As to inquiries about business, finances, job or career, this placement prompts us to contemplate what helps keep our material world together. Is your job steady? Can you count on those you work for or those who work for you? You will probably do well when the economy is prosperous, but are you prepared for leaner times? Can you endure the cyclic drought of slow business? What can you do to ensure your continued success? If you are asking about career advancement or making an investment, this reply cautions you against anything that is risky at this time. Aim for stability.

Obviously, health and healing will be furthered by stability. Before you try new things, new diets, or new activities that may impact your health, make sure your basic energy is strong and vital. Also, if you are working on helping others to heal, first get their base energy secure, and then work on increasing their health potential. What is it that you can do that will prove the easiest way to help them ground thems'elves? It is possible also that one must consider consuming only simple foods, implementing a basic healthy diet with no frills. This is a back to basics approach.

As to questions having to do with one's spiritual path, one's magical life in the world, one is called to reflect upon how one may live in the world without compromising one's dignity and spiritual values. Also, one must consider if one's life is stable in the world, for if it is not, it makes pursuing a spiritual path more difficult, although not impossible if one is truly a mage, but it does tend to consume a lot of energy and draw one's attention away from the spiritual until one sees and realizes that the material and spiritual worlds are not separate things, but one thing seen separately. Still, what helps you keep going on your path? What success in magic assures you that it is still worth doing? What regular (ritual) things can you do to help with that? They don't have to be elaborate things. They can be quite small magics. But it is important that they are regularly performed, habitual almost, but without becoming empty, unthinking and unfeeling action.

THE SACK OF GIVING

Getting the Large Stone in the outer dimensions of the Sack of Giving indicates that generosity is a stabilizing force in your life. Act prosperous. Give whatever you can, as much as you can and this will serve to help bring your life into balance and stabilize whatever situation you may be encountering. Giving gifts is like adding pontoons to the side of a shaky boat. It helps keep it afloat. Broaden your links and your connections and create an atmosphere of people being thankful to you, of feeling you are a bonus in their lives. Bring gifts whenever you visit someone. Give gifts to those who visit you.

If you are asking concerning love, romance, relationship, marriage or friendship, this reply from the oracle advises you to give gifts and tokens of appreciation. If you don't have much, try regifting. But it is important, here in the outer realm, that you give something material as well as offering friendship, love and maybe good advice or a tip about this or that which may be helpful to the person. This magic is centered on a physical object, so give something, even if it is small. Make it something magic.

If the issue has to do with business, finances, job or career concerns, then things will be furthered with just a little bit of investment. It doesn't take much, but if you wish to secure your position and keep it going, make an offering. This can even be a stone, a coin or some other object that you have enchanted. Hide it in the office, or wherever you wish to receive money or notices of success, and let it radiate its powers there. Actual gifts to coworkers or your boss, employees, or costumers, is also favored, particularly if you have done a little bit of magic on these things you are giving. The important thing is to give and, in that way, open the metaphysical door to receiving. This is magic, but it is a magic that has a very definite material basis. You are anchoring your success with the object you give and you are establishing your success in the eyes of the Universe.

Questions about health and healing are well aspected here, if you offer something material with your healing. Perhaps you wish to do supplements, or tinctures or some other remedy, but it is important that you instill these offerings with healing enchantments, for this will extend your auric realm into the material world more widely and this will help bring balance and thus healing into your life and the lives of others.

As to your spiritual and magical life, your path into the higher dimensions of realization and your evolutionary development, this place is very good for donating to the poor, for giving to some non-profit organization, but also to tithing to your coven, vortex or the members thereof. Invest in your group, even if you are just bringing them some good food. Give tokens of magic to the elfae you happen to come across. All this will serve to bring your spiritual life into balance and thus help establish your path as a successful manifestation in the world. You are making your magic real by doing so. You are making Elfin real.

THE PHILTRE OF TRUE LOVE

The Philtre of True Love is always beneficial for love and relationship interests. The Large Stone helps provide balance to a relationship and being that it is in the outer dimension, it manifests in material and physical ways. It is not just a matter of attitude but of real people coming or being in your life. This fall of the Stone is surely good for keeping relationships going, but less favorable for starting anything new or making new contacts and there is always a possibility that one will feel stuck in a situation with no way out presenting itself as yet for stability reigns here. But make the most of the situation and you may find that there are benefits you didn't expect.

If your question was directly about relationship, love, romance, marriage and friendship, the aspects are good for securing relationships, but if one is looking for something new, one should go very slowly. Don't rush into anything. It may seem like true love but it will most likely turn out to be true hell if you are not cautious and careful in proceeding. The beginning is especially important for it holds the seeds of all that is to come. Listen well to what people say as an introduction or a response to an introduction. That will tell you quite a bit. Nearly everything will be revealed, usually unknowingly, in the beginning. On the other hand, if you wish to keep a relationship intact, this will serve toward that purpose, however, if you are not really meant for each other, you will still part just at a later date. But don't worry about that. All is working toward you finding the person who is your true love. Sometimes, the Magic must get the wrong people out of the way so we may find the right ones.

This position is very good for enduring business relationships, and the stabilization of your career, job and finances. A raise or increase in income is unlikely unless it serves to create greater stability, but if it comes it would manifest because someone really likes you and wishes to keep you around. This is a movement of affection as much as anything. Positive interactions are vital here. This placement of the Large Stone helps one find business associates and partners that one can trust and count on for the future. That, in itself, is a true blessing upon one's financial life.

In terms of inquiries about health and healing, if the Large Stone falls here, very beneficial and healing relationships will appear in your life leading toward greater balance and endurance for your healing work and your rejuvenation as an individual. You may find someone with whom you can do healing work and find that your efforts in tandem are far more powerful than your power to help heal alone. This is very good for joining and remaining in a healing circle that meets regularly for healing projection.

And if your question was directed toward gaining greater understanding and guidance for your spiritual path and magic life, and the Large Stone landed here, you shall be blest with those who will truly help you on the path and probably you will help them as well. This is usually a mutually beneficial position. This is like two fan boys of the same star or fandom finding each other and sharing their fandom in feverous and joyous delight. The sense that one is closer than ever to the Living Magic of Elfin and Faerie enlightens one's being and sends a surge of energy through one's soul and into one's spirit. And, perhaps best of all, this energy will tend to endure and last for a good while.

THE PHIAL OF EVERLASTING YOUTH

If the Large Stone lands in the outer realms of the Phial of Everlasting Youth, one will experience a reinvigoration of energy coming into one's life from the outside, and one that should endure for a good period of time although, like all cycles, it will not last forever. So be aware of this from the start and make the most of this opportunity as it is presented to you. Being the outer circle, the energy is unlikely to originate from you, but rather is a gift from the Divine Magic and the Shining Ones channeled to you through another source in the world. Still, like all things elven, make it your own.

If you had a question about love, romance, relationship, marriage or friendship, this placement of the Large Stone indicates a revival of energy in your social life. You may meet new people, it is surely favorable for doing so, or be invited to social events and parties. This could be a busy social time for you coming up. If you are an introvert, it is possible that you will receive new information about the subjects you most love, have someone tell you about a new book that turns out to be great. Magic is swirling into your life and it most likely involves and comes from other people.

For inquiries about business, finances, job and career, this fall of the Large Stone favors new ideas, new contacts, and a revival of the old, so that what you have been doing will suddenly show growth and development after a long period of dormancy. And since it is the Large Stone falling in the Phial of Everlasting Youth, this new cycle of financial success will likely endure for a time. It is good for investing. But with a bit of caution. Don't be careless. Invest wisely, but success for your investments are highly favored. And it is even more likely that someone may wish to invest in you. The possibilities for outside financial sources are favorable.

In regards to health and healing, this placement of the Large Stone indicates a period of great energy and activity. If you have been ailing, don't overdo it. You are on the mend, but don't exhaust yours'elf, and as a healer give that advice to those you are aiding to heal. Plus, the possibility of renewed energy coming into your life is very strong. Someone is sending you healing vibrations. Perhaps the healing you have done in the past is now returning to you with thanks from those you have benefited. They say what goes around, comes around and now it is your turn to benefit.

As to your spiritual life and magic, a good deal of magic is coming your way. You have been blest and no doubt you will be uplifted, enlightened and furthered upon your path. You may want to celebrate in some way, but more importantly, keep your magic going. Take what you get, which will be a bit of practical magic, and use it well. Not all at once, but bit by bit, distributing elfin starlight into the world wherever you go.

Chapter 4:
The Small Stone

The Small Stone signifies the burden that one carries in regard to the question. What one's karma is, what is unnecessary to the situation and what one might consider doing away with or eliminating, or the fact that one may consider reducing the amount of energy one is putting into this thing.

Next you may wish to read the oracle interpretation for where ever your Small Stone lands on the board, the Inner or Outer Circle and the Sacred Magical Treasure therein. And if the Small Stone falls in the center of the Inner Circle on the Torch, you read only the first paragraph of The Inner Circle: The Torch of the Eternal Silver Flame of Elfin. And if the Small Stone falls outside the outer Circle in the Elf Horns of Calling, then you read the first paragraph of that section.

The Inner Circle: The Torch of the Eternal Silver Flame of Elfin

If the Small Stone lands upon or significantly touches the torch at the center of the oracle, then you are nearly done with this situation and are finished with situations like this that are coming up due to karma. Continue on but know that this may be the last time you encounter this difficulty. Bring it to completion as successfully as you can and more on into the future.

And instead, if the Small Stone lands on any of the other Sacred Magical Treasures within the Inner Circle besides the Torch, then you read the corresponding treasure below:

THE ORB OF HEALING

When you receive the Small Stone in the inner circle of the Orb of Healing, you are given the power to clear away the limitations and karma from the past, especially those things that are based in the astral, spiritual and magical realms, which means, in great part, in the unconscious aspects of the psyche and thus to clear the way for a more successful future. This is not an automatic thing, however. It won't just happen all on its own. One has to work at removing the inner obstructions that limit one, particularly the limitations of one's mind and feelings. One has to do the inner work and this does take time but every step forward is worth it. Purity of being opens the door to new opportunities and possibilities.

Getting the Small Stone here in the Orb of Healing's inner realms when one is inquiring about love, romance, relationship, marriage, friendship and one's social circumstance, indicates that one may set about healing one's social life and relationships with confidence. However, one seldom gets this placement if there isn't work to be done. Especially, one may wish to consider one's skills as an enchanter. To contemplate one's ability to charm others and interact with them in a positive way, and how one may improve one's skills in social interaction and intercourse. Really, in the long run it is all about personal spirit.

Questions about business, finances, job and career success face limitations from the past, but mostly due to the way people look at things, from people's enculturated points of view that tend to bind one in place and keep one from moving forward. Faced with such stagnant circumstances, one needs to do what one can to clear one's own inner being, removing the threads of attachment that are being used to limit one. There is nothing one can do that will change the outer situation at this time, at least nothing that will make things better. But if one is able to remove the hooks that the outer world has in one's psyche, one can then act on the shamanic planes of being to shift the essential atmosphere and vibrancy of one's financial environment.

As always, questions about health and healing are highly favored in this position, for the Orb of Healing ever promotes healing energy and a healing influence in the world and in this case works to resolve any residual problems or ailments that have just been clinging to one. Like a cold that seems like it simply won't go away. Although, here the ailments will tend to be more psychological in nature, manifesting as symptoms on the material plane, and have more to do with and originate from one's attitudes and feelings. One can give up being belligerent when one realizes that is no longer an effective tool for getting through the world. One can release old resentments, let go of envy and jealousy and the sorrows of having been rejected and fully embrace ones'elf as one is and proceed with self-assurance into a new and revived world. For you are a healer.

And if you are asking about your spiritual and magical life and path, this is a great place for the Small Stone to fall if one is really ready to let go of one's past, of one's personal history as Don Juan advises Carlos Castaneda to do in his Nagual sorcery books, and step into the realms of pure being without any preconceptions about ones'elf or the others around one and deal with life purely as it presents itself, ever ready to take action based upon the trust one has in one's intuition and psychic perceptions.

THE WAND OF WISHING

When the Small Stone lands in the inner circle of the Wand of Wishing, one is called to examine exactly why one wishes for what one desires. Is there something behind this from the past that is no longer actually serving you and your progress as a soulful spirit, as an evolving elfae? The Small Stone is inclined to indicate that this may be so. Surely, a little s'elf examination and reflection upon this issue would not go amiss, whatever the outcome of your contemplations. And examine the wish itself carefully. Perhaps you can streamline your magical request a bit? Make it more practical perhaps, easier to fulfill? Get it down to what is really important and essential to the matter?

If your inquiry focuses on love, romance, marriage, relationship or friendship, then this position is very good for achieving your desires in that direction, however, you may wish to be sure you are not bringing baggage from previous relationships into this situation as well as reflecting upon what baggage that the others involved may be carrying with them. Also, ask yours'elf, what is the karmic aspect of this relationship? Why have you come together, or why are you getting together and how can you utilize this situation to free yours'elf from karmic burdens of the past and move on into the future feeling freer.

Questions about business, finances, job and career are also favorable in terms of getting what you desire in those areas, but the question is, why do you desire it? And what are you going to do with the success and money you obtain? How do you use what you achieve without creating more karmic burdens for yours'elf that you will have to spend another life undoing? Getting what you want is one thing, and wanting what you get another, but making the most of both in a positive way that moves you toward your destiny and quickens your pace is far more valuable than any material benefit.

When you are asking about health and healing, the prospects are very favorable for healing. However, it is most likely that the illness, disease or ailment is a long standing one, has its roots in the past, probably past lives, and needs to be dealt with in a shamanic fashion, which means that it will not be enough to heal the physical body but one will need to work on the psychological body as well for it is odds on that this problem is of a karmic origin. First, rid yours'elf of or advise others to eliminate bad habits that just perpetuate the problem. Look toward the future and strive toward a healthier life. This will serve you and others well.

And if you were making inquiries about your magical and spiritual life, the prospects are good for fulfilling your wishes and your magic, as long as your wishes involve clearing away past karma, purifying yours'elf and making way for a better future without the unnecessary baggage of an inflated ego and its desires. This is good magic, and surely to your benefit, although sacrificing one's cherished prejudices and habits may take a bit of effort.

THE COIN OF THE REALM

Having the Small Stone fall in the inner dimensions of the Coin of the Realm indicates that one will be receiving a burst of energy from the realms of the spirit. Since it is the Small Stone, this energy will be limited either in the amount given or the duration that it lasts or perhaps will come with certain restrains, restrictions or directives attached to it so that one is obligated to use it in a particular way. So, take this energy and do something good with it, something important to further your progress and the advancement of others. If you are not given direct indications of how it should be used, trust your dreams, visions or intuition, even your spontaneous imagination. But make the most of it while it lasts for it is of a limited nature.

If you are making an inquiry about love, romance, relationship, your social life or a friendship, this position of

113

the Small Stone can denote a short period of increased activity in your social life, especially in relation to those with whom one has a magical connection. It is also possible that someone will appear in your life for a brief time bearing a message from the spirit world, or who will participate in your magic for a short time. Make the most of this opportunity for it will filter down into the material world and shed blessings upon your relationships in general. But don't be fooled into thinking it will last, except in the vibrations it creates as you do the magic, which may resonate through your life for years to come.

When you have a question about business, finances, job or career success or your future prosperity, this is a very good and favorable response that indicates that you will soon receive a sign about your future and your success and it will probably come in a form of a gift of some sort. Contemplate the nature of the gift and the way that it comes for in that will be an indication of the message that is being sent to you beyond the mere blessing of the gift itself. But know that the Coin of the Realm is always essentially favorable for one's prosperity even if it is limited as it is by the Small Stone. It is also possible with the Small Stone that there are a few things one must take care of, to get out of way, before one receives the greater benefit that one desires. First, one must clear and set the table before one sits down to the feast.

If you are asking about health and healing, this position of the Small Stone is very good for a brief period, a small window of opportunity one might say, for making real progress in one's health or one's healing ability. It is a good time to make changes to one's diet or to take up a regimen of exercise as long as these are not radical changes. It is much better to do small things, incremental adjustments, rather than attempt to alter one's life habits entirely and all at once. A step at a time is advised.

114

And if you are making inquiries about your spiritual and magical life and path, then this is a boon for you. You are surely blessed and while this will not mean a large change in your life, it does indicate real progress. It is unlikely, for instance, to be the movement and initiation unto a new level of being and development; however, it does indicate a short period of rapid progress on the level that you are currently mastering. Thus, this brings increased Mastery and Adeptship, and that is surely a wonderful thing for you.

THE FEATHER OF TRUTH TELLING

When the Smaller Stone falls into the inner regions of the Feather of Truth Telling it is a sign that the facts of one's karma and fate will be made clear. You needn't wonder why such and such is happening, or why you are currently stuck, or why you are compelled toward this or that, because the reality of the situation will be revealed to you. Since this is the inner realm, this information will come to you from the spirit world, in terms of a dream, vision, intuition or synchronicity. Heed these communications from the spirits for they are striving to explain things to you and help you understand, for it is only by accepting and understanding the truth that we can act to change things for the better.

If you were asking about love, romance, relationship, marriage or friendship, this placement of the Small Stone indicates that there are issues from the past that bear upon the present circumstances. If one is to progress in the relationship, these issues have to be addressed and spoken to, about, acknowledged or dealt with in some fashion, otherwise they will haunt the relationship into the future, if they have not been doing so already. These ghosts of the past need to be exorcised. Really, exorcised. A bit of necromancy and necromagery would not be uncalled for.

When inquiring about business, finances, job and career, this position of the Small Stone indicates that one needs to seek the truth in the past. The answer to your question resides in what has come before, what has led up to this situation. In order to move forward and progress, it surely helps to know what has brought you to this moment, the direction things have come from and thus are traveling in and the limitations that the past has placed upon the situation. This is not a good sign for money and career directly, but if you apply yours'elf to understanding the forces that you have to deal with, you will know what you need to do to move things in the direction you desire. Although, perhaps the first thing is just slowly removing the obstructions that have attended this situation, like baggage filled with unnecessary things, for there is likely to be debt or other responsibilities that need to be addressed before you progress onward.

As to questions about health and healing, one is dealing with long term issues, Post Traumatic Stress Syndrome, or congenital difficulties, inherited traits, or issues arising from someone's lifelong habits. One may heal ones'elf or help heal another, but if these issues, which in the inner circle are primarily of a habitual and psychological nature, aren't addressed, the dis-ease will merely arise again. It is important to treat the source of the disease, which is essentially karmic and spiritual in nature, and not merely the symptoms.

And when your inquiries have to do with your spiritual and magical life and path, this fall of the Small Stone indicates that you should do everything that you can to clear away your karma as you understand it to be but also to clear away any residual attachment you have to things of the past that no longer have any real relevance for your life. This is your spiritual life, your life in the magic, and your true being is one of magic and light. Release your desires, your attachments to the insignificant aspects of the world, your need to prove yours'elf to others, your kneejerk reactions to the prejudices and misconceptions of others concerning you and your magic. Release it all and move forward into the realms of magical fulfillment.

THE MAGIC MIRROR OF REFLECTION

If the Small Stone lands in the inner realms of the Magic Mirror of Reflection it is a definite sign that one needs to examine one's part and responsibility in what is going on or what is about to happen to make sure that one isn't dragging irrelevant and unrelated issues into the situation that have more to do with ones'elf than with anything that is really going on. Do you have your response prepared before the person even speaks because you have imagined what they are going to say and aren't really listening to what they are actually trying to communicate? Clear your mind, purify your heart and be open to the simple reality that is before you, then you can proceed into the future with understanding and a much greater chance of success.

Questions about love, romance, relationship, marriage, one's social life or friendship are positively aspected here if you are certain that you are not carrying the baggage of the past into the relationship and certainly not into the future. Let that old stuff go. This is especially true of your attitudes and reactions that no longer serve you. Does the person you are involved with or dealing with in this situation remind you of someone from your past? Perhaps looks like that person? They are not the same person and while their presence may remind you of that person, like the sound of something that sounds like a dentist's drill reminds you of the dentist, this is a different relationship. Let it develop purely and on its own. Don't bring unnecessary past experiences and perhaps traumas into it that have no real relation or relevance to this situation. Because this is the inner realm, you can use your magic to clear the air more easily and quickly than you can transform the material world. Burn some sage, wave your feathers around, clear the psychic atmosphere and move into the future feeling freer.

Inquiries about business, finances, job, and career success suggest that one consider the astral atmosphere behind this issue. Not what appears to be going on, but what magics helped formulate this movement in your life, or perhaps lack of movement. Believe us when we tell you, there is magic behind what is going on. Perhaps it is the fulfillment of old magics you put into motion ages ago. Surely, other people's magics are involved as well. How do you get them to harmonize and work things out to everyone's benefit? For unless that happens, the situation will be in perpetual conflict on the astral planes bringing one obstruction after another. Only when you move things toward a future that profits everyone will all the various magicians involved lend their support, even if they don't consciously know what is going on, which most folks don't, for their magic is instinctual rather than truly conscious.

If you are asking about health and healing, then reflect upon the powers you possess for healing. You have made it this far, and thus have healed again and again. You can use that same energy to heal once more or to share it with others so that they might heal their own s'elves. Naturally, you wish to remove any images and ideas that interfere with your healing and healing abilities. Be positive. This is a meditation. Every time a negative thought comes up about your health or your ability to heal, note it and let it pass. Chant an inner mantra of healing energy. Put your powers into the positive and healing aspects of your life and let the healing continue. Increase your healing powers with regular practice.

When the question has to with your magical and spiritual path and progress, it is important that you reflect upon your entire magical life as far back as you can remember it. This is a good time for recapitulation and the examination of your life from its earliest magical stirrings and even back further into your previous lives and incarnations. Remember, your early life, up until your first Saturn Return at about age 28 to 30 is an encapsulated version of your previous lives. Rather like televisions shows that start with: previously on ____. So, how did you get here? And where do you wish to go? Answering these questions will tell you how to proceed.

THE SACK OF GIVING

If the Small Stone falls in the inner dimensions of the Sack of Giving it is an indication that making offerings to the spirits, even if these gifts are limited by your circumstances, will prove beneficial if your offering is sincere. It is genuine feeling and intention that is important in the realms of the spirit not the material value of the gift. While some people put out milk and honey or other gifts for the fair folk, and others offer incense or food and flowers to the various spirits and demi-gods, remember that these spirits also manifest through the world so giving to others who remind you of these spirits is also an effective means of making offerings to them. Find someone who has the qualities of the spirit you seek to evoke and give them a gift sincerely in place of the spirit with that spirit in your mind and heart and this will be the same as gifting to the spirit hirs'elf.

When you are asking about love, romance, relationship, marriage, friendship or one's social life, this position of the Small Stone favors putting bits of magic in the places and settings where you wish to meet people or where you regularly meet with these individuals. You can give gifts to the individuals if you wish, but again being in the inner realm this is really about making offerings to the spirits. Create magical items, such as rocks, crystals, amulets or even spirit papers (paper upon which you have inscribed the sigil of a particular spirit), energize them with magic and hide them in these places of meeting or possibility. This should prove effective for your needs.

As to inquiries about business, finances, job and career success and prosperity in general, the Small Stone with the Sack of Giving indicates that small gifts, rather than large ostentatious ones, will be effective. Also, small investments are favored but not large ones. And thus, it follows that small, regular magics, little rituals and quick but frequent magical circles will prove to be more efficacious than one large and long ceremony. Here we are creeping up on success because making a swift run at it will not work at this time. This is incremental magic and while each bit may seem small and insignificant, they will add up to something great.

Questions as to health and healing will benefit from small and fairly persistent healing efforts. Diet and exercise are of course important, but again because this is the inner realm we are looking more at the power of energetic working upon the astral planes and the planes of spirit. Exercise your magic, give the spirits a steady and wholesome diet of healing and positive thinking. This will alter things for the better for you and everyone who is involved with you or close to you.

If you have questions regarding your spiritual path and magical life, then give to the spirits. This is the time to invest your energy into the spirit realms. Do your magic. You can try to shift things all at once, but this is unlikely to have much effect. It is like a cup you are filling with water, it will just spill over and be wasted in this case and it is quite possible you just don't have all that much energy at this time to invest. So, do no more than you reasonably can, considering the limitation of your circumstances and personal energy. Small bits of magic will actually be more effective in the long run than great endeavors. But, put out the energy, little though it may be. This is the right thing to do and will move you surely toward the higher reaches of illumination and enlightened being toward which you aspire.

THE PHILTRE OF TRUE LOVE

The Philtre of True Love ever acts to unite one with those who are a right fit and here in the inner dimensions, it has particularly soulful and spiritual and thus also magical significance. In other words, it brings together those who can accomplish the Great Work together, who will further thems'elves, each other and all about them, and thus shift the world toward a higher and better vibration. The Small Stone, however, indicates that there are things in your life, most likely arising from the past, and quite likely in the lives of those who you will encounter, that need to be purified before you can move determinedly in to the future.

If you have a question about love, romance, marriage, relationship, friendship or your social life, this fall of the Stone indicates that you are very likely to encounter those with whom you have some "history". This is the time and opportunity to forgive, to let bygones be bygones, to clear the air so that you, at least, if not they, can more on into the future without a psychic atmosphere of ill wishes, regrets and hard feelings following you. And if they are unable to make the transition, at least you will have made it yours'elf and can finally and fully leave them behind. If they wish to wallow in the past that is their business but it is no longer yours if you are genuinely determined to move on and release these past threads of connection. If you are asking about new relationships, this position is very promising if you have released the energies of the past.

If you had an inquiry about business, finances, job or career energy or possibilities for prosperity in general, this position is very good for forming new connections to spirits

121

and allies on the astral planes of being that can help you with these intentions. However, it is even more potent for renewing spirit connections from the past, of clarifying your connection to the spirits and demi-gods you have encountered or been involved with in your past, even if you are merely biding them goodbye as you move on into the new. Farewell gifts and messages of praise will be appreciated even if you are abandoning your previous faith for something that will prove to be more prosperous for you. You don't need to hate the past or denigrate it to leave it for something better.

For issues that involve health and healing, the answer here is to spend time with healing spirits. Find demi-gods or other personages who have a healing reputation who can aid you to free yours'elf from the issues, particularly psychological issues, that affect your attitude and outlook on life and spend time with them, purifying yours'elf or those who have come to you for your healing help and freeing yours'elf and others from the enculturation of your earlier life that is often derived from the experiences of the past. Visualize healing yours'elf fully. See yours'elf entirely healthy. Become complete and whole.

As to inquiries that specifically are about one's spiritual and magical path and direction, this placement of the Small Stone decidedly says that one should let go of the connections to the past and move toward those that can help one advance, those who, most likely, are more advanced on the path and to seek their aid and association. In this placement of the Small Stone, one simply lets the past go, which is to say one doesn't reflect upon the past or even act to purify it, one just moves on and allows the past to fade away into insignificance. By putting energy into the new, one accumulates numerous experiences on this higher level of manifest being and the past becomes smaller and smaller in comparison until it is but a distant memory remembered only for cautionary purposes like a dead-end sign saying don't go this way again.

THE PHIAL OF EVERLASTING YOUTH

When one receives the Small Stone in the inner circle of the Phial of Everlasting Youth, one is called to examine one's upbringing, one's earliest life and perhaps even intuit those things that influenced one's life before one began to think clearly or even to remember. There is something there, isn't there? Deep in your heart, your soul, the unconscious aspect of your mind? You need to look within, but more than that you need to feel within. Doing this will provide the answers you seek.

Inquiries about love, romance, marriage, relationship and friendship and one's social life in general, find response in looking at one's habits, especially habits that one has developed from one's early life but also in examining one's outlook on life formulated at that time. This is the inner realm so it often has more to do with magical, spiritual and psychological development than moves one might be able to make in the world. Get your inner life in order, clear up the things from your past and particularly your formative years that have been haunting you and limiting you in relationship, examine your enculturated attitudes about marriage, romance and friendship and start afresh, then things will develop as you desire.

Questions about business, finances, job or career are answered by looking at one's work habits and one's attitude toward and about money from one's earliest life. Needless to say, one's early life is a recapitulation of previous lifetimes and thus one can look at it to see one's development through successive lives. In doing so, one can understand the karmic limitations that one has encountered as evidenced and reflected in that developmental period. Thus said, it should be clear that the solution to any problems in the financial arena in your life are ultimately ones that can be resolved through magic and most particularly the magic of your own outlook, spirit and attitude.

If you are inquiring about health or healing, this fall of the Small Stone is very powerful for recalling your youth and using the sense of being young and vibrant as a healing vibration. If you were sickly when you were young and overcame it, be assured that you will heal again. If you never quite mastered your health, look to your past to understand the karmic aspects that may be behind this condition. If you can see the truth in this fate, you may also find a way to improve your health through energy work and magic, but first you must understand the true source of the ailment, which here in the inner circle would not be germs or a bodily disorder, which are really only symptoms, but the spiritual energy behind the disorder. What lesson does this suffering teach? How does it move your spirit toward greater power and illuminated being? Perhaps your destiny is to be a healer and this illness a challenge you set in your life in order to strengthen your healing ability.

As regards to questions about your spiritual life and magical path, this position of the Small Stone very clearly indicates that one needs to get back to the enthusiastic, child-like attitude with which one first started one's path, when one was open and ready to absorb and try new things and to perpetuate that attitude and approach to one's path and magic. There may be things, habits that one developed in one's early exploration of magic that need to be corrected and changed, eliminated or let go, but make doing so easy. Don't struggle with these habits. Let them fade naturally as you enthusiastically move into a new era in your spiritual life and concentrate on your positive vision of your life in Elfin and your powers as a wielder of magic.

The Outer Circle:
The Elf Horns of Calling

When the Small Stone falls beyond the outer circle, be very careful. There are situations and people that want to keep you stuck in this mess forever. Don't be tempted. Don't engage. Let them continue in the mire if that is their desire. It is unlikely that you will be able to help them and it is probably best if you just get on with your life and leave them to their dysfunction.

And instead, if the Small Stone lands within the Outer Circle, then you read the corresponding treasure below:

THE ORB OF HEALING

Getting the Small Stone in the outer realms of the Orb of Healing is a wonderful indication that things will be improving, particularly that things that have been wrong a long time, or past difficulties, or long-term problems will finally be resolved. There still may be a bit of effort required to clear one's karma but the prospects for successfully doing so are great and it is likely that something that has been bothering you or interfering with your life for ages will, at last, begin to fade away.

Questions concerning love, romance, marriage, relationship and friendship are also favored for improvement. In long term relationships, you may find people, finally, forgiving each other for past sorrows and trespasses. Obstacles that have been in the way of new relationship will also be falling away so that one may get on with one's life and find those who will be healing and beneficial to one's life and development. Whatever the problems have been, resolution is coming and one can breathe a sigh of relief.

Inquiries about business, finances, job and career will

similarly be rewarded with a new opportunity to release ones'elf from the burdens and difficulties of the past, of limitations that have been holding one back, and of people who have been obstructing one's path. There will be an opening of the way so one may proceed into the future with confidence. Since this is the outer dimensions of the Orb of Healing, it is particularly good for things that involve the material world and material acquisition.

If you are asking about health and healing, clearly you will be pleased to know that issues that have been plaguing you for ages, perhaps your entirely life, will finally find relief and will gradually heal. The Orb of Healing is especially strong and powerful in this instance and you may proceed with your healing efforts with increased confidence and assurance that things are moving toward improvement.

Spiritual and magical questions are blessed with the fact that one's karma, or part of one's karma, is being cleared and purified. One may very well feel lighter, brighter and more powerful and potent as an individual. Don't overdo things. Give it time to heal, but also don't go wild and create more negative karma to deal with. Still, some issues from the past will depart and new potentialities for your path in magic will be entering your life. You can stop looking over your shoulder and gaze into the future with greater assurance.

THE WAND OF WISHING

Receiving the Small Stone in the outer dimensions of the Wand of Wishing is very favorable for obtaining what you wish and desire in a material way, but you need to ask yours'elf in procuring what you desire are you decreasing or increasing your karmic debt. Also, in a very simple practical way, how much stuff do you really need? Is this just more junk that you will have to store or carry around? Is this really useful to you? Does getting this genuinely serve you, or is it just another weight to bear?

If you are making an inquiry concerning love, romance, relationship, marriage or friendship, this fall of the Small Stone is favorable for acquiring your wishes in terms of love but it is quite possible that getting involved with this person or persons will necessitate a lot of material acquisition as well. There is karma here, but mostly having to do with the use or misuse of material goods. Because it is in the place of the Wand of Wishing, you are in luck, but the Small Stone may make this whole relationship or process of developing this relationship a load to bear and you may just happen to find yours'elf saddled with someone else's junk as well, or perhaps, having to move all their stuff around. Still, maybe it will be worth it. Some relationships are.

Financial issues, questions about business, job or career are very well aspected here because it is the outer realms of the Wand of Wishing and is powerful for obtaining any kind of material goods and success. However, remember that this is also an opportunity for you to help clear yours'elf of the karma of the past. If you use what you obtain well, if you distribute it wisely, then you will be securing your future in a positive way that is unlikely to create unnecessary and unwanted problems in the future. Karma always seems to be about the past, but it troubles the present and casts shadows upon the future, like dark clouds on the horizon. Have a future of clear skies and rainfall that creates rainbows.

As to questions about health and healing, this position is quite positive for physical healing. However, if the problem stems from the past, most likely in terms of bad habits, it is important that you cease doing the things that have created this situation. And being the Small Stone, while it is favorable for healing and, in fact, healing is almost guaranteed, the process of healing and thus establishing health, may take a bit of time. There are issues to be dealt with. There is a process to be followed. There is a step by step progression of healing efforts and energy and it is important to see things through completely. Rather like the doctor telling you to take a prescription until it runs out, so too, this healing needs a full cycle of development and effort. And remember health is not a one-time deal; a regular practice of healing and the establishment of a healthy lifestyle is vital to continuing health.

This placement is not primarily about one's spiritual life and magical path, however, anything to do with freeing ones'elf of the burdens and debts of the past and of purifying ones'elf by paying off one's karma, so to speak, affects one's spiritual and magical development. But ask yours'elf, what do you wish your life to be like in the material world? And is that in harmony with your ideals, spiritual aspirations and principles? Does it help you become more powerful as the enchanter, magician, witch, wizard, shaman, you know yours'elf to be? And in becoming such, what duties and responsibilities will you shoulder in terms of the world and the people in the world?

THE COIN OF THE REALM

When the Small Stone lands in the outer reaches of the Coin of the Realm, one is likely to find small gifts and benefits coming one's way. The Coin of the Realm always favors prosperity but due to the Small Stone it is limited in nature, either because of karma/fate or merely the cyclic nature of energy, which with the Small Stone is nearly always at low tide. So, don't expect a great deal, however, these small things may add up to something appreciable in time and even though the energy is limited, this is still a positive outcome for you and much to your benefit and wellbeing.

If you have an inquiry about love, romance, marriage, relationship, friendship or your social life in general, this position of the Small Stone favors an exchange of gifts. Give small presents, but most of all, reciprocate any gift or positive energy anyone puts your way. Don't accept anything without giving something in return. This is the most important aspect of this position. Give back. Even if it is a little thing. Even if you can't give as much or offer the quality they gave you, reciprocate.

Questions that have to do with business, finances, job and career are well aspected here because the Coin of the Realm rules business and money. Again, the Small Stone may limit the abundance you receive. It may make it come in bits and pieces rather than all at once, but the profit will come and this is all to the good. Small investments may also be considered, but this position doesn't favor a large output of money and, more than likely, you will not have the wherewithal to invest a great deal anyway.

When asking about health or healing this placement of the Small Stone is very favorable for healing but slowly and surely. Small sessions of healing will be more effective than an outpouring of a lot of energy. It is better to approach health and healing on a constant day to day basis than to simply think one potent healing ceremony will do the trick. It may, but only for a limited period of time. Slow but sure progress is much more likely to have permanent results than a major surge of energy.

As to inquiries concerning one's spiritual and magical life, path and progress, this fall of the Small Stone denotes gifts of magic coming to you from the spirit realms. Perhaps you will find a feather or some other magical object. Perhaps a bit of money on the street. This is all to let you know that the Shining Ones support and nurture you and are doing all that they can to help to deal with the material plane as you progress toward initiation on the subtler planes of being. It is possible that some synchronicity will occur. Some meaningful and unexpected coincidence. Whatever happens, look at it carefully, as though it is a dream or a vision you need to analyze and understand. The truth will be revealed there.

THE FEATHER OF TRUTH TELLING

If the Small Stone falls in the outer circle of the Feather of Truth Telling there is sure to be some revelations about what is going on, what is behind what is going on, and what people's real intentions and motives are behind what they are doing, beyond what they claim they are up to. It is quite possible that knowing the truth will help you truly understand people, for it is not just the current facts that will come into focus, or even the immediate past, but what is behind it all and this may provide some real insight into the situation that you can use to find a path out of it, if that is what you need, and on to greater success.

Concerning questions relative to love, romance, marriage, relationship and friendship, this position of the Small Stone may produce revelations of a personal nature. Don't be surprised if people start confiding secrets to you that they haven't told to anyone else, or to few others. And you, yours'elf, may find that you have an urge to unburden yours'elf, share your inner feelings, clear your conscience of the past and its regrets so that you may move on into the future with a clearer heart and mind.

Business, finances, job and career inquiries will also find response in the past. Whatever you ask, the answer is in what formed itself into the present. Look to the source. Examine what is behind this situation and you will uncover the means to make it better. We expect you wish greater financial success, progress in your career, perhaps a raise, an improved situation and prosperity. Then, listen well. The Truth is about to be uncovered. You may not like it entirely, but it will answer your question and you can then act appropriately.

Are you asking about health and healing? There are issues from the past that you must deal with, but since they will now come to the fore, it will be hard to ignore them. Take this opportunity and do what you can to promote healing in yours'elf and others. Karma is often spoken of as a debt one must pay, a burden one's must bear, a limitation that can only be purified through sacrifice. But here we are speaking of healing your karma or someone else's karma. Since this is the outer realm, this will take more than good wishes, a positive attitude and positive thinking. This will demand real action in the material world. But, healing can occur. However, first comes understanding.

As to your spiritual and magical life, and questions regarding them, this response indicates that magical and spiritual secrets, perhaps quite ancient secrets of power and mystery will be revealed to you. This, of course, sounds like a wondrous thing. And surely it is. However, it also brings tremendous responsibility. Are you truly ready for so much power? Are you prepared to use the ancient secrets well? You may exult inside, feeling quite good about yours'elf for having been offered these secrets to power, and that is not a bad thing, but a more sober approach to these powers may be in order. Certainly, this is so as you initially begin to use them. First, compose yours'elf and then proceed into this new future and greater realm of activity with all its increasing possibilities.

THE MAGIC MIRROR OF REFLECTION

If the Small Stone lands in the outer dimensions of the Magic Mirror of Reflection, some truth will be revealed about your life and the reasons for the obstructions and limitations that you may be currently encountering. Also, you may find it to be very revealing if you listen to what people say about you and understand that they are really talking about themselves. You are the Magic Mirror of Reflection and they are seeing themselves in you, projecting their issues upon you and understanding you and quite possibly judging you from their own inner perspective, experience and viewpoint rather than understanding you from your own point of view and experience.

When the Small Stone falls in this position in response to questions about love, romance, marriage, relationship, friendship and one's social life, it suggests that you would do well to study your interactions with others carefully. Are you getting what you want out of these relationships? Are they progressing as you wish them to? With the Small Stone progress will be limited and slow, to be sure, but there still should be some progress. If not, then examine why you seemed to be blocked. Is this due to you and your approach, attitudes and behavior, or is this really something to do with the other person and the way they are? When someone says to you the problem isn't you, it's me ... take them at their word. Ultimately, it is them. And yet, examine your own life and approach thoroughly, for there may be things that you can improve that will help with future relationships and social encounters.

If you had an inquiry about business, finances, job or career or your future prosperity and prospects, this landing of the Small Stone tells to you examine the situation carefully before proceeding. Don't invest in anything until you have gone over the books carefully, read relevant reviews, investigated the situation down to its core. Keep your expectations low. This is unlikely to bring great financial or career success with this placement of the Small Stone but slow progress can be made, preparatory moves can be set up, but this is not the time for a major push or effort of any kind.

Questions relative to health and healing require reflection on the background and source of the ills one is seeking to cure but also a humble and modest as well as realistic appraisal of one's healing abilities is in order. You may not be an all-powerful person who can heal every disease instantly, but still you have healing powers, however large or small, and it is important that you exercise them so they will grow and become more potent. It is possible you are dealing with congenital diseases or issues that have been building up for a long time and are unlikely to be cured quickly but still do the healing work and let time do its healing as well.

And if you are asking about your spiritual and magical life and progress upon your path, this placement of the Small Stone urges you to consider and examine your life in the world as it relates to your spiritual life. These are not separate things. Your life as a spirit, as an elfae enchanter, magician, witch, wizard or whatever, is intimately tied up with your manifestation in this world. If your magical life only takes place upon the astral and imaginal planes and dimensions, then consider how you may materialize your spiritual life as you proceed through this world. Make your magic real. Live your elfin life. Progress is likely to be slow, but steady effort will bring results.

THE SACK OF GIVING

When the Small Stone falls in the outer realms of the Sack of Giving, one is called to be generous, as generous as one can be, especially toward those one may have harmed or been prejudiced against in the past. This is a form of unannounced and unspoken reparation. This is a matter of making amends as best one is able. Give what you can. What you can afford. This is not a matter of giving till it hurts, as the saying goes, but giving till it heals. And especially, it is about combining your own past feelings of hurt and grievance to the money or gifts that you donate. If you are giving your old clothes to a charity, for instance, use magic to attach your past karma to the clothes so they become a form of scapegoat. Scapegoats, in the past, where symbolically loaded with people sins and let go into the wilderness. Let your past karma go, along with those material things you no longer need that others may make good use of.

If you are asking about love, romance, marriage, relationship, friendship or your social life, you may find that bringing small gifts and offerings will be well received. Don't overdo it. Don't be ostentatious. That would probably not work out well and would tend to arouse suspicion more than friendship. Instead, give small things that the person wants or can use and do this every time you visit them or they visit you. Pay close attention to their interests and endeavor to make your giving in keeping with their inner wishes. Instill a small charm into the gifts, just a wee bit of magic, not to control them but to soothe, nurture and attract them. On the other hand, if you are asking: will so and so ever leave me alone, give them a gift as well, also charmed so that they will find other people and places much more attractive and wander off out of your personal demesne of Elfin.

Inquiries about business, finances, job and career or one's future prosperity require a bit of investment. Very small investment. Nothing large at all, and probably since you have gotten the Small Stone here, it is unlikely you can afford large investment at this time. But small infusions of money or resources into your future is a good thing. Even better is a regular savings of some sort. Save up for the future. Add little bits of money as regularly as you can. Again, nothing much, perhaps just put your change into a jar each time you have some. But save up and imagine your future success as you do so. In this way, you can watch your prosperity grow.

If your question concerns health or healing for yours'elf or someone else, this is a good time to give gifts of healing. Do small things for yours'elf or others that will heal their spirit and their soul and thereby help heal the body. Comfort foods might be in order, but only in the most limited fashion. Remember this is the Small Stone. The importance of setting limits upon indulgence cannot be underestimated. Yet, if one is overly strict upon ones'elf or others, the spirit and the body will rebel. Thus, small indulgences are to be allowed, and may prove quite beneficial, in disciplined fashion.

When asking about your spiritual path and magical life and progress, the Small Stone falling in this place denotes that one needs to foster and nurture those beneath one. Those that are struggling to lift thems'elves up. And particularly those who are very much like you once were, or are dealing with issues that you dealt with when you were on their level of initiation. Doing this will prove beneficial to you and to your progress which will then have a more solid and wider base of support and you can proceed more quickly, easily and surely into those realms of magic and spirit that you desire to enter.

THE PHILTRE OF TRUE LOVE

With the landing of the Small Stone in the outer realms of the Philtre of True Love, one is advised to do small spells, little magics, in order to increase the feelings of good will and frasority (combines fraternity and sorority and is an elven word and concept) among those around one and those with whom one would like to become involved or associated. Remember, with the Small Stone one needs to limit ones'elf. S'elf discipline is vital here. These enchantments are like perfume. If you put on too much it will repel rather than attract. Subtle is better. Just a whiff of mystery will do the trick.

If you had a question about love, romance, relationship, your social life or friendship, the Small Stone landing in this place represents good fortune in love but in a small or limited way. Or, it may be that it will come in bits and pieces or will be something great that is coming, but it will be a short while before it arrives. The important thing is to know that things are moving in your favor as far as love and relationship are concerned. Do not try to hurry things faster than they are inclined to go. Let Nature take its course and all will work out to your benefit and satisfaction.

If you had an inquiry about business, finances, job or career success, perhaps about your future prosperity in general, then this fall of the Small Stone is very good for establishing good connections and contacts, for creating an atmosphere of mutual trust and liking, but it is not directly favorable for money. Yet, good connections can lead to opportunities and that is what we are looking at here. One thing leads to the other, so while the money may not be immediately forthcoming it can be the result of your actions if you play your cards right. Shore up your business relationships and prosperity will follow.

As to questions of health and healing, perhaps of longevity, when the Small Stone lands here significance is placed upon being around and finding those who are positive and healing for you. Don't let people drag you down. Find right company so you may proceed on the path in a positive way and seek out those who are healing so you may also heal and in doing so help others to heal. And remember, while you don't really need someone's permission to project healing energy toward them, you can't, you just can't heal anyone who doesn't really wish to heal. Make your energy count. Don't waste it upon those who don't really want it.

Your spiritual and magical life and path are both benefited when the Small Stone falls in this position, if you keep in

136

mind that true spiritual advancement tends to be slow. Fast development and instant elevations are not inclined to last. You must make these powers your own and that is best done when you are in the company of your kindred who are also striving to advance on the path. However, because it is the Small Stone, you are unlikely to be able to spend as much time with them as you desire. Or perhaps you will connect with those with whom you can really harmonize, but they live at a distance and you can only see them now and again or only connect through the internet. Still, make the most of what is possible and continue on and this will prove to be to their benefit and to yours.

THE PHIAL OF EVERLASTING YOUTH

If the Small Stone lands in the outer dimension of the Phial of Everlasting Youth, it is a sign that things may be difficult in the beginning but that if one perseveres everything should work out in the long run. None-the-less, pay close attention to these early movements for all that follows will unfold from them and you don't wish to belabor your efforts with unwanted problems that will appear again if you don't deal with them or act to avoid them from the very beginning. Thus, move carefully. Make sure everything is taken care of and proceed into the future with assurance that if you are thorough now, you will have much less to deal with later on and this is all to the good.

When asking about love, romance, marriage, relationship, friendship and one's social life, this position of the Small Stone is favorable for new relationships or a new start to old relationships, or a renewal of relationship and friendship, if one enters the situation with genuineness and sincerity. Hidden agendas will eventually come out to haunt you, if they exist. Be sure that for your own part you are approaching this relationship in an honest and pure way, otherwise there will be difficulties later on. If the others who are involved are not totally sincere or have unseen motives, this will also come out in time and prove to be a problem, but it will mostly be their problem if you have been honest in your approach.

In regard to questions about business, finances, job or career, this fall of the Small Stone indicates that one is probably trying to progress, perhaps even to invest, but with inadequate funds or energy to do so. Be wise. Don't borrow more than you can pay back. Be reasonable. Work within your budget. Be practical. Move forward with your design but in a conservative fashion. It may bring but small success at first but this is a stepping stone into the future, whereas if you attempt too much too soon, you will merely find yours'elf being washed away in the river of failed and overweening ambition.

If your inquiry has to do with health and healing, this placement of the Small Stone is a good sign that healing will occur, but that one needs to continue the healing work even if one appears to get better immediately. Don't let the disappearance of the symptoms fool you into thinking that there is no more work to do. This ailment may be deeper than you think and may have its roots in the past. Continue your energy work on yours'elf or others for a good while after things have seemed to get better. This is about a fundamental transference of energy and the creation of health and longevity and both those things are long term endeavors.

Questions in reference to your magical and spiritual life and path are favored here even though this is the outer circle of manifestation, which tends, for the most part, to be less spiritually oriented and more about practical materialization. Yet, there is a good possibility that one is entering a new era of one's magical development, and it is likely that one is coming into contact with new people who will bring fresh ideas and magic into one's life. You could be joining or getting involved with a new coven, or as we elves call it, a new vortex. But, be careful, don't drag your old habits into this new arena and wind up making it exactly what occurred before. Don't repeat the same mistakes you did previously, and be cautious about getting involved with the same sort of people over and over again as some people do when they choose mates that abuse them, only to leave that person and find another abuser. Be sure this is an authentic step up for you, a true entry into a new realm of magical and spiritual development and then all will turn out for the best.

"Elves love surprises, thus while we often have the power to look into the future, we don't always choose to do so."

"Elves see science as a form of wizardry. It is true that many of those who believe in science don't believe in magic, but nearly all magicians believe in science and elven magi think science is quite magical."

"The Elves say:
We are soul and spirit dancing together.
The voice in your head is not you but other.
Listen for it has much to say.
But the silence is even greater for there
resides the echo of all that is, was and can be."

Part Three

. . . Feathers

Like the sticks and the bones, the feathers could possibly extend over more than one area. The quill point would indicate where the question is heading and the feathered end the background and origins of the issues concerning the question. Also, feathers will tend to fall on the inside or outside of the feather. What does the inside represent to you? What does the outside mean? On the bird, one tends to shed water and be mostly what the outside world sees and the other, the inside, is closest to the bird's body. How may this affect your reading?

Chapter 5:
The Light Feather

The Light colored Feather symbolizes one's blessings in this situation, particularly large blessings, important blessings that may alter the situation dramatically. It is a sign of great luck and the grace of the Shining Ones.

The Inner Circle:
The Torch of the Eternal
Silver Flame of Elfin

With the landing of the Light Feather significantly touching the image of the torch in the inner circle, you can count yours'elf lucky, for you are truly blest, are guided by the Shining Ones and need only heed the dreams, signs and omens they send to you. What luck!

THE ORB OF HEALING

If the Light Feather lands in the inner dimensions of the Orb of Healing then surely things will get better for you overall. This denotes a period of progress on all fronts, but most especially in healing or repairing any situation that has had problems or is currently in need of improvement. While one may move forward with this and venture into new realms and directions in one's life, its power really is in fixing what has broken or setting right what has gone astray. And because this is the Light Feather, this should be relatively easy to do for the spirits are with you.

When you have questions about love, romance, marriage, friendship and your social life, this fall of the Light Feather is great for renewing relationships, setting right what may have gone wrong, working on what has been spoiled (as the *I Ching* says), and setting a new, more fruitful and productive course for old relationships. Make amends. Heal the rift that may have arisen between you and those you cherish. Renew your vows. Revive old relationships. Find new interests together and make progress by repairing what is already working, but just not working quite as well as it may.

If you are inquiring about business, work, finances, career, or the possibility for prosperity in the future, this placement of the Light Feather favors a return on investments made long ago that seemed to have been a loss. Finally, your ship comes in. It may not be a big ship, but it will surely be better than no ship at all and at least it is still afloat when you thought it may have been lost at sea. Any effort to improve the situation you already have going should prove useful and will bring rewards in a relatively short time. You may breathe a sigh of relief.

Questions about health and healing, about your life and health in the future, find a favorable response in as far as an immediate improvement of your health in the present. This is not a bad sign for the future, but not necessarily a good one either. Its emphasis is more on revival and revitalization in the present. If you use this energy now to put forth healing energy, that will surely affect your future, particularly if you make these healing practices a continuing regimen of wellness and rejuvenation.

As to your spiritual and magical life and path, this position of the Light Feather lifts the weary spirit and stirs the soul with wonder. Feel the power of the spirit world, of Elfin or Faerie, radiating into your life and being; and absorb the magic and the enchantment. Spells for your benefit have been cast by the Shining Ones, so stretch out your arms and let them flow over you and into you, lifting you up and carrying you on the winds of Elfin. You're beginning to levitate. Can you feel it?

THE WAND OF WISHING

Getting the Light Feather in the inner circle of the Wand of Wishing is incredibly powerful and a great blessing upon your life. This is the time to make your wishes, but especially wishes for your soulful and spiritual development, the evolution of your spirit through the Universe and through the magical dimensions and not necessarily wishes that have to do with your temporary desires in the material world. This has to do with the advancement of your essential being, what is usually called your higher s'elf, your magical nature and its progress toward life in Elfin and to becoming one of the Shining Ones.

If you were asking about love, romance, relationship, marriage, courtship, or friends, this landing of the Light Feather indicates that all your wishes in their most blessed form will come true. You may not get fulfillment for the desires of your ego impulses, but your true needs will be met as far as relationship and soulful connection and if you are wishing to find your true elfae kindred and companions on the path of magical and spiritual fulfillment then you are definitely on the right track and what you need will come to you in due time at precisely the right moment. Of that you can be certain. They may not appear immediately, but they are on the way or you are being drawn to them and you just need to continue to desire and search for them, for that desire is the compass and magnet by which you will find them, as you will surely do.

If you had an inquiry about business, money, work or career, this position of the Light Feather will fulfill your desires and plans in as much as they are in accord with your true needs and development as a magical spirit. If an avenue closes to you, it is because you are meant to go in another direction. Everything in the material world is leading you toward where you need to go as an elfae being once you have made a genuine and sincere wish to be and discover your true inner nature and being. All else are just details. Your true career is a magical one, everything else in your life, particularly your life in the financial arena, is just the means of getting there.

When asking questions regarding your health or your healing abilities, this position is fantastic for creating healing in your life and in the life of others. See yours'elf as a powerful healer. See yours'elf as having the ability to bring someone back to life who has just died. Imagine yours'elf with miraculous powers, for that is the direction that you are destined to go. You just need to continue to do your healing work as best you are able and your powers will continue to grow.

As to your spiritual and magical life, that is what this position is all about. Do your magic. This is surely the time to do so. If you wish for something in the material world, you can certainly do magic to obtain it but remember most things that manifest in that realm are temporary and illusionary; so, keep the big picture in mind and make every little thing that you do a stepping stone toward that greater realization of your elfin being. You are becoming ever more wondrous but it does take effort on your part. So, set your spells, charms and enchantments in motion and let the magic happen.

THE COIN OF THE REALM

The Light Feather's fall into the inner regions of the Coin of the Realm brings luck and blessings upon your life, often in the form of prosperity, which may manifest in the material realms as money or other material goods, but which in these more subtle realms indicate a profusion and abundance of energy, magic and activity. Invest this energy well and it will profit you greatly. Now is the time to make progress toward your magical and spiritual goals, setting a cycle of abundance in motion.

Questions that have to do with love, romance, relationship, marriage, friendship and your social life are well aspected here and you should be receiving benefits in those areas in your life. Not necessarily material goods, but increased love, affection, connection, communion and loving intercourse in all its various forms. These relationships are particularly bountiful when they have spiritual and magical dimensions to them. Help lift each other up and this will bring added benefits in the future.

If you are making inquiries about business, financial success, job or career, then this placement may not be as powerful a response as you may wish except for the fact that the inner workings and connections regarding these things are positively increased. You may not see the results on the material plane for some time to come, but there are hidden powers at work that are seeking to move you in the right direction, fulfill your magic and get you what you need in order to do what you need to do. Have faith, this is actually all in your favor, although that is unlikely to be easily perceived at this time.

When you are posing a question about health or healing then this placement of the Light Feather surely favors healing work and may very well indicate that others have projected healing toward you. A loving mother's prayers will be coming to fruition. The best wishes made for your sake are finding receptive ears among the Shining Ones and surely this will prove to your benefit and wellbeing. In the meantime, continue with your healing practice. This is nearly always a good thing to do.

Your magical and spiritual life are most affected by this fall of the Light Feather. The bounty of spirit and a soulful connection are increased here and you will have all that you need for putting forth the magic and enchantments necessary to bring about your true will in the world. Do you seek Elfin and your elfae kin? They feel you in the etheric planes and are turning their eyes toward you and although they may only see the horizon in their material vision, in their imaginal sight, you are there and thus you will draw ever closer to each other.

THE FEATHER OF TRUTH TELLING

When you receive the Light Feather in the inner realms of Feather of Truth Telling, one is particularly lucky and blest. The resonance of the feathers together awakens profound things in your inner life and while this is mainly a psychological and spiritual event, it will surely have effects in the material realm as well. Because it is the Feather of Truth Telling, this blessing in your life will most likely arrive as a realization, an awakening, a revelation. You may discover something about yours'elf, your direction in life, your spiritual path or some other thing that is important to you, especially in a feeling way. This will be the truth, surely, which may appear painful at first, but it will prove to be to your absolute benefit in time. So, embrace this truth, for it is the key to greater understanding and to mastery upon the subtle planes of being and to moving easily through the realms of Elfin.

If you posed a question to the oracle about love, romance, relationship, marriage, friendship or your social life, this reply indicates that something will be revealed to you, perhaps some secret, in fact, most likely some hidden information in regard to you and others or you and some particular other. This is a good thing. This will give you an increased ability to understand and influence other people or the particular individual you are asking about. Use this power responsibly, or it will rebound on you and turn from a blessing into a curse. On the other hand, if you use it well, the spirit world will reward you with more knowledge in the future and others will trust you with their inner secrets as well.

If your inquiry concerned business, finances, job or career success, this position of the Light Feather brings an inner understanding of your situation. You will either see or figure out a path to success in your current position or its hopelessness will be uncovered and you will feel free to go elsewhere. And if you feel you have nowhere else to go, you are wrong. The way will be opened, for this is a blessing, the path illuminated. The Shining Ones, the higher spirits of Elfin, are shedding their light upon your life and they wish you to succeed, perhaps even more than you do.

When your question has to do with health or healing, you shall feel as light as a feather as this blessing is revealed and you will know that on the higher planes of being you are composed of starlight and you are energy immortal. This will certainly be healing for your body, but mostly this is healing for the mind, soul and spirit. Your true body, your energetic body, your body of light will levitate when this blessing surrounds you. Use this energy to heal yours'elf and others and it will be multiplied manifold.

And if you are posing a question in reference to your spiritual and magical path, your life in Elfin and the realms of Faerie, then know, beloved, you are one of us and we will always seek to draw you closer and closer to the inner circle of revelation and enlightenment, for you are manifesting the radiance of Elfin in your life and in your heart and its radiance will be left like footprints glowing behind you as you pass into the Mysteries of higher enchantment.

THE MAGIC MIRROR OF REFLECTION

If the Light Feather falls into the inner circle of the Magic Mirror of Reflection one is called upon to count one's blessings, to express gratitude for all one has received, for the blessing of being alive, of being an elf or fae or other, for all that one has and all that one is about to receive, for one is about to be blest some more. It is possible that your life hasn't seemed to be such a blessing to you, yet still, you have been blest by the Shining Ones. The fact that you are reading these words is evidence that this is so. Reach out your hands, your heart and your mind to the Shining Ones in return and they will embrace you and draw you into their circle of magic and enchantment and cast a spell of bounty upon you.

If you had an inquiry about love, romance, marriage, relationship, friendship or your social life and its progress, this placement of the Light Feather asks you to realize the blessing that is your relationship to the spirit world. The wonder that seeps into your life from your connection to Elfin and Faerie, the bounty of your imagination and your ability to use that bounty to make your relationships more wondrous still. There is magic in the air. Look about you. Can you feel it? Blessings are falling like raindrops. Time to dance in the rain.

When you have questions concerning business, money, job or career or pecuniary success in general, then reflect upon what you have, what you have been given and how you can make your life and the world a better place by using your blessings well. Being the inner realms, this is not necessarily a response that indicates material benefit and direct financial gain and yet, there is an abundance of magic and energy that you can use to feed the spirits and thus achieve, with their assistance, all that you desire as far as financial and economic success. But what is it that you truly desire? And why?

Inquiries about health and healing are well aspected here, but what is it that needs healing? Is it your mind, your body, your soul, your spirit, your relationships? This is a place for shamanic healing. For dancing, drumming, chanting and the evocation of the spirits in order to alter the atmosphere of your life and the lives of others. Invoke healing. Draw it into yours'elf and radiate it outwardly. Feel it within and then contemplate the world and your life from this space of healing. Revelations will come.

What would you ask of the spirits? This is surely a good time to do the asking? Seek a vision. Do tarot or some other form of divination. There is a treasure awaiting you in the spirit world. This is a treasure hunt of spirit. Reflect on this. There are blessings as yet unfound, untapped, a source of gold and jewels of magic that you may find if you can just sense that they are there. So yes, continue onward, you are not wasting your time doing magic. Your ideas about spirit and the spiritual realm may be mistaken at times, but you are not mistaken in pursuing the life of magic.

THE SACK OF GIVING

The Sack of Giving ever indicates alms giving and the sharing of one's wealth. With the Light Feather this rebounds to you greatly, but because it is in the inner world of the Sack, the return will most likely come in the form of magical or spiritual energy and power. Also, because this is the inner circle, the giving may best be done by giving to the spirits, leaving offerings about for them. Still, it is important to understand that the spirits manifest in the world, often through those who are "off with the faeries", or the homeless or the disadvantaged, so gifting to them, is giving to the spirits. See who next calls out to you for help and be as generous as you can. It will all return as magical power and potency.

When you are asking a question regarding love, romance, marriage, relationship, your social life or friendship, this fall of the Light Feather favors the gifting of energy and the activity of spells and enchantment as a way of giving. Don't do your spell to get; do it to truly help, enlighten and further those that you are interested in. Do magic to make their life better for them, in the way that they desire as long as it is truly beneficial to them. Let the magic be responsible for bringing you benefits in return. Don't reach out to get anything. Don't strain for a result. Let the Light Feather descend upon your life when it is ready to fall, and feel it caress your soul as it passes.

If you are inquiring about business, finances, job or career success or your future financial prospects, the Light Feather falling in the inner realm of the Sack of Giving indicates that you should invest your energy freely, but without expectation of reward. This is the power of community service. Help out. Give to others. Share your time with those who are in need. Act to make your world a better place to be and the spirits will respond in time. But don't hold your breath. They will probably not send the energy back your way until you have forgotten that you did these deeds and have moved on to other things. Give for the sake of giving. Give from the heart for the Sake of Giving.

Inquiries about health, healing and longevity will find a positive response. The Light Feather surely promotes healing and healing work. Particularly, if it is given freely. Do some pro bono healing and this will radiate back to you as healing energy. Give as much as you can for it will all beam out into the world, of which you are a part, and everyone will benefit thereby. What greater blessing can there be than that?

And if you are asking about issues having to do with your magical and spiritual life, you are indeed lucky, for the Light Feather is ever a sign of a blessing and a boon upon your spiritual life and magic. If you should find such a feather in the near future, use it in your magical workings. Place it upon your altar, or magic table as we elves call it, wave it over burning sage or incense to purify your environment or to help spread the magic about. Put it in your hair, like a merit badge, and wear it about, for you have earned it. You are beloved of the Elfin spirits and you need but continue on your path and they will help you whenever and however they can.

THE PHILTRE OF TRUE LOVE

Getting the Light Feather in the inner realms of the Philtre of True Love is a blessing for soulmates, star mates, weldlinques (elven concept of two people becoming one) and soul bonding. While it has a potential romantic aspect to it, the spiritual and magical influences in the inner dimensions make it more potent in terms of finding those with whom you can carry out your mission in this lifetime and perhaps your destiny for lifetimes to come. Still, such relationships of spirit often have a physical component to them, so we can't rule that potential out completely. At the same time, the important thing here is to understand that those who are part of your team, so to speak, your sorcerers' group, your elven adventurers' party are drawing closer and if you are not already in contact with them, you surely will be soon.

If you posed a question concerning love, romance, relationship, marriage, friendship or your social life and activity, this is certainly a powerful response, although its meaning has to do with your long-term development rather than any transitory associations. In fact, this may be an indication that you need to let go of casual relationships that

153

aren't going anywhere, and surely never will, so you can embrace those that are really meant for you and with whom you can accomplish something meaningful and substantial. It is time to stop wasting your time. Duty calls and your purpose draws nigh.

If you a posed an inquiry about business, money, job or career success and progress in a material sense in the world, this response suggests that you spend your money on those things that further your progress as a spirit, as an elfae or otherkin, as a magician, wizard, witch, enchanter and to invest in your future, your true future and in those who are a part of that future. Be sure you have all the supplies you need for the adventure you are surely about to embark upon. On the other hand, if you don't have much in the way of money in order to get what you need, it will probably be coming to you and most likely through your association with those who are part of your quest, your quest-mates so to speak.

Inquiries about health and healing should find response in the fact that adventure is healing. Being with those with whom you are truly meant to be, is healing as well. Being on the path, doing what you were always meant to do fills one with life and magical potency and the thrill and excitement of the quest. There are few things as healing as the revival of one's spiritual and magical being, the connection to the Divine Magic and the Shining Ones and the knowledge that one is linked to them forever in loving association.

When you have asked a question about your path and your magic and you get this response then you are truly blest in your associations. Your kindred are close to you or are drawing nigh and as Sherlock Holmes would say, 'the game is afoot,' which always bought back life into his soul, awakened his spirit and surely put color in his cheeks. Listen to Buffy Sainte-Marie's song of Leonard Cohen's poem *God is Alive* and you will get a sense of what we mean.

154

THE PHIAL OF EVERLASTING YOUTH

The blessing of the Light Feather in the inner realms of the Phial of Everlasting Youth grants one longevity, vibrant aura, youthful spirit and the sort of energy that one might expect from those who have just fallen in love. It is reviving to the spirit and while this is the inner circle and doesn't necessarily denote direct movement on the material plane, an enthusiastic spirit is bound to radiate outward and influence all that it touches. When religious folk talk about being born again and the sense of renewal and revival that this gives them, this is the sort of energy of which they speak.

If you had a question that was oriented to love, romance, relationship, friendship, marriage or your social life, this indicates a new cycle of activity in those spheres and even more so a sense of hopefulness and a rejuvenation of the atmosphere and feeling surrounding relationships. This is a new day and one is filled with the feeling that everything is looking up, that those one is meant to be with have arrived or soon will, and that these relationships may go on forever. You may rightly sense that there is an eternal bond between you and those who share this path with you. And this, beloved, is not just a feeling but a reality.

As to business, finances, job or career success, this placement of the Light Feather often sets one to looking into new avenues, new prospects and new ventures and also, new people with whom to share these adventures. There is a blessing here, but the blessing comes from the fact that one senses that one's path and life course and work are all combined and that life is more fulfilling when one does the type of work one enjoys doing and is able to support ones'elf with one's creative endeavors.

Healing and Health are surely benefited by this position for it brings the quick healing energy of the young and strong and the power of spirit to spread and share that energy with others. You have the energy, now you just need to continue to do the healing. Unlike those who feel they are drained after doing healing work, here one is revived by one's healing efforts and has even more energy after doing a healing. So, continue healing and let the healing spread. As we elves say: Healing is Contagious; Pass it Around.

As to your spiritual life and magical path, this fall of the Light Feather denotes the wisdom of innocence and the power of a youthful spirit. Be ever open and ready to learn and share and the thresholds to greater experience and power will open to you, the Shining Ones will smile upon you, and you will be blest with the knowledge that even as you grow older in body, you are getting closer and closer to those realms where one is ever young.

The Outer Circle:
The Elf Horns of Calling

If the Light Feather lands beyond the outer circle, then you should know that while luck is coming in your life, it has not arrived as yet, or not fully arrived, and it will take some time to fully manifest. But have faith; it is coming. The fact that others may be getting in the way and interfering is a minor consideration.

THE ORB OF HEALING

The Orb of Healing in the outer realms produces pronounced improvement on the material plane, especially when the Light Feather, which tends to uplift and lighten everything it touches, is involved. Whatever your concern, this should make things better. Accept this gift from the

Shining Ones with an open heart and a realization that some luck has come your way particularly as it has to do with improving your situation. It is not a powerful indication for starting new things, unless those new things are a continuation and advancement upon what has already been going on, but for fixing those things that may have gone a bit astray, it is potent.

If you had a quandary about love, romance, friendship, marriage, relationship or your social life, then you can feel certain that things will be getting better for you even if that means that the old relationship will pass away and a new and improved one will begin. Some things are just not worth keeping as much as we'd like to cling to them, like a toddler desperately grasping a tattered security blanket that has long since seen its day. Still, the possibility of a relationship you currently have reviving is not out of the question, although some faith is required in as much as one needs to accept whatever does happen as being part of one's destiny. Then all will be well as it was always meant to be.

When you are asking about business, financial concerns, job or career prospects then you will be happy to know that things should be getting better in that arena and all you really need to do is make the most of the opportunity to set things right when you have the chance. This is surely a periodic development. No cycle lasts forever, but if we are aware of this fact we can make the most of the moment as it presents itself and in that way be ready beforehand for the shifts that will surely come in the future. Distribute and save while you accumulate and you will have all you need, a cushion so to speak, for leaner times.

If your inquiry had to do with health and healing, well then you are especially blest, doubly blest by the healing influence of the Orb and the blessings and boon effect of the Light Feather. You may feel like the Shining Ones have reached down and lifted you up a bit, as though you are levitating just a fraction off the ground. Spread healing now that there is almost no resistance. The veil between the worlds has grown thinner for the moment and you can draw down the power and potency of the healing aspects of the spirit realms and unite it with the dimensions of Nature and enhance your healing energy thereby. Do this now!

As to inquiries having to do with your spiritual and magical path and development, your destined evolution, the way is opening. Make as much progress as you can as long as this energy lasts. You are getting deeper and deeper into the realms of Faerie, the inner realms of Elfin, the shamanic planes of being and the point is to just keep going as long as you can until the world and its responsibilities drag you back again to take care of the things that you came here to do in the first place, but for now, keep flying. You can worry about landing and what to do once you land, later.

THE WAND OF WISHING

With the fall of the Light Feather into the outer dimensions of the Wand of Wishing, one obtains great magical power to achieve what one desires in whatever area one chooses or in every area, to manifest one's vision into the material world and to actualize one's dreams. What is it that you truly will? You have the power to achieve it, but consider also the consequences. What will change in your life when you get what you want? Wish carefully, as the admonition advises, and look to the long-term effects of your magic. Work toward what will last for in the long run only that which is harmonious with and which benefits everyone involved will have a permanent and positive effect upon your life. As the elves say, seek not for yours'elf alone, but for your others, also.

It is possible that you had a question about love, romance, relationship, marriage, friendship and your social life, and this also finds a positive response here and a real opportunity to improve what is going on in your social life, and to create a situation that is better for you and for all with whom you are involved. At the very least, be prepared for a bit of excitement, an increase in social activity or the appearance of someone who can get things moving and get things done. This is what you want, isn't it?

There is a blessing for business, finances, job and career prospects as well, so you should have or be able to acquire what it is that you need to carry out your will and your mission upon the Earth. The tools you need are forthcoming. Use what you have and more will come. Your needs will be provided for and the energy, in terms of material benefit and goods, will surely be made available to you. Make the most of what you have and you will certainly get more.

When your inquiry has to do with health and healing, you need only wish to heal and be healthy and do what is required on the material plane to make it so, which is to say, have a proper diet, exercise and reduce those indulgences that wear upon your health. And most of all, do your healing work and exercises, your qigong, reiki or whatever your practice may be and let the healing flow into the world, circulate around and return to you so you can send it forth again in an endless circle of rejuvenation.

As to your spiritual and magical life and path, this placement of the Light Feather gives you all the power you need to advance upon the path. In fact, receiving the Light Feather in this position is an indication of advancement. It is your diploma, so to speak, your graduation present. It is everything you need to begin upon a new and higher level of development. Continue on, you are clearly on the right path.

THE COIN OF THE REALM

The fall of the Light Feather in the outer circle of the Coin of the Realm is assuredly a lucky sign for those with money concerns. It brings blessings in regard to money, is good for gambling even and a beneficial influence for investments. It helps one gather together the resources to accomplish what one needs to do in the world and to further ones'elf and one's others. Use this opportunity well and the benefits will continue on into the future.

When you have a question about love, romance, marriage, friendship and your social life, this placement of the light feather brings benefits in terms of material goods but is not, in and of itself, a good sign for feelings, emotions and connections between people unless those relationships are very money oriented. Be cautious of those who only like you when things are going well for you financially. You may not care, but don't count on them being around when the cycle moves the other way.

As to business, finances, job and career, as we said, this is surely good for the financial concerns but doesn't necessarily bode well for connections, interactions and business relationships. However, if all you are concerned about is making money, then this is a perfect response and energy for you. Therefore, be glad for the money but don't be heedless when dealing with others.

If you are asking about health and healing, this response is good if you need money for herbs, medicine, the right food for your diet, exercise equipment and so on, but doesn't affect health directly unless having money makes you feel healthy and certainly there are people who get depressed when they don't have money, and surely most of us feel better when we do have enough to spare and share.

While spiritual questions and issues about your magical

160

life and path may seem contrary to financial concerns, there are those who relate the ability to make money with one's magical potency. Certainly, being able to provide for ones'elf is a significant spiritual issue, and having the magic to draw money to ones'elf does indicate first degree initiation, however, this is just a temporary period of bounty, like the autumn when the harvest comes in and it is not, in and of itself, a sign of personal magical power but rather of a blessing from the Shining Ones. Still, using it well does test one's wisdom and that is the challenge for one's spirit.

THE FEATHER OF TRUTH TELLING

When the Light Feather falls into the outer dimensions of the Feather of Truth Telling, it creates a harmony between them that is very beneficial for the truth of what's going on in the world around you to be revealed in a way that will bring blessings into your life and prove to be of great value to you and your path through the world. Realize that whatever comes out, whatever is discovered will eventually prove to be to your benefit. Hold on to that realization and all will be well.

If you had an inquiry about love, romance, relationship, friendship, marriage or your social life and prospects, the Light Feather is very positive if you are willing to share yours'elf and your feelings and become a little bit vulnerable, without allowing yours'elf to get hurt, which takes a good deal of strength and s'elf confidence. Open yours'elf up to others. Reveal the truths of your inner being. Let those you care about know about your elfae or magical path and spiritual life. Let them have a glimpse at who are really are and desire to be, and this will open the way to them revealing something of thems'elves to you.

If your question has to do with business, finances, job or

career success or future monetary prospects, this position says that something will be disclosed to you shortly that will prove very helpful to you in this regard. Use this information to guide your financial decisions and follow the path to success. This is surely a boon for you and it may very well lead to more information of significance if you do a little research. This is probably only the tip of the iceberg. As the saying goes, follow the money.

When you are asking about health or healing or longevity, this fall of the Light Feather denotes that healing will come from being truthful with yours'elf about your life in the world. Take a realistic look at your life and your path through the world. Don't be afraid of what you see. Don't hide from the truth. Knowing where you actually are is only the starting point. From here we move on to Elfin and we do this through healing. This is a blessing of healing. As light as a feather caressing your brow, relief will come.

Questions about one's path, spiritual and/or magical, find a blessing here from being honest about ones'elf in the world. You don't have to put up a false front all the time. There are people with whom you can be real about yours'elf and your true elfae nature and with whose help and support you may venture onward, each reinforcing the magic of the other. Live your magic in the world. Be the elf, fae or other you truly are. It doesn't mean you have to announce yours'elf to the world. But it does mean you need to be authentic within yours'elf. Express your elfae nature. Let others give it a name if they wish to do so. But be real. Live your magic.

THE MAGIC MIRROR OF REFLECTION

When the Light Feather falls into the outer realms of the Magic Mirror of Reflection, it is a good time to ponder one's life, one's blessings and most of all what one might do to share one's blessings and make the world a better place for everyone and in doing so secure one's own future benefit and prosperity. One may therefore wish to contemplate the nature of luck itself, its seemingly fickle attitude toward most folks, the way it seems to adore some select individuals nearly always and what enchantment they used or was cast upon them that caused that to be. How does one create luck? (See our book *The Keys to Elfin Enchantment*).

Questions about love, romance, marriage, relationship, friendship and one's social life pose a question in return: how does one get lucky in love? How does one increase one's power of enchantment? How does one create a loving and healing environment? There is benefit to be found in examining these things. That is the point. Honest reflection upon one's life will produce blessings in itself. Once you see the truth, you can proceed with great power.

If you wanted to know about business, finances, job or career success or your future chances of prosperity, this is a good time to plan for the future. What is it that you really want for yours'elf in a material sense and how may you obtain it without creating bad karma that would only drag you down again in time? You may have tried to puzzle this all out previously, but now, with the influence of the Light Feather, you will be blest with insight and a way will open for you. But you will need to look for it. A quest is in order.

Perhaps you were asking about health and healing, in which case there is benefit to be found in a close examination of your life, your daily routines, your habits, lifestyle, your environment and everything that can bear upon your health. If you are working at something that is bad for your health, find another way to make money. Don't make excuses; make a change. Your health is important. Just ask the old folks. Perhaps you feel you have no choice, but fortunately with this placement of the Light Feather a choice should manifest.

163

And if you are inquiring about your spiritual life and magical path, this is a good time to pause and meditate. Open your heart and mind and let the powers of the Earth, the Shining Ones, the Elders of the Eldar illuminate your mind and soul. Accept the blessing of their grace upon you and then proceed in the direction of the light and radiance of Elfin.

THE SACK OF GIVING

If the Light Feather flutters down and lands in the outer reaches of the Sack of Giving, then generosity will prove very profitable to you. You are blest and blessings will surely descend upon you and your life. But, if you then take these blessings, which will most likely manifest in some material form, and share them with others, you will be setting a cycle of bounty in motion that will return to you manifold and bring you blessings of prosperity potentially for years yet to come. Share your wealth and you shall be richer still.

When asking about love, romance, marriage, friendship, relationship or one's social life and prospects, the Light Feather indicates that gift giving will prove effective in moving things forward. However, this is not random gift giving but magical gifting. Put a spell or enchantment on every item that you give. Not a spell designed to get something or move things in a particular direction. Not one of those *come to me* spells that you might find Hoodoo practitioners doing, but a simple blessing spell. An enchantment designed to make life better for the person you are giving it to purely out of the kindness and goodness of your heart. Then, leave the rest to the spirits and you will surely find blessings coming to you in return.

If you were inquiring about business, finances, job or career success and prospects for the future, then you are certainly lucky to receive the Light Feather here, but even luckier if you make donations to worthy causes, or make investments into good projects. Be a patron of the arts or other things of value to society. Don't invest just to make money. Invest because you love the things you are investing in. Don't buy art because you think it will increase in value in the future. It may do so, but most likely not, unless you are really lucky, which with this placement of the Light Feather you clearly are, but buy a particular piece of art because it appeals to you. Then you can't lose, even if the artist never becomes well known you will have something that will bring beauty and wonder and perhaps inspiration into your life for years.

When asking about health and healing, the Light Feather brings relief into your life. It brings healing, rejuvenation and revitalization. Use this energy to help others to heal. Spread the healing as widely as you are able. Radiate healing, beam it into the world, particularly into your immediate environment. Let the healing spread like a contagion of wellness and the benefits will rebound upon your life bringing greater healing still. Keep the energy going as long as you are able to do so and this will be rewarding for everyone.

Inquiries about one's magical and spiritual life and path are similarly awarded with the bonus of the blessings of the Light Feather. But, make progress now while the energy is to your advantage. The way is opening. Pour your spirit into your magical life. Do magic. Be enchanting. Let the abundance flow from the purity of your soul into the hearts and lives of others. Help those who are also on the path to advance and find their way. That is your chief mission now, to foster the progress of others on the path.

165

THE PHILTRE OF TRUE LOVE

If the Light Feather descends into the outer dimension of the Philtre of True Love, it brings blessings for your love life, your relationships in every area of your life and especially a lightening, in terms of relief in your life, for every association, but particularly those that have long term significance for your life, your path and your destiny. This draws together those who should be together, who are meant to be together, both in a personal and transpersonal fashion. These will be your kindred of spirit and of soul.

When you have a question concerning love, romance, relationship, marriage, friendship and your social life, you are obviously in luck in terms of this response. This is not only beneficial for relationships in general but has even greater promise for relationships that are long lasting or which will endure a long time. This moves relationships toward a deeper and more profound connection.

If your inquiry involved business, money, job or career success, this placement of the feather is lucky in terms of business relationships, especially ones of long standing, or developing relationships that will last, but is not a good sign for money overall except as business connections favor financial success. Deal with those you know and trust. Don't take chances on those you don't really know or you are unsure you can trust.

Questions concerning health and healing have a favorable response in as much as good relationships, relationships that you know you can count on, are good for one's health and wellbeing. If you are experiencing health difficulties, hang around with those that make you feel better. Visiting old friends can be helpful, but particularly being around those who are sympatico to you, that share your vibration, your interests, your path, and your vision.

And if you were asking about your magical and spiritual path, then this position of the Light Feather favors finding those that share your path and who can help you upon the way, share the quest with you, be part of your frasority (fraternity and sorority), your fellowship of the ... whatever. True friends upon the way sharing an experience that will last in one's heart long after those involved have gone their separate ways, so that one will always feel connected to them throughout one's life and throughout lifetimes to come.

THE PHIAL OF EVERLASTING YOUTH

When the Light Feather descends to the outer realms of the Phial of Everlasting Youth, one is blest with a period of increased and very youthful energy. This feels a great deal like falling in love. One is with filled with lighthearted enthusiasm and feels like life is wonderful, everything finally makes sense in the world and all will turn out as it has always been meant to. Use this energy while it lasts because, like youth itself, it will pass away.

If you had an inquiry about love, romance, marriage, relationship, your social life in general or some friendship, this fall of the feather denotes a positive time for relationships, a blessing upon your life that comes to you through relationship and an opportunity to improve your friendships and social life overall. If you were waiting to ask someone out, this is the time to do it. It doesn't guarantee a positive response but it does guarantee that if the person turns you down it is really for the best and something or someone even better will come into your life. So, take a chance, for something good will come of it no matter what they say.

When asking about business, finances or job or career prospects, the Light Feather landing in this place indicates a spring-like renewal of financial and business activity and prosperity. It is good for investment and taking a bit of a chance. But remember, it is just a cyclic event, just a bit of a spell, and it will not endure forever. So, make the most of it while it lasts. Don't over invest. Don't be like some naive youth who plunges into danger without thought of the morrow because sHe (she/he) feels invincible. Don't totally throw away your wisdom, experience or caution, but know that the time is favorable and if all else looks favorable as well you can take the plunge and won't have to regret it.

As to questions concerning health, longevity and healing, this placement of the Light Feather, revitalizes your life, rejuvenates your personal energy, gives you the juice that you may use to heal yours'elf or to help others heal and is surely a blessing for a renewal in your life on all levels of being. Let your personal feeling of being filled with life flow from you into those around you, into your environment and let healing issue forth.

And if you are asking about your magical path and spiritual life, this response points to a renewal in your magical activity and spiritual development in the world. For a short while, at least, you will have a lot of magical energy at your disposal. Do magic while the energy is alive and vibrant and eager to be dispensed. Later, this increased charge of energy will pass. But if you have done your magic, have released it and send it forth at this time when you have the juice to do so, it will come back to you when you need it again. So, spread your enchantments far and wide while the 'mood'/blessing is upon you and let the magic do the rest.

Chapter 6:

The Dark Feather

The Darker Feather designates small blessings. They may not change the situation greatly but they will have a positive influence on it and ease your way toward the mystical realms and realization of Elfin. It will not change the essential circumstances that you are dealing with, but it will tend to make things go better.

The Inner Circle: The Torch of the Eternal Silver Flame of Elfin

When the Dark Feather falls touching the torch in the inner circle, it means that the Shining Ones and the spirits and powers of Elfin are sending you a boost to help you progress on the way. This will not be large events but little things, subtle things and will ease your path. Just a squirt of mystical WD40 or a drop or two of magic oil.

THE ORB OF HEALING

The fall of the Dark Feather into the inner realms of the Orb of Healing signifies small blessings and improvement in one's life, particularly in the healing of the body, or relationships or situations in one's life. This will not bring about a radical change of any sort, nor will it make a great deal of difference to your life but it will make things better, relieve tension and set things going a little faster or easier. This energy will not last, nothing does, but it does indicate a temporary reprieve. It is like breaktime in the workplace, a short pause between work periods rather than the end of the day or the end of the work week.

If you had a question about love, romance, relationship, marriage, friendship or your social life, then this is a good sign for small developments. It is unlikely to indicate love at first sight, but it could denote an accidental meeting that later occurs again, and then again until something does develop. If things have been difficult in relationship, this may indicate a small improvement, not a total change in the way you are interacting with each other, but none-the-less, a chance to move things in the right direction. It is a step forward, even if only a small step forward.

Questions concerning business and financial issues or one's job or career, also find the opportunity for making things better, although again a large change is unlikely and any effort to make big alterations will most likely find that the energy is just not there for doing so and is therefore unlikely to succeed. One would not wish to attempt anything new on a large scale for such endeavors would surely peter out in time and while the beginning might be strong the follow through and endurance is likely to be poor. Enthusiasm will only get you so far. On the other hand, radical changes often arouse resistance whereas small changes are seldom even noticed.

When you are asking about health and healing, then you are certainly in luck, even though the healing may only be a minor improvement, it does move things in the right direction and if you rest and don't push things the possibility of greater healing may come. Do small healings. Do them frequently. Create a habit of healing and healing work. This is a good thing and definitely to your and everyone else's benefit.

Inquiries about one's spiritual path and magical life, one's progress toward mastery and advanced initiation are met with encouragement to continue on the path, keep doing the magic and one's spiritual practices day to day. This is a sign of success and advancement but not so much that one might feel that they have leveled up, so to speak, but it still represents progress on the level one is currently working on. Continue on the path and greater success will certainly come to you and that is the point really, endurance and perseverance will bring great success in time. And in a very real way, endurance and perseverance are the ultimate goal.

THE WAND OF WISHING

If the Dark Feather lands in the inner circle of the Wand of Wishing, one can be certain that while one will receive a series and perhaps a variety of small blessings, that one of those blessings, at least, is a diamond in the rough. Examine these blessings carefully for within them is some great and potent magic or at the very least you can parlay them into a powerful magical spell that will fulfill your wishes.

Questions about love, romance, relationship, marriage, friendship and one's social life find a positive boost in this response, although due to the fact that it is the inner circle, it is much more inclined to bring blessings to relationships that have a spiritual and magical component to them than those that are merely passing associations in the outer world. This is the blessing of knowing spirits, of being in contact with the Shining Ones and the elves of the more subtle dimensions. No doubt this will affect your life in the material world, but its true meaning has to do with your spirit and its progress through the lifetimes. There is magic here in making contact with the spirit realm, although, unless you actually know what you are doing, the Ouija board is not advised for this communication. Still, the Elf Queen's Daughters were adept in using it, so if you are as well, its use is surely not precluded.

When your inquiry is about business, finances, job or career success, this position of the Dark Feather favors pursuing jobs and using your money in a spiritual and socially conscious fashion. If you are working at a job or career that is not in tune with your beliefs, your soul and your spirit, you may have a small window of opportunity to make a change. At any rate, keep the eternal in mind and use your money as though you were going to live forever in your current body. Make your money count.

If you were asking about health or healing, this placement of the Dark Feather, decidedly brings health and healing energy into your life and the lives of those with whom you share your healing energy. This healing is, for the most part, a healing that derives from the power of a strong spirit and a calm and tranquil soul. The spirit world is sending healing your way and you, in turn, may send healing its way, which is rather like opening a savings account of healing in the spirit world. The healing energy will be there when you need it. And while these may not be large deposits, particularly with the influence of the Dark Feather, they will add up if you keep depositing.

As to your life of magic and spirit, this development, while a small movement, is assuredly a great one. You now have some influence on the astral planes and the realms of spirit. The spirits are listening to you. You may not be deemed as greatly wise as yet, but you are someone whose words are taking on increasing import and they are being heeded. This is surely a good thing.

THE COIN OF THE REALM

The fall of the Dark Feather into the inner demesne of the Coin of the Realm denotes a bit of luck regarding financial concerns, but mostly on the planes of spirit and magic. In other words, you have extra magical energy to use, just like a birthday card with money in it that has been sent to you from the Shining Ones and while it is not a huge amount, if you spend it wisely and well it will certainly be to your ultimate benefit and will aid you in your progress toward Elfin/Faerie, the realization of your true s'elf and, in time and probably indirectly, your success in the material world.

If you presented a question regarding love, romance, relationship, marriage, friendship or your social life to the oracle, this position of the Dark Feather is very favorable for doing small magics and sending out love, healing and blessings to those you love or whom you'd like to affect and influence in the positive way and this magic will surely rebound to you in a beneficial fashion, improving your social life and relationships. It will help change the way people feel about you and move them to look upon you from a more favorable point of view.

Naturally, this is a good position for business, for the Coin of the Realm favors financial success and with the blessings of the Dark Feather this is all to your benefit. Being in the inner realm the effect is more atmospheric than material. It favors increased energy in business and a sense of bullishness in pecuniary dealings. But don't overdo things. This is the Dark Feather and while positive, its powers are limited. Secure your success. Progress slowly. Advance with caution but with a knowledge that things are moving in the right direction.

When you are making an inquiry about health and/or healing, this placement of Dark Feather is excellent for healing emotional trauma, mental disturbances and from that the physical body. It is good for curing the soul and the spirit. Apply your healing powers, and if you can do so, do it as a gift, a blessing given to others for the benefit of a better, more elven world. And if you are asking concerning your own health, this position is great for stirring your spirit, for a powerful spirit is an immensely healing energy.

And if you were making inquiries about your spiritual path and magical progress, the landing of the Dark Feather in this position is very favorable in terms of receiving blessings from the spirits. The Dark Feather is a boon sign, but usually limited in nature, but the Coin of the Realm boosts that energy a bit more so the blessings you receive are somewhat larger than they would otherwise be. However, due to the fact that this is the inner realm, its effect will still be mostly in terms of magical and spiritual energy and since you are making an inquiry related to those subjects, you are in luck. Undoubtedly, some wondrous bit of magic will occur soon, most likely in the form of a synchronicity.

THE FEATHER OF TRUTH TELLING

When the Dark Feather lands in the inner circle of the Feather of Truth Telling one is called to listen carefully to the spirit realms for a message will be coming to you that is to your benefit. Mostly likely, it will come in subtle ways or through small things, and the revelation is unlikely to be life changing but it will help improve things for you and while it will be but a small truth that is revealed, only a piece of the puzzle that is life, it will help you to connect to other pieces and get a better idea of the scheme of things. It will increase your power in little ways but still that is all to your advantage.

If you had an inquiry about love, romance, relationship, friendship, marriage or your social life, the Dark Feather in coordination with the Feather of Truth Telling will open the way to relationship through incremental steps and an increased understanding of the situation, how to achieve what you desire in relationship and more than that a greater insight into people and what it is they desire, what motivates them and how you can influence them with this knowledge. Use this insight well. It will help you, without doubt, but remember, there are still vaster depths to be revealed. You've dived into the ocean and seen under the water, but you haven't yet been to the bottom of the sea that is the inner psyche of the individual. That will take deeper understanding and definitely more time.

If you posited a question regarding business, finances, job or career development and success, this fall of the Dark Feather may indicate realizations about others around you with whom you have financial dealings. It is unlikely to directly affect your financial situation but it will give you insight into commercial interactions and you may thus increase your ability to achieve success in business because you will have a greater understanding of how business works or at least how a particular enterprise you are involved in functions. You will see the keys to success and that is worth more than money.

When you are asking about health and healing this position of the Dark Feather is good for a superficial understanding of what ails a person and what to do about it. You may see their symptoms and understand what disease afflicts them, but you are, as yet, unlikely to be able to see the true cause of this disease, the inner aspects of their soul and spirit that permitted it to occur in the first place. But don't worry about that now. Just project healing energy as best you can and while this may not be a permanent solution for their spirit, it will at least patch them up enough that they can get a little farther down the road of life.

And if you were inquiring about your spiritual path and your life and progress as a magician/enchanter, then this placement of the Dark Feather brings you a bit of luck. But be honest with yours'elf. Don't overestimate your progress. Be realistic about where you are and move on from there. Those who claim they are more advanced than they truly are, are just making fools of thems'elves. And if you are not honest about where you are, how can you possibly find the way to where you need to go? This is but small magic. But it is magic you can use to your advantage or to the advantage of your kindred, if you are realistic about its power. This power is a minicar, not a race car. But it will get you there. It is a donkey not a race horse, but again, slowly but surely, you can use it to get to where you wish to go.

THE MAGIC MIRROR OF REFLECTION

As the Dark Feather floats down and lands in the inner dimension of the Magic Mirror of Reflection, one has a chance to contemplate one's life, especially one's spirit and one's progress through the lifetimes and to know that while things often happen slowly relative to the quickness of our imaginations, one has been blest and is progressing on the path to Elfin. Look carefully and you will see a bit of magic coming your way from the spirit realms. Use this magic now. It has a time expiration date on it. Stir the cauldron and let the spirits do the rest. Do you see? You are blest.

If you posited a question having to do with love, romance, relationship, marriage, friendship, your social life, or your compact with the spirits, this placement of the Dark Feather bids you look to the positive side of every interaction, for by doing so you will also find a pathway to success and an opportunity to move things in the direction you desire. This is an atmospheric realm. A realm of ambience and feeling. Don't over-think things. Clear you mind and feel what is going on and you will find the way.

When your question involves business, finances, your job or career advancement, or your prosperity in general, this response is favorable in terms of getting a little aid from the spirit realms. They are unlikely to alter your situation entirely. This will be but a small boost for you. Apparently, the challenges you face in this realm are an aspect of fate and s'elf development. They are meant to make you stronger and better at what you do. Also, the time is just not right as yet for major changes, but if you continue steadily onward in association with the elfin spirits, things will progress in a favorable fashion and while you may not get everything you want as yet, you should surely be pleased to be advancing.

As to your health and healing, this is a good time to analyze what is going on. This is a positive aspect for seeing your strengths, both in your physical body and in your spirit and healing abilities, to identify them and improve and augment them in everything you do. Increase your healing power and particularly increase your connection to the realms of Nature and Spirit and the harmonious and healing energies that reside there. Get out in nature for a while. It will do you good and then reflect on this question.

If you had an inquiry about your magical path and spiritual development, this fall of the Dark Feather indicates slow but sure progress. Small blessings will pile up and bring a bit of wonder into your life. Reflect upon the meaning of a kiss on the cheek from an elven princess or prince. Consider yours'elf and your progress as a spirit, but don't think too long or too deeply. A quick cursory examination will do just fine. Here we are just refining things. Doing minor tune-ups. Major changes are not needed nor beneficial really, or even possible at this time. Make the most of what you have and continue onward toward the Magical, Wondrous and Sacred Realms of Elfin.

THE SACK OF GIVING

When the Dark Feather falls into the inner region of the Sack of Giving, one is urged to give alms. Not a large amount, surely. Small gifts will do and surely small blessings will come to you in return. You can give more if you wish, but the returns will still likely be limited at this point. And, in fact, if you wish to wait for these little boons to arrive first, it is perfectly okay. It is just that upon receiving this grace from the Shining Ones, it is wise to spread the good luck about and share it with others and that will certainly prove to be to your further benefit. This is magic in motion. As we say, small magic, but it is important to keep it moving. Keep it flowing. Like lifeblood it needs to circulate.

If you had offered a question about love, romance, marriage, relationship, friendship or your social life, this position of the Dark Feather says two things. One, this is a good time for you in relationship. It does not indicate significant developments, but it is positively in your favor and things are evolving in the light of your best interests. And two, give gifts. Give tokens of appreciation, but mostly offer something the individual desires in as much as you can do so. This will in time bring you what you desire. The movement is unlikely to be quick, but it is a sure and dependable development.

If your inquiry posed concerns about business, finances, job or career development and success, or your future prosperity and financial possibilities, this fall of the Dark Feather presents opportunities for small investments. This is not the time to do any large investing or big financial moves but the atmosphere is great for shifting your pawns and minor pieces upon the chess board of life. You are really preparing for something greater in this way, but the time for big moves just hasn't arrived as yet.

When you have an inquiry that involves health and healing, you are blessed with a period when it is very beneficial to do healing work. The response is unlikely to be great, but by continuing to put out healing energy, the atmosphere will eventually shift and people's attitudes toward you will be influenced toward more positive thoughtforms.

Here we are not altering the body so much as the mind and disposition. The healing is more atmospheric than material in manifestation.

As to one's spiritual life and magical path, the landing of the Dark Feather in this position is great for advancing upon the spiritual and magical path by making offerings to the spirits, by doing small spells, by keeping your spiritual practice going, particularly as it involves helping others to advance and learn upon their own path. This is the gift you have that you can give that will further them and you. Share your wisdom. Share your help. If you can, share the burden they bear and by doing so make the world a better place, a more elfin place, a more magical place for everyone.

THE PHILTRE OF TRUE LOVE

As the Dark Feather lands in the inner circle of the Philtre of True Love one may feel their soulmate drawing closer and surely those who are meant for one's spirit, one's magic and one's evolutionary development will appear, at least for a while, but certainly in a way that increases one's knowledge, understanding and power, and guides one further, farther and deeper into the realms of Elfin and Faerie. And, the realization of your own true nature will be reflected in those that really love and admire you and seek to nurture your evolution.

With questions that involve love, romance, relationship, marriage, friendship or your social life, this position of the Dark Feather attracts your soulmates, star-mates and others with whom you have or will have an intimate spiritual and soulful connection. Being the Dark Feather, which is a minor blessing, it may be that this is just the beginning. You may pass each other on the street, or share a time together at a gathering, and note a connection between you but not be able

179

to keep the connection going, at least, not for now. This, for the time being, is a relationship of distance as far as the material world is concerned, testing your true connection to each other. If you remain true in your hearts, time, fate and destiny will eventually bring you together.

If you had an inquiry about business, pecuniary concerns, job or career success, this placement of the Dark Feather temporarily reveals to you those who may help you succeed in the world, as long as your financial success doesn't impede or block your spiritual and magical progress and your evolution on the subtle planes of spirit manifestation. This is the time to make these connections stronger for they will in time demonstrate the means by which you may succeed in the world while doing those things that you truly love and which are in harmony with your spirit and your soul.

Inquiries about one's health or one's ability to heal, or the health of some loved one, will find that this is a small opportunity to do a bit of healing based upon true connection and genuine affection and sympathy for another. This cannot be faked. Or really, it can be faked but will be lacking in any power. The connection between you and the one you are helping to heal or who is projecting healing energy to you must be real and based upon a genuine sense of spiritual relatedness and compassion. Otherwise, you are just wasting your energy and going through the motions. And as it is, this is a power of short duration. Use it while it lasts.

And if you are asking about your spiritual path and magical progress, this is certainly a good sign that indicates you will shortly make a connection to a spirit that will give you a boost and help you upon your way. Again, with the Dark Feather, this is unlikely to be a major advancement, but it is a boon for you and it is real magic with which you can do something that will shift your life in the direction you wish to go without making a major change in your life at this time.

180

Still, it can lead to something greater and that is what is needed at this point.

THE PHIAL OF EVERLASTING YOUTH

With the fall of the Dark Feather descending into the inner dimension of the Phial of Everlasting Youth, one is blessed with a revival of energy, particularly in the more refined realms of spirit and magic. It is not that your body has gotten younger in reality, but that you will feel mildly thrilled, excited and rejuvenated in your spirit and this surely will affect your body in a positive way. This is a bonus of magic and power. It is not a large nor greatly powerful boon but a blessing, none-the-less, and one that can be used to further your life, particularly your magical and spiritual life and path.

If you presented an inquiry about love, romance, relationship, marriage, friendship or your social life to the oracle, this reply indicates an improvement in the mood and atmosphere surrounding relationships. If you are wise and subtle, you may take advantage of this positive mood and ambience to heighten your relationships, but cautiously. Push no farther than the first resistance and then retreat a bit. Progress can be made here but not far. Take the easy way and advance but with a bit of casual joy. Don't rush, skip. Don't march forward, dance. And perhaps in doing so you will create even greater delight and will attract more luck to you.

When you have posed a question in regards to business, finances or your job or career success and advancement, this position of the Dark Feather will not have any direct affect upon your financial life and career, however, it will tend to revive your own energy and determination to succeed. The blessings here come in your own ability to progress, albeit slowly and incrementally, toward your goals. This is a favorable situation, just not one that will shift your material circumstances quickly. But it will tend to make you far less likely to be depressed or to give up easily. The future looks hopeful.

Questions that center on health and healing will find this a great energy, although not immense, for doing healing for yours'elf and others. While the Dark Feather is not powerful, this position is exactly in tune with longevity, vitality and an energizing of ones'elf and one's ability to heal. This is a steady downflow of life energy from the subtle dimensions into the more material ones although its primary influence is in the revival of personal spirit. Thus, it acts primarily against depression and promotes enthusiasm. This is not a downpour but a light spring drizzle.

If you were asking about your spiritual life and magical path, this landing of the Dark Feather renews your energy on the path and gives you a boost of magic. You can use this to make progress upon your path and surely this indicates advancement and evolution, even though it would not be something that constitutes a profound experience. It is simple progress in a steady fashion in keeping with a somewhat Zen perspective on life.

The Outer Circle: The Elf Horns of Calling

With the fall of the Dark Feather beyond the outer circle, there are blessings that are coming to you. Not big blessings, but more likely a sort of a small bonus, but it is being delayed by the intercession of others and by intervening events. It could be that it will be overshadowed by these events but if you look carefully the blessing is there and you can use it to improve what is going on and thus make things better in small ways.

THE ORB OF HEALING

When the Dark Feather lands in the outer realm of the Orb of Healing, one is blest with a period of revival and revitalization for one's physical body in particular but also its influence sheds a healing light on every aspect of one's life but especially those areas that have power to improve one's material wellbeing. These are real manifest benefits, although limited, that come into your life, not simply an improved outlook on life, although it may very well lead to that.

If you posited a question that had to do with love, romance, relationship, marriage, friendship or your social life, this response of the Dark Feather indicates contact, connection and beneficial encounters of a wondrous nature. This is just a passing phenomenon, and may not last, but the feeling may endure and the connection can possibly develop in the future if you continue to nurture it. There will most likely be touch involved. Be receptive and respond in kind and on the same level as the person seeking to connect with you. Be aware and go no further than the moment allows. Bide your time and save some for the future. Leave them wanting more.

When you had a question that involved business, finances or your job or career success, or perhaps future possibilities for prosperity, this placement of the Dark Feather brings about improvement in your financial life. This should even bring you a bit of money as an unexpected bonus. It is definitely positive for relieving debt and setting your life on a stable financial course. Thus, things should improve in this area all around.

Inquiries about health and healing that find the Dark

Feather here are especially lucky, for the Orb of Healing increases the power of the Dark Feather in regard to healing overall. So, any healing work or magic that you do will be increased in its power and its potency. Do the healing. Let the healing happen. Feel the healing in yours'elf, your life and your environment. This is truly a blessing.

And if you are asking about your spiritual and magical life and path, this fall of the Dark Feather is good for making progress in small ways upon the material plane. It is especially good for fixing things that have gone wrong or if you have strayed from the path it is an excellent and favorable time to get back upon it. Or if others you know have fallen from the path and need a little help returning to it, this is a great time to aid them for it will bring blessings to them and you.

THE WAND OF WISHING

If the Dark Feather descends into the outer realm of the Wand of Wishing your dreams will come true, although only in a small and limited way and/or only partially. The Dark Feather rules small blessings and a little bit of luck, so don't push it. Nothing will be achieved by trying to force more out of the situation than it is capable of giving. Still, this is a positive response for you and one that should bring real material benefits, only of a limited nature. Still, small magics can lead to great things if you are patient and do your best with the blessings that have come to you.

If you had a question about love, romance, relationship, marriage, friendship or your social life in general, this landing of the Dark Feather brings real luck and movement in a positive fashion in terms of relationship. This is not the big stuff. It is not an aspect that would be positive for 'popping the question', so to speak, but it does signify real progress in your social world with small blessings manifesting. Perhaps you will have 'a moment' with someone. Just a passing connection but one that feels really good and special. Something spiritual manifesting in the mundane world. Who knows what it could lead to in the future, or if it will lead to anything at all, but still, even if it doesn't, it was a special moment.

When you are posing a question relative to business, money, job and career success, or your future prosperity, this is a good sign that you will get a bit of an advancement, a small bonus may come to you, probably not as much as you hoped or most likely not as much as you fantasized and desired or deserve, but still, it's good to get it. Make the most of it and it may become more. This is business after all and using money well and encouraging it to grow is what it is all about. So, count your blessings along with your increased income.

Inquiries that have to do with health and healing find real healing of a slow but sure nature in response. A boost of energy may come to you. Don't exhaust yours'elf and drain it all away. Be wise in using this energy. Like making love, don't be in a hurry to get it all over unless you don't really want to be doing it in the first place. Make it last. Stretch out this healing period as long as you are able to do so. Do healings in short sessions. Not enough to wear you out, but enough to move things along in the direction of greater health. Give healing like you are giving treats to children. Just a little bit at a time.

When you are asking about your magical life and spiritual development and get this placement of the Dark Feather, you can use little magics and actions in the material world to mirror your desires and visions on the subtler planes of being. As Above, So Below, or in this case As Below, So Above. Make your elfin life real in the world. You may be limited in how much you can do but do your best and this

185

will prompt a response from the spirit world and from the Shining Ones and this may very well bring you more blessings still. For the life of the elves is blest, and luck, while sometimes small, is often bountiful.

THE COIN OF THE REALM

With the Dark Feather landing in the outer dimensions of the Coin of the Realm, one may expect a bit of luck with money, in particular, with business and with the possibility of the acquisition of material goods. This is not great luck. If you were a gambler, it would be good for doing a small bit of gambling but then quitting as soon as you were ahead. It would not be wise to chase this wee bit of luck for you will never catch it. Accept the small grace that is offered you, be thankful and be on your way.

When you have asked a question about love, romance, relationship, marriage, friendship or your social life, this fall of the Dark Feather indicates that small blessings may come to you in this area, in fact, it is quite possible someone will give you a small gift, some token of their appreciation. It will not be anything great or grand and surely not expensive, but if you accept it in the spirit with which it is offered, you will surely be making progress in relationship and in your relations overall.

Business, as we said, and financial matters, as well as job and career advancement are favored here, although in small ways. This placement of the Dark Feather is unlikely to signify anything of great importance in these areas, but these small successes may certainly lead to something greater. So, accept the benefits that are given to you with appreciation, even though they may seem unimportant and insignificant, and make the most of them, for in using them to their fullest you are telling the Universe to send you more.

186

If you asked about health and healing and got this response then this is definitely good sign for healing, although it may cost you a little bit, but it will be worth it. Whatever you spend in terms of your health will rebound to you in wellness, and with this placement of the Dark Feather, you are most likely to get a discount on supplements and other items that promote healing in your life or support your healing efforts. Also, you may receive material benefits for the healing you have projected to others in appreciation for your efforts. It may not be much but it will be a genuine boon to your life. And if you receive it with the right attitude, that in itself will be healing to you.

If you are making inquiries about your spiritual life and magical path, this fall of the Dark Feather indicates that small blessings will come to you, wee signs, little rewards for your steadfastness, subtle indications that you are on the right path. These are not the peak experiences that many look for, nor the pivotal revelations that will totally alter your life and give you some profound insight but rather these are minor blessings that none-the-less will help you upon the way and encourage you to endure and continue with your magic. It is a step forward on the path and that is what counts.

THE FEATHER OF TRUTH TELLING

If the Dark Feather lands in the outer dimension of the Feather of Truth Telling, the truth is going to come out and it will definitely be to your advantage, if not immediately then surely in the long run. So, embrace this revelation, for it is to your benefit and you will profit thereby. While it may not be the entire truth that is revealed, it is, none-the-less, a thread that you can follow to discover even more.

If you had a question relative to love, romance, relationship, friendship, marriage or your social life, this position of the Dark Feather indicates the disclosure of some secret or secrets that will give you greater understanding as well as increase your success in personal interactions. They say that the truth can hurt, but here it will blow away the obstructions that have been coming between you and another and while it will not heal the situation instantly, it will open the door to a better and more satisfying connection. Proceed with a certain amount of delicacy and caution, but proceed.

When your inquiry concerned business, money, job or career success and you get this position for the Dark Feather, it is probable that you will learn a trick or two that will help you on your way. There are things that we learn that can increase our financial success, and one of these secrets will be revealed to you or you will somehow discover it on your own. But the important thing is to take advantage of this opportunity and while it is unlikely to make a large difference immediately, in the long run this may prove very beneficial to you.

When you are asking about health and healing, this position of the Dark Feather in coordination with the Feather of Truth Telling, at least gets you to the root of the problem. It doesn't heal in and of itself, however now, whatever ails you or some other, the source of the illness should become clear and with the boon aspect of the Dark Feather the possibility of healing is increased. So, analyze the problem and carry out your healing practices. The time is favorable for improvement.

Questions about one's spiritual path and magical development finds the way being opened and the path made clear. If you have been uncertain, this revelation should erase your hesitancy. You can proceed with confidence because the way to Elfin/Faerie will now be made more obvious to you, at least for now. Signs will come. Heed them and proceed deeper into the realms of magical manifestation.

THE MAGIC MIRROR OF REFLECTION

The fall of the Dark Feather in the outer realm of the Magic Mirror of Reflection suggests that examining your blessings, no matter how small, will be of great value to you. Like the saying: Count your blessings, this is a good idea. Count your blessings and you may find that you have far more than you realized and that you can weave them together into a greater magic still for surely, though small, they are all connected through you. It is a little like gathering up your pennies. If you have enough of them, they can add up and if you don't have enough as yet, keep collecting.

If the Dark Feather lands in this position in response to a question about love, romance, marriage, relationship, friendship or your social life, this says that you need to look to the little things to find the answer to your question. Don't look at what seems to be going on overall, but rather concentrate on the details. It is in the bits and pieces, the snatches of conversation and things overheard that the answer will come to you. And remember, there is a blessing for you in this somewhere. You may have to look carefully to find it, but it is there.

When the questions concern business, money, career advancement or job issues, this reply indicates that if you look carefully you will see there is a small window of opportunity opening up for you in these areas, but you have to look closely, remain alert and ready to seize the chance when it comes. Somewhere amid the mounds of activity and data, the sheets and forms, it lurks and you just need to go through them to find it. Whether such a small gain is worth your time is up to you to decide, but the opportunity is there.

As to inquiries that revolve around health and healing, this placement of the Dark Feather favors healing energy but not so much that it will make a great difference quickly. Rather, this position suggests that you accept the healing energy that

189

is given you, however small, and then consider how you might make the most of it for yours'elf and your others. Surely, healing is a good thing, no matter how little it might be and like microscopic germs but even more subtle, healing vibrations may also grow and spread. How do you spread the healing? You get the vibration humming through your life.

Oh, beloved elfae kin, what blessing this to be together again, upon the path, upon the way, making magic every day with nights enchanted we do sway to the sounds of kindred singing, of faerie gently winging, of elves now starlight flinging, bringing such grace into our lives. Consider this, Elfin is all around us and if we find it within us, we will realize we are there and have been all along. Smile, beloved, this is a blessing true.

THE SACK OF GIVING

When the Dark Feather lands in the outer circle of the Sack of Giving one is advised to give small things. Not great gifts and not a lot, but tokens of appreciation and magic. Here, truly, the feeling involved is more important and valuable than the gift itself. If you wish to give more, of course, you may do so, but it is not advised at this time. Your generosity will most likely be met with suspicion as to your motives if you give too much. Small things are better. Leave them wanting more. And consider that you may give token gifts each time you see them, although Behaviorism tells us that giving rewards every time is not actually as powerful as rewards given intermittently.

If you posed a question about love, romance, relationship, marriage, friendship and your social life and you get this response, gift giving is definitely a plus to bring about small blessings and improvement in relationship. It will not have a large effect and giving more will not cause a greater response, at least not one you would want. The idea here is to shift things gradually. Rather like taming a wild creature. Any sudden moves will cause it to bolt. Here we are making small offerings and nudging slightly closer as we do so. The point of this exercise, however, is to get them edging closer to you as well.

Of inquiries about business, finances, job or career success or your future prosperity, this fall of the Dark Feather indicates that small things can be done, minor investments, fractional changes but it is not time to do anything large or that involves a huge risk. This is calculated risk time. This is increase through increments. Don't get us wrong. The atmosphere and influence of the Dark Feather is positive. It is just not very powerful.

If you had concerns about health or healing, then this placement of the Dark Feather is positive for healing, but not for quick healing. This is a slow healing process. This is a take your medicine or vitamins or supplements or whatever each day as directed until you gradually improve, get stronger and are vibrantly healthy again. This goes for helping others to heal as well. Small healing sessions are much to be preferred to large and powerful healing efforts. It just isn't going to happen all at once and you are wasting your energy if you are pushing it to do so.

As to your spiritual path, your magical life and progress, the Dark Feather is very positive for making slow but sure progress on the path. It favors regular rituals of a day to day fashion. Habits of magic, so to speak. Make your life more magical in small ways. Give daily offerings to the spirits for a while. If you wish your life to be more magical, do more magic. Let magic inform your life with its wonder, bit by bit. There is no need to rush. Enchantment is the art and science of ecstasy. Why be in a hurry?

191

THE PHILTRE OF TRUE LOVE

With the landing of the Dark Feather in the outer circle of the Philtre of True Love a small blessing in terms of love and relationships will surely come into your life. Whoever appears has the power to alter your life in small ways, but certainly for the better and this represents progress for you even while it is just a step or two forward. Be on the lookout for strangers bearing gifts, and for friends who wish to draw closer. This is an opportunity for you and may very well lead to improvements in your material situation.

If you had a question about love, romance, relationship, friendship, marriage or your social life, this is a very positive response that will draw to you those who will make a difference in your life and who are really meant for you. Being the Dark Feather, it is possible that they will come into your life for a brief period, so that you know of their existence, and then out again and then appear again later when the influences are stronger. This could also indicate a brief romance or fling. Nothing that lasts in this case, but something very sweet and wonderful while it does endure. Hugs and kisses of delight, we dreamed of you the other night.

When you are interested in getting information about business, finances or job or career success, this position of the Dark Feather is great for short term success in advancement in those areas, most definitely coming through a connection to someone you know or will meet. It need not even be the strongest connection, just one that you feel good about. Since this is just a limited time offer, you don't have to stress overall about the future. Just take the opportunity when it arrives and do your best with it.

Questions regarding health and healing are also very favorable here, although the energy that comes to you is in terms of healing relationships, which is to say via individuals whose influence is one of healing and who are energizing to you. And, if you turn around and do the same for others, surely this healing will spread out into the world and eventually return to you in time, as all your magic does.

Oh, what a blessing it is to find one's true kindred in the world where it is often so difficult to encounter our kind. Were you calling to them? Wishing for them to come? It may just be a passing encounter. Perhaps just a short time together at a festival. But those moments together are precious and surely inspiring and you will be able to go forth again renewed with faith that your kindreth will return in time, again and again. Such is the life of spirit and magic.

THE PHIAL OF EVERLASTING YOUTH

The placement of the Dark Feather in the outer circle of the Phial of Everlasting Youth is a boon for one's health, one's level of energy and one's feeling of wellbeing. One is revitalized, filled with youthful spirit and enthusiasm and this is a blessing not only for one's ability to get things done but also for one's health and one's body, especially. It is a bit like being a child again, only for a short time. Although, it may also indicate an increase of activity in your life. Things which seemed slow now begin to hustle and bustle about. Take advantage of this energy while it lasts, for it will surely pass in a week or two or a month at the most.

If you had question that had to do with love, romance, relationship, marriage, friendship or your social life, this fall of the Dark Feather is wondrous for a renewal of energy and activity in those areas. There is, however, an innocence to this placement. It is best to let go of all hidden agendas and just hang out with those you love, those you encounter and those you enjoy being around and relax and play for a while. Let the adult games go. Be childlike and just enjoy the moment.

That will bring you luck in the future. Stop trying to get somewhere and just be where you are.

When you ask a question about business, finances, job or career success or your prosperity in general, this position of the Dark Feather gets things going. There should be an increase in business dealings and purchases. This is also a good time for small investments or starting new things but not large endeavors. The power here, while good, is a bit weak and limited. So, proceed into the new, but with caution. Don't take unnecessary risks, they are unlikely to work out. But this is a perfect time for smaller enterprises.

If you had an inquiry about health or healing, this response is certainly positive for healing within yours'elf, helping others to heal and feeling healthy. If you are recovering from an illness, however, don't wear yours'elf out just because you suddenly feel great. Feel great, but still rest. Do what you can to make this energy endure. Don't waste it all at once. Like the old saying concerning money: Don't spend it all in one place; don't spend your energy all at once. Savor this sense of increasing wellness and do whatever you can to keep it going.

As to inquiries about your spiritual and magical path and life, this position of the Dark Feather is a small boon for those areas. Since it is in the outer realm, the indication is very favorable for doing magic, particularly if it involves others, for group interaction is especially beneficial here. None-the-less, the material realm will be stirred around you. The possibility of the arrival of signs and omens is also strong. You may get an offer to join in some magical working or someone's religious service, so join in, even if it is not precisely attuned to your own beliefs. Hold your magic within you and let the magic spread into your life and the world around you.

194

Part Four
. . . Charms

Besides the personal charm that represents you and the otherworldly charm that indicates magic from the spirit world, you might also have charms for your significant others that you use from time to time, or have a charm for some person with whom you are interacting and who may bear some influence regarding the question you have put to the oracle.

Chapter 7:
The Personal Charm

The Personal Charm represents one's personal magical power. These are powers one has achieved and earned and cannot be taken away from one.

The Inner Circle: The Torch of the Eternal Silver Flame of Elfin

When the Personal Charm falls so it is on or principally touching the torch at the center of the oracle, it indicates that your power is being increased. The spirits support you and are uplifting you and especially giving you the power to deal with the situation evidenced by your question. You are literally being empowered.

If instead, the Personal Charm landed within the Inner Circle upon a Sacred Magical Treasure other than the Torch in the center, then you may find the corresponding treasure below and read the interpretation to consult the oracles.

THE ORB OF HEALING

This is surely an indication of one's ability to heal one's s'elf and to heal others, particularly on the Shamanic planes of being, through them and by virtue of one's personal energy and spirit. It urges one to increasingly become a healing influence so that everyone one meets and every situation one encounters is uplifted by one's presence. (Note the Hallmark movies and television show *The Good Witch* for an example of this sort of magical power.)

When you are asking about relationship, love and romance, this reply indicates that your own healing spirit will positively affect the situation. No matter what is happening, be positive and healing about it. If you are asking: will so and so like me or love me or become romantically involved with me, the response is inclined to indicate that this is very likely because you are so charming or have such wonderful magical power of personality. But the question then becomes: are you sure that this is what you truly want? That this person is really the right person for you? Whatever the answer, do what is best for you both, in as kind, loving and healing a fashion as you can.

If your query involved finances or business, then this answer tells you to affect the situation from the inner planes. Use your magic to make things better, to improve the situation. You clearly have the power to do so. You don't need to doubt that fact. Now, you just need to take action or continue the magic you have set in motion, to reinforce your spells and let time and the spirits do what they do.

Obviously, if you were inquiring about healing and health, this is a great response, indicating that meditation, visualization and other healing techniques that function through the mind, imagination and spirit planes, are highly advised and certainly will have a positive effect upon the situation. Heal and do healing.

As to questions involving one's spiritual path and development, this reply urges you to continue to improve and increase your powers, particularly the potency of your personality and your healing abilities. Be a joy in everyone's life. Be an inspiration. Be yours'elf as best you may, ever improving what you do and all will turn out as it should in the best way possible.

THE WAND OF WISHING

Many, perhaps, most responses from the oracle ask us to consider others and our affect upon them, however, this reply directs one to consider one's own magical and spiritual development and how it can be uplifted, improved and furthered. What can you do to increase your charms, your magical power, for from that others will indirectly be benefited. The key is to make all things that increase you to therefore and de facto make things better for others as well.

This is the Personal Charm in the inner realms of the Wand of Wishing, thus its power mostly comes in and from the Faerie realms and the shamanic dimensions. Remember, the spirit world is the true world upon which the material world is formulated. Which is not to say that the material doesn't affect the realms of spirit, for they are intimately connected, but this is the primal realm, the Source where power and magic arises. From here, the world is and can be shaped.

If your question was about relationship, romance or friendship, and in the experience of these elves as professional diviners at least half the questions we've ever had put to the oracles involve love and romance, then the response here says to pursue your own spiritual needs first and foremost in this instance and let relationships develop on their own. Don't do anything directly. It's not necessary. It's not the time and you have more important things to do at this point.

Inquiries about business and finances are to be viewed in terms of increasing your own prosperity at this juncture. Later, when you have increased your own good, you can share it with others. Still, being in the inner realm, this is more about magical and spiritual advancement and increase, more about prophet than profit, and worldly concerns are secondary here. Thus, if you can put off dealing with money matters it is best to do so until this energy is fulfilled. Another situation may arise later and you may have stepped into a somewhat different dimension where the concerns that trouble you now no longer hold sway or have any relevance.

Concerning the issues of health and healing, be healed. You have the power. Energize yours'elf in the astral planes and visualize and, perhaps more importantly, feel your body of light. It is essentially immortal and impervious to all disease except spiritual ones. If your spirit is strong, nothing can harm you.

This is primarily, as we said, a response that speaks to your spiritual and magical development. Use your powers to make yours'elf greater as a spirit. Not as opposed to others. This is about you and has nothing to do with others directly. Be as great as you can be. See yours'elf as another Merlin, Gandalf, Galadriel or Gandhi, Mother Teresa, Dalia Lama or whomever you view to be a high wizard and evolved spiritual being and act from that place of power and magic. Increase yours'elf and your own good and let your magic naturally overflow into the world.

THE COIN OF THE REALM

Upon getting the Personal Charm in the inner circle of the Coin of the Realm, you can feel assured that you have some credit in the realms of spirit. This is like having a savings account in the Faerie worlds, an account filled with magical coinage that you can use and spend to achieve what you wish in the various dimensions. This is surely a sign of good karma or of hard work rewarded to say the least. You've done the magic and now it has accumulated and increased for it is paying dividends. As always, use it as wisely as you can. Invest it in your future, into your magic and, if you will, help others to advance thems'elves upon the path for that is quite possibly how you came this far in the first place.

If your inquiry was focused on love, romance, or relationship then the reply indicates that things in these areas will be furthered if you pour your energy, your heart and your soul into them. Your magic charge is at full. Use this energy to do more magic to obtain what it is you desire. Just be sure that you are following the principles of the light. That you are doing what is best for everyone in the situation. You cannot violate the true will of others without wandering into the dark realms and eventually paying the price for doing so. But then, you don't have to. You have charm. Use it to entice those you desire and if they don't respond then know that they aren't really right for you or the time isn't quite right for you to come together. Be patient. This is about letting your magic unfold.

On the matter of business or financial dealings, then obviously this is good sign. You have a magical power highlighted at this time for attracting prosperity to you. Feel successful. Be successful. Let the spirits do the rest. Really, let the spirits take care of it for you. They are eager to do so.

This is not a bad sign if your question concerned health or healing, but it is not a direct answer either, other than to say that you have the energy in the astral realms that will enable you to effect healing there and that will filter down into the material realm. The emphasis here is on shamanic healing. Drum, dance, do trance work, put forth the healing vibes and subtle changes toward health and healing will occur.

When asking of your spiritual life and path, this response says that you are likely to be uplifted shortly. You are advancing upon the path and you need do nothing more than continue to progress as best you may. You have some spiritual, magical power. Let it radiate into the dimensions and bring you greater luck still.

THE FEATHER OF TRUTH TELLING

When you receive the Personal Charm in the inner circle of the Feather of Truth Telling, one is called to examine one's own powers, how one uses them, the effects one produces in the worlds, particularly the netherworlds, and how one may increase, improve, develop and refine one's skills, abilities and magical powers. It is also quite possible that some truth will be revealed to you, some hidden knowledge, some esoteric secrets that will heighten and increase your knowledge and thus your power.

Questions that are centered on relationship, friendship and romance are best if they have a spiritual dimension. This is the inner circle and everything focuses on the magic and one's relationships in the realms of spirit, spiritual development and one's relationship with the spirits, the Shining Ones and others on the path. Again, one is called to examine one's s'elf and one's magic but also there is an indication that some truth about relationship, either an individual relationship or about techniques of relating in general, will be revealed to you.

This is not necessarily a good sign for business and finances in the world, having to do with the inner spiritual world, however, it may increase your understanding of how to bargain and make deals effectively with spirits in the astral realms and that may redound to your benefit in material terms in time. The worlds are connected and all we do in one realm reverberates through the other dimensions.

Inquiries concerning health and healing are positively favored if one does one or more of a variety of healing practices such as Qigong, Reiki or just meditation and positive visualization. Improve your skills in these techniques and greater techniques will be revealed to you or you will be led to those who can improve your knowledge and powers in these areas.

Of course, one's path, one's relationship on the path and one's relation to the realms of magic are especially benefitted when getting this response as long as you are being honest with yours'elf and others in your magical workings. And certainly, the truth is your ally in those realms where the genuine is valued greatly and the deceptive is but a pale and fading shadow that cannot stand the light.

THE MAGIC MIRROR OF REFLECTION

Upon receiving the Personal Charm in the inner circle of the Magic Mirror of Reflection one is called to meditate upon one's abilities, how one uses them, not simply the immediate effects but the long term and extended effects of one's charm, and how one may best improve ones'elf and one's personal powers. Being in the inner circle, we are talking about how one's magic reverberates through the Universe.

Concerning questions about relationship, romance and friendship, this response suggests that one needs to examine the energy that one puts out and the types of people that it attracts. Are you attracting the right people to you? People that are good for you and for your path? Are your powers helping them on their path?

Regarding inquiries about business, finances and money, you need to ask yours'elf if your magic is truly attracting success and prosperity in your life and, if so, how are you using it? Are you helping others to prosper as well? Remember the magic of sharing and generosity. Invest in others. Invest in the magic and in doing so, invest in your own life and future.

If your inquiry had to do with health and healing, then consider whether your magic and enchantments are healing to you and others, or if you are being drained by your workings or are draining others. Remember, all that you do returns to you. You are ever creating your own future through your magic/your actions, in all that you do. Your magic should be revitalizing for you and all associated with you. If this is the case, then you are blest, indeed.

In response to questions about one's spiritual life and path, this oracle guides one to reflect upon the influence of one's personality in the world and particularly in the shamanic realms. What does your light look like? What is the vibration that you are radiating in and through the dimensions? How may you refine and improve what you do? Is your vibration true and genuine? Or is it filled with static from force, uncertainty and un-clarity? Become your true s'elf and all will evolve toward the fulfillment of your true desires.

THE SACK OF GIVING

Upon receiving the Personal Charm in the inner circle of the Sack of Giving, one is called to consider doing service and particularly spiritual service, as well as to contemplate what special talents and abilities you have that will be of benefit to others, especially others on the path of magic and spirit. How can you use your powers so as to make the world a better, more elven world to live in.

Clearly, you have something to give and most likely it is something very unique and special that almost no one else can offer to the world. You are a vital piece of the puzzle that creates Elfin on Earth and makes the world a more magical place to be and experience. Pour your special magic into the world around you, and into the lives of those you encounter and great benefits are bound to come to you in time. All magic returns to its source like the great and magical salmon of wisdom to the place of its spawning.

When you get this response as a reply to questions about love, romance, relationship and friendship, you are directed to give your energy to those you wish to influence. Obviously, if your question was: will so and so leave me alone, then you need to apply your magic elsewhere in the directions you wish to develop. Are you a musician? A writer? A dancer? A poet? An artist? An actor? Create and offer your creations to those you seek to know. Don't be attached to the response. If you are expecting appreciation or an immediate or direct return, you may be disappointed. The idea here is to give freely, like Santa Claus, and to observe what the individual does with that gift. That will tell you nearly everything you need to know about them and your relationship, or lack thereof.

On issues having to do with business or money, then the response is to give, to invest, but not necessarily directly. Give to charity. Give to a church or other worthy fund. Donate. Further those on the path and let the magic deal with finances on the material plane, altering the atmosphere and situation to favor you. In other words, make offerings to the spirits, to your gods, if you have gods (most elves don't worship gods but we do try to keep a positive relationship with those beings we call the Shining Ones), and most of all give of yours'elf. If you are borrowing from others to give (such as taking the life of some poor animal as a sacrifice), it is not the same and the one who is actually sacrificed or sacrificing will eventually reap the benefit and you will be indebted to them.

On questions about healing and health, this response says that by giving of yours'elf and your energy, you revitalize your being. Good works, in this case especially, promote healing. Remember, preventive medicine is the best, so do good works on a regular basis and this will help increase your powers of longevity. And if you practice the healing arts, focus your energy on others and their healing, especially in this instance by working through the astral planes and the shamanic realms.

205

As to spiritual inquiries and questions about one's path, the reply is very clear, as already noted. Give of yours'elf. Pour your devotion into the path. Improve yours'elf by helping others. Participate in group rituals or events if available. A bit of volunteerism is appropriate here.

THE PHILTRE OF TRUE LOVE

The Personal Charm in the inner realm of the Philtre of True Love is clearly a very positive response to any question concerning love, relationship, romance and friendship. This increases your power to attract others, particularly to attract loving relationships to yours'elf and to draw to you true and loyal friends. On the other hand, it is important that you understand that the essence of this power comes from being true and loyal as a friend and as loving and kind as one can be to all those that one attracts.

At the same time, you should comprehend that with this power you may attract all sorts of people, even those you may not find attractive or who are not quite right for you, but it is vital that you treat them with kindness and respect as well and doing your best to help them find their own direction and path and, in as much as possible, aid them to find those that are right for them. In this sense, you are helping to set the Universe in order so that everything works out as it should for everyone, and this is surely to each individual's benefit.

On queries about money or business, this response points to the fact that one should seek those that one can trust but it also increases one's ability to attract those who wish to do business with you and who are inclined in positive ways toward your financial wellbeing. It is likely that when you receive this oracle that you will be given gifts or that other benefits will come to you. Invest wisely while you can. But remember, since this is the inner circle, the magical circle, these benefits are likely to be of a magical nature or to involve your magic or path.

On matters of health and healing, this answer points toward being with those one loves and, in fact, being in love and being loving, as keys to improving one's health. Thus, right company and association is very important and since this is the inner circle, the company of one's kindred who are on the same magical and spiritual path is greatly advised.

When you receive this in response to questions about your spiritual path, then the answer is clearly to use your charm to find your kindred but it may also indicate that your path will be furthered by those you love and who love you in return. Let love be your magic and let your magic be love and wonders will occur.

THE PHIAL OF EVERLASTING YOUTH

Upon getting the Personal Charm in the inner circle of the Phial of Everlasting Youth, one is called to consider the enduring effects of one's magic and, in fact, how to make one's magic persist and last. What is it you wish to achieve in the long run? Where do you see yours'elf and your magic in lifetimes to come? Are the issues you are inquiring about really relevant to your magical and spiritual life? Or are they just passing fancies with nothing of real importance for you?

When you have asked about love, romance, relationship and friendship, the response indicates that one should seek relationships that will remain and to seek the enduring part of relationships that are just of a passing nature. In other words, act in such ways as to leave a lasting impression of a positive nature. Help each on their path. Give them something of your energy, a spark from the flame of your spirit that will help ignite their own soulful being.

Regarding questions concerning business and finances, one is directed to examine one's own ability to survive and thrive in the world and through the ages. What talents do you have that help you make it and succeed in the world? How can you heighten and improve those abilities? Clearly, you have a charm that helps and protects you. Develop its powers further. There is something about you that attracts success. How can you make it stronger and even more successful?

Issues of health and healing are nearly always dealt with on the shamanic planes of being when the charm falls in the inner circle. Since, it is in the Phial of Everlasting Youth, this is clearly a good sign for health and healing. Use your magic to make yours'elf, your spirit, your body of light even stronger and more resilient. From that, you can affect the material plane and thus your physical body or the bodies of others. Become a permanent healing presence in other people's lives.

On questions of spirit and one's spiritual path, the response says to continue onward. Don't give up. You are making progress and everything you truly achieve, everything that you have truly made part of your spirit, will continue into the future. All genuine achievements are carried forth from lifetime to lifetime. If you have earned it, and apparently you have, it cannot be taken away from you, you can only lose it if you let it atrophy through neglect and non-use. Increase your powers. Like your muscles, they need regular exercise.

The Outer Circle:
The Elf Horns of Calling

If the Personal Charm lands beyond the circle of the oracle, it means that all your efforts are currently in vain. You might as well save your energy. Others are distorting what you do and at this time there is little you can do about it other than wait for the atmosphere to change. Be patient, your time will come.

If instead, your token landed within the Outer Circle, you may find the Sacred Magical Treasure below that the Personal Charm has landed upon and read the interpretation to consult the oracles.

THE ORB OF HEALING

If you have received the Personal Charm in this place in the outer circle, it indicates that you have some real healing skills that you have developed in this or previous lives or both that you can use to repair or improve the situation surrounding the question you have asked. The fact that it is the Orb of Healing tends to indicate that some rejuvenation or revitalization is necessary concerning this issue. Strive to make things better.

If you were asking about romance, friendship or relationship issues then the indication is that you can use your Personal Charm to make things more harmonious and satisfying. You have the power, the power of Personality, to achieve what you want in this situation. You don't need to force things; in fact, force is the opposite of what you need; enchant those around you. Why make things difficult when it can be so easy? Also, ask yours'elf if the people around you are good for you. Do they contribute to your healing? Are they a positive life influence? Are you good for them?

Regarding inquiries about business, finances and money in general, the oracle says that you have everything you need to move forward in the world and that particularly you have the skills and abilities that you need to succeed. Use your personal power. Let your light shine. Attract money and success to you. You can do it.

Of course, matters of health and healing are particularly highlighted here as this is the place of the Orb of Healing. But you may wish to examine your personal life. Are you getting enough exercise? How is your diet? Does it contribute to your wellbeing? You surely have personal healing power but are you supplementing it and reinforcing it with good habits?

On spiritual questions, this response denotes a need to further develop your personal healing abilities. You've got skills. You've got magical power. Now, it is time to make them better and stronger. The path is not stagnant. Increase your skill. Enlightenment is not an end goal but a continuing process. The development of our s'elves and our magical abilities are also near infinite in nature. There is always more to learn, always things we can improve. The path of Mastery is never ending. Do your best and the best will come to you.

THE WAND OF WISHING

When you receive the Personal Charm in the Wand of Wishing in the outer circle, you are particularly blest and the chances of success for the question you have asked is greatly heightened. Make your wish. Do your magic. However, know that its energy is more powerful in the exoteric world than the esoteric one. More likely to take effect in the material planes than in the subtle ones, although they are intimately connected.

If your question concerned friendship, romance and relationship, then once again, set your magic in motion. You have the power to achieve what you will and, perhaps just as importantly, the time is ripe. Wave your magic wand. Let your enchantment unfold then sit back, relax and watch it all come to pass in time.

Business, finances and financial dealings are also favored here. Again, use your power to set the world in motion. Attract money and prosperity to yours'elf or toward those you wish to benefit. Whatever you invest at this time will likely bring rewards to you. The important thing is to follow your true wishes, your true path, to do the things that will further your inner ambitions, which is to say, doing what you love to do in order to make money is accented.

Health and healing will come about if you use your healing powers. Energize yours'elf. Radiate your personal energy. Visualize the results you desire. Wish for healing for yours'elf or others, pour healing into the world. Use the magnetic power of your hands and heart to beam out healing power.

Inquiries about one's spiritual life and path are less highlighted here, unless you are thinking of taking direct action in the world. This is not necessarily favorable for meditation or personal revelation, but if you are going to do a public ritual or work on your sanctuary or just donate energy into the world to make it, and thus you, better, then proceed with confidence, the Shining Ones support you.

THE COIN OF THE REALM

Clearly when one receives the Personal Charm in the outer circle of the Coin of the Realm one is due some luck that will most likely manifest in a material fashion, which is to say money or other things of value will come to you, most likely unexpectedly and perhaps in ways utterly unforeseen except by this oracle. You are attracting benefits in your life and whatever is most valued in the world in a material sense, which is to say actual objects, are working their way toward you.

If you gamble this may be the time to do so. However,

remember this is your Personal Charm and not the Otherworldly Charm and thus skill is a factor here. The time is right but it is not pure luck but ability that holds sway. So, pick games that are based on skill not luck alone.

If your question was directed toward love, relationship, romance or friendship, then this is also a good sign, but the indication is that you should give something of value to those you wish to influence. It is quite possible that someone will give you something worthwhile, but that is a minor consideration, the important thing here is for you to donate, gift, re-gift and thus make the atmosphere for forming relationships more favorable.

When asking about business and finances, you are, as we said, in luck. You have the magic touch, at least for now and certainly concerning this issue. If you are wise, you will take what you receive and re-invest it, use it well and it will pay dividends in the future. You seem to have a knack for financial dealings.

Inquiries about health and healing are not directly favored here, however, you should have the money with this response to get what you need for the remedies or medicines that will heal you or your others. Sweat equity may be part of this, but the important thing is that you have or will get what you need.

As to your spiritual path, this reply indicates that real benefits will accrue from your path. The object or objects you receive are less likely to be money than magical items. Just as King Arthur was given the magical sword Excalibur, so you may be gifted an object of magical power and significance that will increase your influence and ability and help you on the path.

THE FEATHER OF TRUTH TELLING

Upon getting the Personal Charm in the outer circle of the Feather of Truth Telling, one is called examine ones'elf in the world and in particular how one uses one's powers and the effects one produces in the world. Good intentions, while important, are not enough. The results of your magic are also important. What effect are you having on others and their lives and what is the effect of your magic in your own life and path? Be honest with yours'elf.

At the same time, this response says that if you have used your magic well, then greater truths will be revealed to you. No one will be able to deceive you, especially in reference to the question you have asked of the oracle. Examine the situation carefully and all that is hidden will be revealed. Falsehoods will be exposed.

In issues that involve relationship, romance, friendship and love, the oracle directs you to use your powers directly, truly and purely. Be genuine with others and all that is artificial will be made clear. Plus, your charm will inspire others to be genuine as well. This will surely rebound to your benefit as well as theirs.

When one is inquiring about business and money, this response indicates that honest dealing on your part will compel others to do the same or failing that it will expose their deception. It is not, in and of itself, a money-oriented reply. Before investing or spending, one should examine the situation carefully. Be sure that everything is as it should be, as it seems and as it is presented.

Health and healing are favored here, however, once again, one needs to be honest with ones'elf about one's habits, diet, etc. Are you really doing what is best for your body?

In terms of one's path and spiritual life, the oracle directs one to be as open as possible about one's path. Perhaps the

213

time has come to reveal to those who are ready that you are an elf, faerie, witch, wizard, etc. Stand strong in your beliefs and have faith in the validity of your path.

THE MAGIC MIRROR OF REFLECTION

When the Personal Charm falls in the outer realms of the Magic Mirror of Reflection, it suggests that one should meditate upon one's powers and how one uses them in the world. What effect do you have on other people? Are you encouraging them to better thems'elves? Are you helping them along? Or are you only out for yours'elf and your own benefit and wellbeing? Surely not. How do you create win-win situations in which everyone is benefited?

Also, what are your true powers? This is to say: not what power you may have because you temporarily hold a position of authority over others, but what is the power or powers of your personality? If you didn't have any direct worldly power, what could you achieve on your own, just using the power of your personality? Can you make friends easily? Can you influence people? Do people immediately like you and have a good sense of your being when they meet you? And how do they feel after they've known you for a while?

On questions concerning relationship, love, romance and friendship, the answer is quite clear. Your charms will have the desired effect. But reflect upon what this means for the other person. Are they truly meant for you? Are you what is best for them? Be clear about what you want to happen and what you intend. Remember, you are a magic wielder, your word is your bond. If you pause and think about the person or situation, all shall become clear to you.

In reference to inquiries having to do with business and finances, again, you have the power to influence people toward what you want, but you also have the power to reflect upon the situation and see to the depths of the matter. Therefore, examine the situation carefully. What can you do to make things work better, more smoothly, to increase the potential for success for everyone involved in this situation.

On questions about health and healing, the oracle says that you have the power to heal, but first pause and contemplate what the source of the illness may be. Don't just treat the symptoms. Get to what is causing the problem to arise. You wish to heal this permanently and this you can do if you deal with the roots of the issue. And, most of all, be healing to those around you. That is really the best way to heal yours'elf.

As to your spiritual life, you should consider how your powers in the world advance your spiritual development. Are your material life and spiritual life directly and intimately connected? Which is to say, do you live the life magical, elfin and spiritual in the world? Or, are you like so many people who separate their acts in the world from their religious beliefs so that they do whatever profits them during the week and are only religious on whatever their holy day happens to be? Integrate your life and your psyché and advance swiftly thereby to the higher realms of magic and the inner realms of Elfin.

THE SACK OF GIVING

When the Personal Charm lands in the outer reaches of the Sack of Giving, one is directed to give of one's s'elf to others. Pitch in as best you may, but most of all give what you have in abundance and by doing so inspire those around you to do the same. Encourage people, empower people, lift their spirits, arouse their courage, let them know that they have what it takes, that they can do it and all that they need to do really is to persevere and to keep trying.

You can, of course, give material things. This, after all, is the material realm and signifies your life as an elf, fae or magician/enchanter in the world. You can give money or your time or some other thing but since it is your Personal Charm, your magic, in this place, it is most important that what you give is a positive attitude and an example of how one's goals can be accomplished, demonstrate how one can successfully follow the Elven Way in the world.

On questions about relationship, romance, love and friendship, the answer is that you need to put more of yours'elf into the relationship. Don't try to force things. Let the subtle power of your personality have its effect. Give of yours'elf without expectation of return. Give freely. Give generously and go about your business. Your gifts are a magic that will work their way into the situation to help it and make things better. There is no guarantee with this response that a person will like you or get involved with you, but remember, if your gift of magic doesn't work with a particular individual you are interested in, it will find its way and guide you to someone with whom you can find fulfillment.

When the question concerns business or money, this reply advises one to invest, particularly one's energy and effort, in the situation. Give what you can contribute and this will further things in a positive way. This may be a well that needs to be primed. And since this is the Personal Charm, it may be what people need is your leadership, your enthusiasm and to see your own devoted effort to make things better.

Regarding an inquiry having to do with health or healing, this is an indication that you have the power to heal yours'elf, this situation or another person, if you would just put out the energy to do so. Contribute what you can to healing. Be healing. Radiate healing. Charge an object with healing powers that you can use when you need to do so, or give it to another to aid with their healing or place it in a location that could use upliftment and healing.

If you are asking about your spiritual life and path, then this response says that you should consider putting energy into your vortex (elven name for coven or sorcerer's group), especially into encouraging others on the path, of setting an example for them and dedicating yours'elf once again toward leading the life elfin with as much enthusiasm and vigor and joie de vie as you are able to manifest. Let your elf light shine unto the world.

THE PHILTRE OF TRUE LOVE

Receiving the Personal Charm in the outer reaches of the Philtre of True Love indicates that you have the power to attract to yours'elf those who are right for you. This is the power of the soul at work and the influence of your personal magic unfolding in the world. It is likely when you receive this response that synchronicities, particularly meaningful coincidences that have to do with relationship or which come through those you know or meet unexpectedly, will occur and this will provide revelations for you.

This is the attraction of those who are meant for each other, of those who are sympatico, those who hum together when they are near to each other, their vibrations singing in unison, their energy alive and awakened by each other.

Thus, if your inquiry concerned love, romance, relationship and friendship, this is a great sign for you, especially for drawing to you those that will further you in your life and who may be your soulmate or possibly your friend for life and beyond. Even if you should part in time and go your separate ways, you will remember this relationship forever. This is a sign that you are ready for your soulmate to appear. The time is right. If you have already met your soulmate, then now is the time to do something great together.

Concerning questions about business and finances, again the indication is that you will attract the right people that you can trust to do business with, who will profit you financially or give you the information or hints that you need to do so and who may prove to be business partners and friends from now on.

When one's inquiry is about health and healing, the indication is that friendship is the key to healing. Your Personal Charm, your true friendship and genuine affection for the individual will prove to be healing for them. And vice versa, if it is you who needs healing, if it is your health you are inquiring about, then being around those who really care for you is the solution. It is also possible that the information you need, the particular diet, or remedy or other healing regimen will be revealed to you by someone who really cares.

As far as your spiritual path is concerned, this reply says that you will find those who are good company, right company for your path, but it is important that you trust your own feelings of attraction. Don't get involved with someone just because they seem to be treading the same path if you aren't really attracted to them as a person. Trust your reservations. Trust your instincts. The true elven path is one of love and friendship. Find friends you can count on and your path will unfold and be revealed to you.

THE PHIAL OF EVERLASTING YOUTH

When the Personal Charm lands in the outer realms of the Phial of Everlasting Youth, one is advised to look at the situation afresh, with the eyes of a child so to speak, without expectation of any sort, or any assumptions about what may happen, as well as to put aside one's preferences and aversions and to view the situation as if for the first time, as an outsider considering the question might do. You may wish, however, to retain your essential, pure and innocent wish for the outcome you desire.

Also, renew your charm, which is to say, do something to revive yours'elf, renew your energy so that your spirit shines (and here we are using spirit in the sense when someone says so and so shows a lot of spirit or they had a very spirited exchange of ideas). Make yours'elf a welcome and positive addition to every situation.

If you were asking about love, romance, relationship or friendship, then this response bids you to do something new. Get out of your habits. Look at the question in new ways, but mostly do new things, do something to revive and refresh the relationship or your approach to relationships. Go places you haven't been before. Get out of the comfortable rut and take a bit a walk on the wild side to liven things up.

If money or business is the theme of your inquiry then you may contemplate what you can do that is different that will improve your finances but also think about what you can do that will keep the money coming in or keep the business thriving. Don't think simply in terms of the new, the different and original, but also consider the lasting and enduring. How do you make it work and keep working? Don't look at just the short-term fix but a permanent solution to what you desire.

On inquiries about health and healing, this is a very positive reply, but one that particularly emphasizes play as a remedy for ill. Laughter, joy, and having a good time are the cure here. Liven things up. Bring a bit a fun to bear and revive those who have been feeling ill and awaken the youthful spirit in your own s'elf and this will induce healing. Games, role playing, hobbies or whatever floats your, or the individual who needs healing's, boat will serve the occasion.

Being in the outer world, this response when the question is directed towards one's path or spiritual development says that one should explore new avenues in one's path but even more so suggests you ask yours'elf what you can do to revive the feeling of excitement, revelation and enthusiasm that you felt when you first awakened and discovered your path. How do you get back that feeling and keep it alive?

Chapter 8:

The Otherworldly Charm

The Otherworldly Charm signifies powers that one has been granted but that one has, as yet, not earned. The Shining Ones are giving you extra power in this situation but you must make it your own through practice and perseverance.

The Inner Circle: The Torch of the Eternal Silver Flame of Elfin

When the Otherworldly Charm touches the torch at the center of the oracle, it means that the powers that have been loaned to you are now becoming your own. You have done well and you have earned for yours'elf that which seemed only temporarily granted. This is surely a good sign for you. The degree to which the Charm rest upon the torch indicates how great this power will be.

If instead the Otherworldly Charm landed within the

Inner Circle upon a Sacred Magical Treasure other than the Torch in the center, then please read the corresponding treasure below:

THE ORB OF HEALING

The Otherworldly Charm combined with the Orb of Healing beams healing energy into our lives. In the realm of the Torch, the inner dimensions, it signifies healing energy coming into your life from the Elven realms, from Elfin and from the Shining Ones. It is particularly a sign of spiritual healing, or mental and emotional healing, but which, none-the-less, affects one's physical being. It is the power of mind over matter in terms of one's physical wellbeing. And is surely a blessing upon one's spiritual life.

If your inquiry involved relationship, then doing what is most healing toward ones'elf and one's others is recommended. Take the high road, the path of spiritual upliftment and evolution and accept the other for whom they are at the moment and nurture their spiritual development. This doesn't mean, as some may interpret it, that one should force one's views on others, or attempt to coerce others into what one thinks is a more spiritual life. This is about a joyous acceptance of ones'elf and allowing others the freedom to go in the direction they choose.

If your question had to do with business or finances, the answer indicates that doing what is most loving and healing in the situation will help alter the atmosphere to one that is more conducive to success in the world. Although, it may indicate one should simply leave things be for the time being and concentrate on one's spiritual life.

Thus, if your question concerned healing, then this is a great sign to get, denoting that a spiritual attitude, a joyous disposition, an energetic spirit of being, the rejoicing of life and happiness will positively affect your situation and make everything more likely to succeed.

And if you asked about your spiritual life, your elven path, then the answer is to heal, to be healing, to channel healing energy through your life, to open yours'elf to the healing vibrations of Elfin and allow its radiance to fill you and when you do, the path shall be revealed to you.

THE WAND OF WISHING

The Wand of Wishing is about being able to fulfill one's wishes. When one gets the Otherworldly Charm in this place it gives one extra magical power to achieve what one desires and since it is in the inner realm the indication is that the realms of magic, the elfin realms and one's relationship to them are especially highlighted. What is your wish for Elfin? What is your wish for yours'elf in Elfin? What is your wish for your kindred in Elfin?

No matter what your question concerned, this is a positive sign. It suggests that fulfillment of your wishes is near and that you just need to wish, use your magic and enchantment and let the spirits, let the otherworld and its magic, do the rest. Are you done? Did you wish upon an elven star? Blow spells upon a dandelion? Have you waved your magic wand around? Now it is time to let the magic do its part.

If you were asking about relationship then this indicates that those relationships that are most magical and most spiritual are to be preferred. This response speaks of *right company* and the need to associate with others on the path as well as do your best to help, share with and guide those who are your kindred. Also, it urges you to let go of those relationships that lead you astray or simply don't fulfill your spiritual needs and purpose. Remember, you have a destiny, a mission to accomplish. If it is romance you are seeking, you will find it among those who are also on the path of the Elven Way. Seek the company of other enchanters.

If one's concerns are of business or finances, this response from the oracle encourages one to do one's magic. Set the world in order in the elfin realms and they will affect one's success in the more mundane realms. Most folks believe that everything that happens in the world arises from the material world, but the elves believe that the worlds are interconnected, like a string, and you can pull on one end or the other, but both will affect what is going on. As Above, So Below, As Within, So Beyond. Pull the string in the realms of spirit and draw money to you or perhaps much more importantly draw to you those things that you need to further you on the path.

Questions of health and healing find this reply indicating that the power of positive thinking, which is really in a way what placebo magic is about; the will to heal, is a vital factor in healing. Visualize healing. Draw healing light into yours'elf or those who need healing. Practice Reiki or some other healing modality. We are not all powerful, but we do influence the world and when it comes to ours'elves and those close to us, our powers are much greater, particularly in this case as one is favored by the time as indicated by the Otherworldly Charm.

Questions concerning one's spiritual path and growth are especially favorable here. Most likely a promotion, so to speak, is coming to you. Not a mundane promotion. Not a matter of titles or prestige necessarily but a real increase in magical/spiritual power. It is possible that the Shining Ones have lent you this temporary boost in power to see what you do with it. Use it well and it may become a permanent possession, a real ability and skill and a part of your nature. Make it your own.

THE COIN OF THE REALM

The Otherworldly Charm in the place of the Coin of the Realm is a decidedly good sign if one is asking about finances. However, here in the inner realm it is not so much about money and financial success in the world but concerns energy and success in the nether realms. You should ask yours'elf: what is the Coin of the Realm? What do the spirits value most? What can you give, barter or trade that will make your way easier in the shamanic realms of being? Whatever it is, a bit extra is being given you. Use it to make progress on your path and all will go well.

If your question involved love and romance, then the oracle asks you what is the Coin of the Realm of romance, especially in inner world of spiritual romance and relationship. Why, it is love, kindness, consideration, loyalty and friendship. Be true to your relationships. Fulfill the spirit of the relationship, keep your vows and great benefits will come to you.

As to health, this gives you a bit of healing energy and some power of a spiritual sort. What can you get or give that would be healing to yours'elf or others? Use your energy to heal. You have extra power as a gift from the realms of Elfin. Share it. Spread it about. Exercise your healing powers. And give to those who have been healing to you. Appreciate and recognize the wondrous gifts you have been given. Reciprocation is an important elven value.

And if your inquiry had to do with your spiritual and magical path, then the spirits have deposited a bit extra into your account. Perhaps you can use it to pay off some of your karmic debts. Perhaps you wish to invest it those things that will pay off in the future. Quite possibly, you will be able to afford certain magical items or tools that you previously couldn't.

THE FEATHER OF TRUTH TELLING

When you receive the Otherworldly Charm in the inner circle of the Feather of Truth Telling, it signifies that you need to be honest with yours'elf about yours'elf, your life, your ambitions, your shortcomings, your desires, and whether your actions further your spiritual life or whether they are leading you and/or others astray. If you don't do this with complete candor you may very well lose the blessings and aid of the Shining Ones. It is also quite possible that the truth or some important truth or facts will be revealed to you. Secret knowledge may come to you. Deeper truths of the Universe, of magic, may be revealed. Don't ignore this truth, embracing it will help you, your magic and your life greatly.

Regarding matters of romance, friendship and relationship, one must ask one's s'elf if the relationship furthers one on one's path or not and also, are you helping others to be their best s'elves and to evolve. What is your magical and spiritual connection to those others? How may you proceed together to best utilize the blessings and powers that the Shining Ones have granted you?

If your query involves business, success or financial matters, then you need to examine your feelings, attitudes and relationship to money particularly concerning the issue or issues about which you are directly inquiring. Also, you must be honest in your dealings. This response cautions us against underhanded tactics and illegitimate business practices. You just won't get away with it so don't even try and if you are already involved with something shady, it's time to straighten things out. Thus, also look into the netherworlds, the astral planes and be sure that those you are dealing with are on the up and up. If not, the truth will be revealed. If your feelings and instincts are telling you something may be wrong, they are probably right.

In questions concerning health, the indication is that you

225

should do magic to improve your health, particularly your psychological, psychic health so to speak. You've been granted the power to do so, therefore now is the time to use that power purely, clearly and honestly.

As to questions directly about your path and your magic, the Otherworldly Charm makes the path clear. It dissolves misunderstandings, shows you a light through the mists of Elfin, and reduces doubt and uncertainty. See truly, the way opens.

THE MAGIC MIRROR OF REFLECTION

If you get the otherworldly charm in this position it is an indication that you must examine yours'elf, particularly your magical and spiritual s'elf in keeping with the question you have asked. This is the magic mirror that speaks truth that one may not wish to hear but also shows one not only what one is but what one can be, which is to say what one is in potential.

If your inquiry had to do with love or relationship or friendship or marriage, then examine yours'elf carefully, look at the relationship for what it truly is and ask yours'elf is this really what you want, does it fulfill your needs and is it genuinely the best thing for everyone involved?

When the question concerns business or finances, it indicates that one must think this situation over carefully and consider all the possibilities, particularly if it involves investment of any kind. Caution is advised. Don't be heedless. Proceed with knowledge. Base what you do on factual reality.

On the issue of health, this reply indicates that you need to see beyond the surface. Health is not merely skin deep, nor is it simply a matter of physical wellbeing. How is your spirit in this situation? How you feel and your psychological attitude also affects what is going on. In fact, here a strong spirit is key and vital to good health and healing.

Are you the elf you truly wish to be? Who you know yours'elf to be? Are you manifesting your most elfin s'elf, your highest s'elf? The otherworldly charm can help you do just that and the magical mirror of reflection can help you see the truth of your being. This is your magic, your path, and any question concerning it finds that continuing on the path is the right thing to do.

THE SACK OF GIVING

Upon receiving the Otherworldly Charm in the inner circle of the Sack of Giving, one is cautioned to use the extra energy and power that has been lent to one from the spirit realms and the Shining Ones, for the use and betterment of others. Be generous with this power. Help all you can help. Don't worry about what they will do with what you have given them, just give with best intentions and leave them to the responsibility for their actions. Nor need you worry about reciprocation. The return may not be direct, but you will receive benefits from your actions in due time. All you put out will come back to you. This is a law of life and of magic.

As to relationships and romance, well, clearly it is time to give to those you love. Give presents. Especially, since this is in the inner realm, be generous to those on the spirit planes. Give magical energy. Reward your allies and the spirits that serve you in an openhanded and handsome fashion. Burn candles. Do chants, or whatever it is that you do to energize the spirit realm.

If the inquiry had to do with business or finances, then the indication is that giving energy, pouring magic into the realms of spirit, will have an effect upon the material plane. Visualize what you desire and in doing so be magnanimous and munificent in your dealings. Give alms of spirit and give to those who are begging on the street. This will return to you multifold.

Regarding questions concerning health, this definitely points toward using your abilities to heal others. However, it also indicates that by helping others, by giving to others, you will be healed. Here we are speaking of the joy of giving in a very direct way. We might speak in this instance of the healing benefits of giving. But especially we are speaking of the spiritual benefits of giving. You are becoming nobility in the otherworldly realms.

In regard to questions concerning one's spiritual path, this reply is a clear indication of the need to give, to pitch in and help, to pursue one's path with a generous attitude and a determination to invest one's life energy into one's spiritual development. You need to proceed wholeheartedly. Dedicate yours'elf to your path fully. Aid those who are also on the path, give bountifully of your time and energy.

THE PHILTRE OF TRUE LOVE

When you receive the Otherworldly charm in this position in the inner realms, it is an indication that your powers of enchantment have been heightened and that your relationships and your ability to connect with others on the shamanic realms are positively enhanced and empowered. This is not so much about love and relationship in the mundane world but of making allies and achieving your will through enchantment in the realms of magic and spirit.

If your question concerned relationship, then this is a good sign, although again, it is a sign more of connecting with spirits, djinn and elementals than it is about romance. However, if you ask about romance it is an indication that romance can be affected through the realms of Elfin and

Faerie and thus this greatly strengthens your power to use spells and enchantment to connect with others, particularly if that connection has a magical and spiritual aspect to it. To use this power to draw love to you is, by its very nature, also drawing your destiny and attracting those that will influence and quicken your progress as a spiritual being.

If your inquiry had to do with wealth, business or finances then the indication is that you may successfully bargain with spirits in order to achieve your will concerning those matters. Remember to keep your promises and to pay what you have offered to the spirits, and also, be as generous as possible. Act wealthy, be wealthy in a giving way.

On questions of health, this reply denotes the significance of attitude and spiritual development as a key to longevity and a healthy and healing life. The saying: you are as young as you feel, is relevant here. Personality and spirit, by which in this case we mean your essential spirit and joie de vivre are the key factors to healing. When doctors say that a person is healing because they have a strong spirit and a will to live, they are speaking of this energy.

And if your question had to do with your spiritual life and development then be assured the Shining Ones are sending you energy that you can use to further your life and your destiny. The magic is with you and all you need to do is love life, love magic, love your kindred, love Elfin and revel in the love that the Divine Magic holds for you.

THE PHIAL OF EVERLASTING YOUTH

Getting the Otherworldly Charm in the place of the inner circle in the Phial of Everlasting Youth is a great sign for one's spiritual life and for energy affecting one's healing and especially the aging process in a positive way, keeping one young looking and youthful in expression and spirit. One is simply filled with life and lives life to the fullest. It gives a sparkle to one's eyes and a bounce to one's step.

In questions concerning romance and relationship, this helps the relationship to endure, to stay fresh and alive and filled with joy and happiness. This is particularly the case if the individuals involved share a spiritual path of some sort or share a common interest. Opposites may attract but they don't always stay together.

Relative to business or finances, the oracle indicates that keeping things new and fresh is advised. Introducing new products or ways of doing things is recommended, and new investments are also positively highlighted as long as they are in keeping with what is just and fair for everyone, which is to say one needs to think of win-win situations.

Naturally, if your question concerned health, this is a very positive sign for good health and healing, particularly for the power of magic (or prayer for those who pray) or evocation to have a healing effect upon one's s'elf or others. It also gives one the power to influence others toward healing, especially concerning the healing of the mind, emotions and psyché. Thus, its power is more toward psychological healing and the healing of emotional traumas than of physical healing but the two are deeply connected. One's presence, by its'elf, has a healing effect upon others.

And if one is asking about one's spiritual path, the response indicates that one would do well to involve ones'elf with and help those who are new to the path and to aid them in their progress. One will receive great benefits from doing this.

The Outer Circle:
The Elf Horns of Calling

When the Otherworldly Charm lands beyond the circle of the oracle, it means that the powers you were granted are now fading away. If it still touches the circle in part, it means that these powers are just beginning to fade and you may be able to revive them. On the other hand, it may very well indicate that you have completed the mission that has been assigned to you or for which you volunteered, and now you don't need these powers anymore.

If instead, the Otherworldly Charm landed within the Outer Circle, then please read the corresponding treasure below:

THE ORB OF HEALING

When getting the Orb of Healing in the outer circle, it is a wonderful sign for healing of one's body. Also, it can indicate developing various modalities for healing ones'elf or helping others to heal such as Reiki, Qigong or elven healing methods or simply an improved diet and regular exercise. This is surely a blessing and that the otherworldly charm is involved means you are getting the support of the Shining Ones for healing and improving your health and particularly for radiating healing into the world for the benefit of others.

If your question had to do with business and finances, or romance and relationship, the indication is that efforts to use this extra energy, this otherworldly charm to improve one's relations with others concerning these areas, promises the possibility of great success. Do what will make the situation better. Remember, this otherworldly charm is a bonus. It won't last, so use it well while you have it.

In terms of spiritual matters, this a good indication of

healing energy coming into your life from the ethereal realms, from the Elfin realms of magic and spirit, and it is likely that a sign will come to you, one that involves healing in some way. Listen for words of healing. Pay attention when someone speaks about healing for that is the indication, a sign or an omen, that healing will be coming to you.

You may also wish to create your own Orb of Healing, or some other talisman dedicated to healing in the material realm and charge it with healing energy now that the spirits favor this and you have the energy to do it. This is a propitious sign for creating healing magic.

THE WAND OF WISHING

When you receive the Otherworldly Charm in the outer realm, in the dimension of the Wand of Wishing, this indicates that you not only have been given some extra power and authority of a magical nature but that you need to do something with it. To do magic, to wave your wand, to set things in motion and use that power while it lasts in order to fulfil your dreams, visions and wishes.

If your question had to do with relationship, romance, or friendship then it is likely that you are dealing with someone who sees you in a very favorable light. In fact, it may designate someone who may idealize you and see you as being greater than you actually are currently. Thus, there is a responsibility to not only act toward the fulfillment of your dreams but also to take in account the needs and wellbeing of this individual. Don't take them for granted. Remember, anyone who sees you as being special must be a very special person.

If the inquiry concerned business or financial matters, it is possible you will get an investor interested, an inheritance or otherwise have something extra that you can use to pursue your dream job, business, etc.

On the matter of health, this response indicates you should take up doing or, perhaps, not doing those things that affect your health. If you learn of things that can make you healthier, you have a responsibility to begin doing them. This place indicates action and revelation. Act upon those secrets that have been revealed to you. Also, this place can indicate that there is an aura of vitality that surrounds you. It gives you a sense of being alive and filled with energy. Again, make use of this while it lasts.

And if your question involved spiritual matters, this is surely a blessing upon your magical and spiritual life. It enables you to bring the power of the ethereal realms into the mundane world and to affect transformations thereby. Make Elfin real in your life and in doing so, you will be making it real in the lives of others as well.

THE COIN OF THE REALM

In matters of relationship and romance, this is a good sign of real benefits coming through relationship. If you were hoping to marry into money, well, it looks like you may get your wish. At any rate, relationships will prove to be financially and materially productive, providing real benefits and an increase in your material wellbeing. Connections should be very productive at this time and if they are connections that involve your magical elven spiritual path then that is even better.

If your question concerned business or finances in the world, then you are in luck. This is a great response indicating that the magic will attract money and financial success to you. Whatever magic you have done in the past for financial success is beginning to take effect. The spirits are with you and acting in the world on your behalf.

As to questions concerning healing or health, this is not directly an indication of healing per se, unless you find a shopping spree healing or a sudden financial windfall to be physically regenerative. It does tend to indicate that whatever expenses you have for healing services should be less than you anticipated or that you will receive unexpected help in paying for them.

As to spiritual matters, this response indicates that you need to establish yours'elf in the world in some way. First Initiation involves the first chakra and one's confidence and ability to survive and prosper in the world. However, since this is the Otherworldly Charm in this position, it denotes that the spirits will help you get established. Maybe you need to create a sanctuary, or create an altar, if your magic uses altars (which most elf magic does not) or buy some magical tools or set up a place where the kindred can meet, create an elven sanctuary. What is your spiritual ambition in the world? Pursue it and the Shining Ones will help provide the finances necessary.

THE FEATHER OF TRUTH TELLING

If you receive the Otherworldly Charm in the place of the Feather of Truth Telling, it indicates that some esoteric truth is being revealed to you and particularly in this place, which is associated with the Elven Horns of Calling, it will be a truth that connects you to other fae, helps you draw them closer to you, reveals something about them, or guides you to them. This is a gifted power, so use it while it lasts and make the most of it.

It may be that you will be able to see the Elfin reality that exists within and yet lays upon the normal world of seeming. It could be that you will be able, at least for a while, to see who is or isn't elfin and what sort of elfae they may be.

Although, we caution you about projecting that idea upon them except in the most open and casual ways. Let them tell you who they are in Elfin, what sort of elfae they may be. Don't insist upon your own interpretations of them. Let them express thems'elves fully.

But it may also be the case that they will be able to see you for who you are for a brief period. To get a glimpse of Elfin through you and feel drawn to the Otherworldly aura you project. The truth of your magic is being revealed. They may possibly see your etheric elf ears or faerie wings or whatever.

If your question concerned relationship, this is a good sign for being open and for others trusting you enough to be open to you as well. Be trustworthy with their souls, spirits and imaginal beings, and help them manifest their true s'elves in reality.

If your concern is about money or business, this is an indication that some secret will be revealed to you that will aid you in that pursuit or that you will meet someone who will help you make the right connections. There are things to learn, things that will be disclosed and this will open the way for you financially.

If your inquiry had to do with your health, then things that will help you heal will be unveiled. There are secrets of healing that shall be yours. Embrace them and use them well.

Or if your question had to do with spiritual matters then this reply would indicate finding right company, those who will further you as a spirit and a soul, finding your star mates and fellow members of your vortex, your energetic gathering of elfae spirits. We are not merely saying that you should look for such individuals, but that they shall be arriving soon.

THE MAGIC MIRROR OF REFLECTION

Receiving the Otherworldly Charm in the place of the Magic

Mirror of Reflection in the outer circle points toward the need for an examination of how one uses one's magic in the world. What one does with the power that Elfin has granted one, the power that comes as a result of one's association with the Faerie realms, and the effects that one produces through the use of this power. What do you wish to achieve? What are the results of your magic? Are you taking everyone's needs into consideration?

In terms of romance, love, marriage or relationship, this response says to examine your relationships carefully. How does your relationship with Elfin affect your relationship with others? Are you bringing magic and enchantment into their lives? Are you making their lives better? Is your relationship to others a blessing for them and for you? That is ever the question because that is ever the Elven Way. But also, can you reveal your true s'elf to them. Or do you need to hide your elfae nature from them? And what does that say about them?

Concerning business or finances, this reply suggests you should contemplate the unseen elements in the situation. There is more to what is going on than simply mundane pecuniary concerns. There is magic behind this. There is purpose unseen by most. The Divine Magic is working through this situation. What is required of you to fulfill your purpose, your mission, in this instance?

If your question concerns health then you may wish to consider whether your magic is generating energy, that is giving you energy, or draining you. Are you giving energy to others or sucking from them? If you are not being revitalized by your magic and your connection to the Elfin realms, then something is wrong. Don't stress. Don't try to force things. Let your magic be easy and near effortless. Magic should be like weightlifting, where it exhausts you a bit when you work out but makes you feel better and strengthens you in the long run. And elven magic, which is enchantment, while taking effort, should be fun and enjoyable. Rather like performing in a play and then receiving a standing ovation.

And as to spiritual questions, the reply is: make your magic real in the world. Use your powers to improve your life and the lives of others and in doing that you will have done something truly worthy that will reverberate through the world and your life. Thus, the answer to your question is positive if you use your magic well and negative if you have been abusing or misusing your powers. Examine yours'elf and you will know what to expect.

THE SACK OF GIVING

Getting the Otherworldly Charm in the outer realms of the Sack of Giving directs us to use our energy liberally and well. Give gifts, give magic, give your time and energy, invest in your life in the world and invest in those you know, love and whom you think might by bettered by a positive infusion of life and magic. Give real things if you can, even if they are tokens, and instill magic and enchantment within them. The point is not the material value of the object but the magical charge that comes with it. This is not to say that you shouldn't gift something of value if you can afford to do so but this is primarily about energizing other's lives. What you are really giving them is magic.

In terms of inquires that have to do with relationship and romance, well, the response is clear. You need to prime the well, so to speak. Give gifts, but especially magical gifts, which is to say gifts that have meaning, not only gifts that bear meaning for you but also and more importantly gifts that have meaning for the individual you are giving them to. Give them something that they want, need or desire. Something that they have longed for, as long as it doesn't bring them harm or lead them astray from their true path.

If you are asking about work, business or finances, then the answer again is offer gifts. Bring donuts for your employees, coworkers and bosses or whatever works for you, your situation and, of course, diet. If you don't have coworkers or a boss, this is a good indication that you should consider investing a bit. The spirits seem to favor this. If you gamble at all, this is a good time to try your luck, but don't be foolish, don't overextend yours'elf; if you win take the win and withdraw, don't keep chasing it.

On matters of health and healing, this reply denotes the value of doing something good for yours'elf. If you are thinking of changing your life habits, changing your diet for the better, dieting to improve your health, then this is a great time to begin and the otherworld spirits will respond with rejuvenation and vitality. This is especially good for giving others something that will improve their health and if they are thinking of dieting or of beginning an exercise regimen and have a hard time doing so, consider joining them and dieting and exercising with them. It is much easier when you do it together.

And on questions about your spiritual path, this guidance directs you to put energy into others. Give help, offer guidance if you can, share your energy, perform public service, help out at your shrine, temple, sanctuary, ashram or wherever. Bring gifts for the spirits, but particularly, bring things that will improve your place of magic. If your temple is the forest or wild places, give magic rocks or other things that will keep the forest pristine and that will nurture its growth but unite your magic with its magic. Or build and leave faerie houses. Wooden statues or figurines that will dissolve into the woods in time will also be fine. But most of all, present offerings to the spirit world.

THE PHILTRE OF TRUE LOVE

To receive the otherworldly charm in this position is a blessing, obviously, for love. It is especially a magic that helps one find one's true kindred in the world and join with them to the benefit and happiness of all. Since to elves, friendship is one of the most important things in life, this also serves to attract those who will be good friends and who will make an important contribution to your life, bringing you energy, direction or something else of value that will further you upon your path. So, if your question concerned friendship, romance or relationship this is an especially potent and positive reply.

If your question had to do with business or finances, then it is a good sign for finding those that you can trust, although it may also be a warning that you need to be sure you can trust those with whom you are dealing. Being the otherworldly charm, it does, however, indicate that your allies and familiar spirits are looking out for your interests.

In terms of health, it suggests that healing comes from being around healing people. Love and friendship are keys to healing. However, there may also be an indication that one can find healing by developing and improving one's relationship with the realms of spirit. Imagine yours'elf in Elfin, Faerie or some other otherworldly realm and let yours'elf be healed in that realm by those that truly love you.

When asking about one's spiritual life and path, this is a strong indication that 'right company' is vital to one's path at this time. Find those that you can associate with along the way, those that are upon the same path, those from whom you can learn, those who will nurture and foster your being and also those that need your guidance and inspiration.

THE PHIAL OF EVERLASTING YOUTH

This is a particularly elven oracle that has to do with the fact that elves often look younger than other folks even as we age. This is surely a blessing in terms of a youthful disposition. The idea that one is as young as one thinks or feels is germane here.

In relationship, this answer tends toward a vibrant personality, an ability to charm others and promotes the idea of using your charms in interacting with others. Develop your personality and all things will come to you with ease. When people really love you, they will do anything for you.

As far as business and financial concerns, or your career success, this is a good sign for an enterprise that will last and endure. It is also a positive sign for a revival of one's financial affairs, a new spring, so to speak, in one's pecuniary interests. Make haste while the time is propitious.

Receiving the otherworldly charm in this position indicates a blessing upon you, this is particularly true if the question concerns health, for this gives you a health boost, a healing energy and power especially for yours'elf but which you may also use to energize others.

If one's question concerned one's spiritual path, this would denote the significance of keeping a fresh eye, an open mind, and a receptive spirit. To ever seek to approach things with a childlike attitude and a willingness, an eagerness, to learn. If you do this, the Shining Ones will generously share their secrets with you. It is nearly impossible to teach anything to those who think they already know everything.

Part Five

... Bones
(or Shells, Seeds, Leaves, etc.)

Bones are, like the sticks and feathers, inclined to fall upon more than one area. Like the sticks, it is helpful if you decide which is the pointing end of the bone, most likely the narrow end, and which the wider end of the bone, perhaps where a joint is. The narrow or pointing end designates the direction things are moving in and the wider end indicates the source of the influences surrounding the question.

Chapter 9:

The Long Bone

T he Long or Large Bone refers to the ancestors and how your ancestral past influences this question. It is an indication of the Collective Unconscious as it manifests in your life. To understand this, ask yours'elf what have you inherited in a psychological and psychic way from your ancestors?

The Inner Circle: The Torch of the Eternal Silver Flame of Elfin

If the Long Bone chiefly falls upon the torch at the center of the oracle, it means that you are likely to become overwhelmed by the influence of the past, by your ancestors and will instinctually move in a direction that baffles your logical mind. That's okay. Trust your instincts; that is the right thing to do in this situation.

If instead, the Long Bone landed within the Inner Circle upon a Sacred Magical Treasure other than the Torch in the center, then please read the corresponding treasure below:

THE ORB OF HEALING

With the landing of the Long Bone in the inner region of the Orb of Healing, an influence comes into one's life that promotes healing and health in a way that removes traumas from the past, that heals emotional scars and bad mental habits that originated in one's early life, from one's family or upbringing, and which have been plaguing one for nearly ever. Now is the time to clear and purify your heart and mind and to make a new start in the world and in your life toward a better, more magical and more elfin future.

If you are especially concerned about love, romance, relationship, marriage, family and friendship, this position of the Long Bone offers an opportunity to clear away the hindrances of the past and to make a fresh start in one's relationship, a new beginning with your family, with old friends and other relations. However, this is less about actually changing relationships and more about altering one's view of relationships, one's feeling in relationship, one's attitude and approach to interaction with others. Spirit rules here in the inner circle, and one's spirit in relationship will determine what occurs and how one deals with it.

Business, finance, job and career questions are also favored here in as much as one looks at the past, sees what has worked for one and what hasn't and makes appropriate changes. This, again, is about one's approach to the material world. What is it you really want materially? What is your motivation for succeeding in the monetary world? Examine your attitudes, particularly as they were instilled in you by your family and thus your ancestors, and decide again, for your own s'elf and path, what it is you really want and why you want it.

Naturally, health and healing and all inquiries related to them are well aspected in this position. Whatever has gone on in the past can now heal and change for the better. Most especially your mental and emotional attitudes may evolve for the better. Also, in this place, you can change the past, so to speak. Surely, your ancestors have been reincarnated many times by now. Send them healing energy. Help them upon their path as it unfolds before them in the present and this will return to you as healing energy and increased healing power.

As to the world of spirit, your magical and spiritual

evolution, this position gives you a chance to clear some karma and move into the future unencumbered. More than that, it gives you the power to heal the karma of your ancestors. You can fix what they have spoiled and in doing so aid them on their path, for you are connected. Just as you have endured the world you were born into due to fate and karma, so can you alter that world for those who are connected to you. Be a better elf or elfae and that will help heal the world and you will venture onward with greater power and understanding as well as the thanks of those who came before you. We are all in this together.

THE WAND OF WISHING

When the Long Bone falls into the inner realm of the Wand of Wishing, wishes long held will start to come true. Even more so, the wishes of your ancestors for you, especially your spiritual ancestors, the ancestors of your path and practice, will begin to take effect in your life. Did you not know that they did magic long ago, before you were ever born that would affect your life? These powers are now coming to fruition. For your own part, this may be the time to do magic for those who are yet to come. Pay it forward into the future for those who are not yet conceived except in your imagination and in the nature of life, which is to say those who are fated and destined to be.

If you presented an inquiry about love, romance, relationship, friendship, marriage or your social life to the oracle, this placement of the Long Bone denotes fulfillment of dreams long held concerning relationships. There is magic here but its effect is mostly spiritual in nature, thus it will tend to manifest as joy, understanding, realization and a sense that things are as they need to be and are moving in the direction they were always destined to move. There is a sense of purpose to relationship and an inner knowledge that the

245

people who are in your life or are in the process of coming into your life are there for a reason and that reason is magical fulfillment of your deepest inner wishes. There is a cosmic connection to what is going on.

If you had a question that involved business, financial concerns, job success or career advancement, this position of the Long Bone brings luck into your life and while it may not directly manifest as money or material things, being the inner realm, it will give you a certain talent for making money, or an insight into success, a tip from a friend who knows or some other bit of information that will serve you and be to your advantage in terms of dealing with the affairs of the material realm.

If you were asking about health or healing, then this position is favorable for being able to heal personally, or to help others to heal, but especially in a shamanic fashion. Its power is more about mental and emotional health than physical healing but they are connected realms and one influences the other. Still, the point here is that there is an opportunity to bring about healing through the evocation of the imaginal realms and to affect the world thereby. Shake your rattle, beat the drum, dance down the spirits and let the healing flow into you, through you and outward into the world.

When you had a question regarding your magical life and path and your progress as an evolving spirit, this position of the Long Bone is very much in your favor and to your advantage. Your aspirations to rise and advance as a spirit are supported by the magic of your ancestors of the path. You, in a sense, are their wishes coming true. You are the fulfillment of their magic and you need but continue on with sincerity and endurance and all that you hoped and wished for will come in being.

THE COIN OF THE REALM

Receiving the Long Bone in the inner circle of the Coin of the Realm brings blessings upon you from the ancestors, usually in a material form, but since this is the inner realm it is less about money per se as one's ability to make money or to successfully navigate the material world. This is a place of spirit and it denotes that you have inherited a strong spirit and ever carry with you the love and support of those who have come before you.

If you had an inquiry that involved love, romance, relationship, friendship, marriage or your social life and activity, this position for the Long Bone indicates a boon upon relationships, particularly upon family relationships or those who will become family to you. Since this is the inner circle, these do not necessarily have to be genetically connected to you. This can be those who are family by spirit. The family one finds in the world and that one adopts or is adopted by. In fact, this position is far stronger for one's spiritual family than a genetic one.

Naturally, if you posited a question relative to business, finances, job or career success or future prosperity, then you are in great luck, for this position is strong for business and money matters. It is particularly strong for interaction with those who are like you as a person, who feel connected to you instinctually, and perhaps those that see you as being like they were when they were young, or those that you see as being like you. Help them so they will help others in the future and you will be the blessed ancestor of spirit.

When you had a question regarding health or healing in this place, the Long Bone indicates that a connection to the spirit world, particularly to your spiritual ancestry, your magical lineage, will bring energy and healing to you. If yours is a tradition of healing, you are practically blest. Healing energy will be coming into your life, especially into your sense

247

of s'elf and your energetic being and this will filter down into the material world giving you the power to heal yours'elf and to help others to heal.

If you were wondering about your spiritual and magical path and practice, the spirits that guide your tradition are looking down upon you and are well pleased. You are one of them. You are part of the family, and they will do all that they can to help you. Absorb the blessings and bounty that they are sending to you. Continue to make progress upon the path while remaining open to their aid and guidance. They will show you the way, although surely you will explore new ways as well, perhaps discover new avenues to spiritual and magical success, and this is as it should be and as they ever intended. They don't wish you to follow blindly but with eyes wide open.

THE FEATHER OF TRUTH TELLING

When the Long Bone falls into the inner dimension of the Feather of Truth Telling, one is likely to encounter a revelation about the spirit world. Expect signs or omens that seem to involve or come from one's ancestors, the Shining Ones, or the Elders of Ancient times. A message has been sent through time and now the moment has come when it will arrive and awaken something within you to stir you in some deep and profound way. It is as though you have waited your entire life for this moment to come and you know now that everything that has come before has been leading up to this moment.

If you presented a question about love, romance, relationship, marriage or friendship to the oracle, this position of the Long Bone suggests that you need to be honest with yours'elf about relationship, about the purpose and motivation of the relationships you have, and whether there is any long-term or even short-term purpose in knowing and being involved with these people. This is a reminder from the ancestors that you are here for a reason. You have a mission to fulfill, perhaps a geis (magical binding or obligation) upon you that obligates you to do or achieve certain things. If the people you are asking about are not helping then you need to move on to other relationships that will aid you in achieving your magical and sacred purpose.

If your inquiry had to do with business, financial concerns, job success or career advancement, this placement of the Long Bone suggests that you look at the situation carefully. There is an unseen spiritual dimension to what is happening. There is a reason you are succeeding or encountering obstacles, although people seldom seek the aid of the oracle when they are succeeding. There are unseen spiritual forces moving things along in order to get you to where you have always been destined to be. Trust in this movement. And be certain that whatever is going on the truth will come out soon and you will realize it was there all along but you are just now realizing it. It will probably be so obvious you will wonder why you didn't think of it before.

Questions that involve health and healing will find that a close look at the past and especially the practices of ancient peoples and their healing practices will reveal something of value to you. Quite possibly, the healing and healthy solution is to be found in a direct, open and pure encounter within yours'elf and your relationship with the ancestors. This calls for a bit of shamanism. Step into the astral planes, the feeling planes, the imaginal planes and seek the answer there. There are elfin healers awaiting you and they will do all they can to reveal what you need to know in order to heal or help others to heal. Beat the drum, bang the sticks, dance the steps that lead to ecstasy and revelation will be yours.

As to inquiries that are centered upon your spiritual life

and magical path, this position brings a boon to you from the past, a gift from the ancestors that will inform and enlighten your way. Pay especial attention to your dreams in the next week or so. If you happen to be someone who doesn't remember their dreams, then examine your daydreams, your fantasies very carefully. There is something within them that speaks of you, your past and your future.

THE MAGIC MIRROR OF REFLECTION

If the Long Bone falls into the inner realm of the Magic Mirror of Reflection, one is called to contemplate all those that came before one, particularly upon the path of magic, enchantment and the highways and byways to Elfin and Faerie. This is the inner circle, thus the spiritual and magical takes precedence over the material world and one's ancestors are ancestors of one's mind, path, beliefs and practices. Reflect upon their contribution to you as evidenced by the lore they've left behind and look deeper still, making the past understandable through the present and vice versa. Styles and practices may change but people and their needs remain essentially and continually the same.

If you had concerns about love, romance, relationship, marriage and friendship, this fall of the Long Bone calls you to consider the background of your relationships. What brought you together in the first place? What attracts you to each other? What is it about this relationship that binds you together? And where do you think these relationships are going based upon where they have been, remembering that history tends to repeat itself and our habits are inclined to limit us to certain behaviors. And, if you don't like the way things have been, what, if anything, can you do to change it?

Or perhaps you had an inquiry about business, finances, job or career development and success. If so, this placement of the Long Bone indicates that you need to look to the past, especially to those who came before you to understand this situation. Who were your mentors? Who were the ideal fulfillment of your aspirations? How can you do what they did to achieve success for your own s'elf. And will doing so incur a great deal of karma? For they may have succeeded in the past, but where are they now? What limitations may they be facing in their current life due to deeds of the past?

Issues that have to do with health and healing, also will be benefited by reflection on the past, but in this case on contemplating who the great healers were and how they did what they did? Is healing and health merely something one inherits? Is one born into this or any particular life with healing ability or with a tendency to be healthy? Or can you truly develop and improve your health and healing abilities by your actions, attitudes and lifestyle? From the even point of view, all these factors have influence in one's life, but what do you feel?

Questions concerning one's magical path and spiritual development find that meditation is recommended. Quiet your mind, let the Universe and the Divine Magic find a place in your heart. Listen to the subtle suggestions of the Shining Ones as evidenced by signs and omens. The way forward in this case may be found in repeating things that you or your spiritual ancestors have done before. Ritual practice is recommended at this point. What are the rituals of your day to day spiritual practice? Improve them but don't abandon them.

THE SACK OF GIVING

If the Long Bone lands in the inner region of the Sack of Giving it points to the ancient practice of making offerings to the ancestors, which is essentially a form of necromagery, in order to receive help and guidance (necromancy) from them. So, if the Long Bone is found here, pay heed to the ancestors. It is time to get in touch with them. Remember them. Honor them and listen well to the inner voice of intuition within you, which is often their voice.

If you asked about love, romance, relationship, marriage, friendship or your social life and got this as your reply, then it is important to remember the past. See what has worked for you before, what hasn't worked, your mistakes and the accumulated wisdom of your family and make offerings and gifts to the spirits in order to move the situation along in a more positive way. Also, you might consider giving gifts to those who remind you of your ancestors, or to spirits that are related to love and relationship.

When you are asking regarding business, finances, or the potential for job or career success or your prosperity in general, this response from the oracle denotes a time when practices from the past are likely to prove successful (or unsuccessful) again. History is about to repeat itself. Know your history. In the meantime, give generously to the poor, the downtrodden, the homeless and those in need. Alms giving is the action of the enlightened rich. Think rich. Act rich and become successful.

If you posed a question that had to do with health and healing, this position brings you benefits from your ancestors. A boost of energy to help you on your way. Whatever their challenges might have been, they survived long enough to get you here. Tune into the energy of health and absorb the love of your ancestors. Only, try to do whatever they did better. Improve your health through your lifestyle. Practice your healing arts and think of those who will come after you, either your genetic descendants or your spiritual and magic descendants. Send them healing so that they will be more successful still and when you return again in another life, they will surely help you upon the way.

When you have made an inquiry about your spiritual life and progress upon the magical path, this fall of the Long Bone indicates the influence of the ancestors in your development. As well as making offerings to the ancestors, it also suggests that you take a closer look at your personal ancestry and your spiritual ancestry for there is a reason you are who you are and who you've become and who you are meant to be. There is a purpose to your manifestation. A quest and a mission for you but also a geas or obligation and duty upon you. Seek a vision, but not a vision gained by trying to see the future but a vision found by viewing the past and the long span of development leading to your incarnation. In certain ways, due to reincarnation, you are your ancestors, or surely some of them. Look within yours'elf and find the way to Elfin.

THE PHILTRE OF TRUE LOVE

With the landing of the Long Bone in the inner region of the Philtre of True Love one can be assured that the ancestors and the spirits who helped bring you into being, love you truly and are supporting your efforts to manifest your magic in this world. Romance may be fleeting but this love is Divine and transcends lifetimes carrying you ever onward. In return, send your love to those who need your aid and support. Make offerings to the ancestors and the spirits with whom you have relationships and set your magic in motion. Its fulfillment may not come for generations but it will manifest in time. Simply make your magic true and clear and all will come to be in the light of Eternity.

When you were asking about love, romance, relationship, marriage, friendship or your social life and prospects, this position of the Long Bone is truly wondrous in terms of love magic flowing into your life. It is up to you to use it well and make the most of it, surely. But the energy is there and if you wish to do a love spell or two, this is certainly the most propitious time to do so. Remember, if you violate the will of others, you have gone astray and are stepping onto the dark side. Be open in your magic and seek those who are meant to come to you. Nurture all that do come, whether they are meant for you or not, and wonderful things will manifest. You may have to send some of them upon their way, but do so with kindness and compassion. Doing this will bring you and them increased luck.

Questions that have to do with business and finances, or your job or career success are not as strong here, however, if you are interested in doing magic to make the right contacts and connections, you are in luck. This is especially the case if you have known these individuals for a long time, or they were known to your parents, or others from the past. The return of those who have connected with you or done business with you previously in a successful fashion is also favored here.

When you have an inquiry about health and healing, this placement of the Long Bone brings healing through those who you have been connected to, loved and liked for a long time. It brings healing to and from the family and it brings healing via love to you from your ancestors by way of the netherworlds. There is magic here for healing and health, but it is important that it is loving magic. Fill yours'elf with the feeling of love and loving and let that feeling carry your healing spells into the world or to those you wish to help heal. If it is you that needs healing, let love be your guide.

As to the spiritual world and your magical life and path, this fall of the Long Bone connects you to the ancestors of spirit in an extremely loving and positive way that will find your magical power and energy increased immensely, at least for a week or two or a full cycle of the moon. Cast your spells and enchantments with love, knowing that the spirits who came before support you in your evolution, development and success. You are beloved unto them and they seek your benefit, upliftment and evolution in all that they do.

THE PHIAL OF EVERLASTING YOUTH

With the landing of the Long Bone in the inner circle of the Phial of Everlasting Youth, one's spirit is renewed especially in connection with the ancestors, the ancient of days, and filled with a sense of connectedness to one's spiritual ancestors and all who have struggled, sacrificed and quested on the path previous to one's own current life. One's inner life is extended, which is to say that one may feel as though one is immortal, or approaching immortality, for one knows that the spirit world is one's true life and one is immortal in that realm. This is surely a blessing for you that connects you with the Shining Ones and the quest of all of life toward perfection and fulfillment.

If you had a question that involved love, romance, relationship, friendship, marriage or your social life, this fall of the Long Bone denotes a sense of connection and meaningfulness in relationship that also inspires you upon the path. You may feel renewed in relation to the spirits that aid and support you and this will filter down into the material world, so even those that aren't upon the path will see you as a person of purpose and integrity, and accord you the respect, often quite unconsciously, that one usually gives to priests, monks, nuns and others that have devoted thems'elves to a spiritual life and calling. You are considered to be a person of note and of subtle yet indefinable power and influence.

Questions about business, finances, job or career success and development, are not as favored here in the inner realms,

255

although it is very good for a revival of one's energy in terms of going forth and being a success in the world. But it is not very strong if one's motivation is merely to make money, or to feed one's ego through financial and worldly success. If, however, one has a true magical and spiritual purpose for attaining money, fame or success in the world, the position of the Long Bone will fill you with determination to endure and continue on toward your goals.

When you had an inquiry relative to health and healing, this is an excellent response for it brings you the healing power of the young, and renews all aspects of your life, but especially your inner life, your sense of being able to heal. This will make you feel like a child or teenager again only with greater experience and wisdom. This energy is so powerful that it will affect those around you and energize their spirits as well and the healing will spread and this is to everyone's benefit.

As to questions about your spiritual and magical life and path specifically, this placement of the Long Bone brings the power of the ancient ones into your life and you will realize that in many ways you are just as they were one time and you, like them, are moving surely toward the realization of your true s'elf and the perfection of your being. You are a bright and shining elfin being and the magic is pouring into your soulful spirit and filling you with wondrous energy and potency.

The Outer Circle:
The Elf Horns of Calling

If the Long Bone lands outside of the outer circle, it denotes the fact that you are losing touch with your past, your ancestry and the spirits that have long fostered your being and sacrificed so that you might have this life and this opportunity. Whether this is a good thing or a bad thing in this situation, we will leave for you to decide. It could be that it is time for you to set out on your own in an entirely new direction.

If instead the Long Bone landed within the Outer Circle, then please read the corresponding treasure below:

THE ORB OF HEALING

With the landing of the Long Bone in the outer realm of the Orb of Healing, one is called to correct the mistakes of the past, to fix what can be fixed, to improve all that one can and in general make things better for ones'elf and everyone else. This position accords with setting things straight, getting things back on track and moving in the right direction. This is a position of overcoming the effects of karma. Here you have a chance to change your life by clearing your karma and the mistakes of the past. Get out that magical broom. It is time to sweep the detritus of the past away forever.

If you offered a question about love, romance, relationship, marriage, friendship or your social life to the oracle and receive the Long Bone here, then whatever has gone wrong in relationship has a chance of being repaired. This is particularly true if what has happened has to do with the past, one's family or the family of the person one is involved with, or the ancestors, which is to say the past history of the family and particularly therefore, one's upbringing. You can do it differently. You can make it better. And even if you can't renew a particular relationship you can start another rather like it, only better.

When your inquiry involved a question about business, finances, job or career success, this position is great for adjusting the situation to your favor. If you have made mistakes in the past, now is the time when you can correct them. Anything that involves your family, your ancestors or your past that affects your financial wellbeing and career, for instance being born poor or impoverished, can at this point be dealt with in an effective fashion so that the future will be better than the past. This is an opportunity to set a new course in a new direction.

Questions about health and healing are especially favored in the placement of the Long Bone, particularly if they involve long term problems, hereditary difficulties, congenital diseases, or illnesses that are somehow due to past life karma. Now is the time when things can be purified, resolved and one's body and health set in order. However, it is important, as you surely know, to support this effort toward change with a better diet, exercise or whatever will keep your health at optimal levels.

And if you were making an inquiry about your magical path and spiritual development, this response from the oracle indicates healing energy coming to you from the past. Your ancestors wish you well. They placed some magic in motion that will bear fruit at this time, helping you upon the way and increasing your chances of success in the world due to your magic (and theirs) and the power of your spirit and your personality. This is an opportunity for you to make quick progress upon the path.

THE WAND OF WISHING

If the Long Bone falls into the outer circle of the Wand of Wishing, one will be blest in a very material way. One's magic, especially magics and spells one cast quite a long time ago, perhaps even in previous lives, begins to manifest in one's life and in the world and certainly to one's benefit, for one's material desires and wishes, at least in part, begin to come true. Things you have long wanted begin to come to you and if this brings you joy and inner satisfaction without depriving others, that is surely a good thing.

When you had an inquiry that had to do with love, romance, relationship, friendship and your social life, this placement of the Long Bone is powerful for bringing you the trappings of love. It doesn't guarantee the feelings and sense of being loved; but if flowers, chocolates, rings, or perhaps sex is what you have been wanting, you are definitely in luck. Relationship and friendship will find a place in your life in physical manifestation. Whether the feelings behind this development are sincere, genuine or lasting is another matter.

If you posed a question about business, finances, job or career development and success, this fall of the Long Bone indicates rewards that have been a long time coming, finally begin to manifest. Your work comes to fruition. It is harvest time at last, and it has been a long season, so it will probably prove to be very bountiful. What you do with this, however, is the important matter. Use it to ensure future success as well and in this way your good fortune will endure. Still, you may wish to celebrate, just be cautious not to overdo it.

When you had an inquiry that involved health or healing, this position for the Long Bone denotes real healing, a genuine movement toward better health and more than likely those things that will bring about that healing state, which is to say medicine, herbal remedies, an exercise program, a new diet or the machinery for exercise, etc. Know that this is a blessing from the ancestors. This is their gift to you. Their love is manifesting in a real way into your life making it better and more enduring. It is a movement toward longevity.

As to a question that has to do with your spiritual and magical life and your advancement upon the path, this position opens doors for you. New opportunities shall arise for you in your spiritual life, new powers and abilities will begin to manifest, or more than likely powers that you have had for a long time will be increased in their potency. The ancestors support you and your efforts. They seek your advancement and success and are with you every step of the way. Continue your mission to become the best that you can be and the world of magic will open before you.

THE COIN OF THE REALM

With the landing of the Long Bone in the outer dimension of the Coin of the Realm, one is benefited in a very material way due to the past, due to inheritance, due to all that has come before. This is a blessing concerning money and material things in particular. But it also brings one luck in a more general sort of way having to do with the material world and success and manifestation within it. More than likely, this is the effect of good karma that has come to you from previous lives and from the well wishes of those you've aided in past lives.

If you offered a question about love, romance, relationship, marriage, friendship, or your social life, this is a very good sign in terms of getting real benefits, financial or otherwise, from relationship or having luck regarding material things in relationship. It is not necessarily a sign of love, romance or friendship in itself, which is to say it is not about good feelings and connection but rather the accumulation of material things due to relationship. How you use these things is up to you but think of the future and the magic you are setting in motion through sharing.

When you have an inquiry about business, finances, job or career success or your prospects for increased prosperity, this reply brings you great news, for this position signals real material benefit, increases your prospects for success and financial gain, and usually indicates money or some other material benefits coming to you. Lady Luck is smiling on you either due to things you have done in the past, or more likely due to the love she has for your ancestors. Your ancestors invested in you, perhaps gambled that you would be more successful in the world, and now things will pay off for you and them, or really for them through you.

Questions about health and healing will find a positive response here, but only in terms of being able to get or afford those things that will promote your health and healing abilities. If money or material gain makes you happy, then you are in luck. This position, in that case, will surely be a boon for your health. And if you take what you get and share it with others it is quite possible that you will bring some healing into their lives as well.

As to inquiries about your magical and spiritual life and path, this placement of the Long Bone sees you being rewarded in very real ways for your efforts and progress upon the path. If recognition is important to you, it is likely to come. You may find you are being promoted within your particular magical lodge or order, attaining some advanced degree, certainly obtaining those things with which you can carry on your practice more successfully. This is like being a violinist who suddenly can afford a much better violin. In itself, it doesn't make you better at playing the violin but still the sound is so much better. You are refining your hum and vibration in your current manifestation and the ancestors are well pleased.

THE FEATHER OF TRUTH TELLING

If the Long Bone falls into the outer circle of the Feather of Truth Telling, one is called to seek the truth in one's current situation, but also to seek the full truth, the truth that is behind the truth. One needs to look at one's own and other people's motivations and also why it is they wish what it is that they desire and why they act the way they do. What is behind what is going on? What forces have been in play from the past? For in seeing the truth and acknowledging it, you just may have a chance of changing the situation for the better for you and others. This may call for a bit of sorcery.

When you had a question relative to love, romance, marriage, friendship or your social life, this position of the Long Bone designates a time when an examination of one's history and one's ancestry may provide some insight into what is currently going on. You may wish to do one of those ancestry DNA tests. You may be surprised. Sometimes our inner conflicts as well as our outer ones have an unseen dimension due to our genetic heritage. It is good to take people for who they are, and not judge them by their ancestors, relatives, and ethnic background, but at the same time, it may very well help, especially in this situation, to know what their lineage is. Can elves and orcs get along? Are faeries and goblins compatible?

If you asked a question about business, finances, job or career advancement and success or prospects for prosperity, this placement of the Long Bone indicates that certain facts will be coming out, disclosures and other revelations about things that have happened in the past that will affect your financial situation. This truth may not seem to be to your advantage at first, but at least now you know the facts and knowing the truth is vital to success. Dealing with reality will give you a true advantage over those who are acting upon illusion and falsehood and refuse to see the situation as it truly is.

If you were wondering about health and healing, this position of the Long Bone indicates that you need to be honest about your own healing abilities and powers, don't pretend to be other than you are but also remember your ancestors want your success. They wish you to go further, live longer and healthier than they did. And if not, then they are some piss poor ancestors, indeed. Discover the truth of the situation and from that you can proceed to heal. It is likely that you will be dealing with issues from the past, but the fact remains, it is time to focus your healing energy and send it forth.

And if you were inquiring about your spiritual and magical life and path, this fall of the Long Bone denotes a time when it would serve you well to be completely clear about who your ancestors were. Especially, in this case, about those who proceeded you on your spiritual path. Be honest with yours'elf about where you are on the path, as best you can tell, and how developed they truly were. Remember, no matter the hype, the legend and the lore about them, they were human beings with their own peculiarities, foibles and weaknesses. Let them become real in your mind, no matter how great or horrible they may seem in retrospect and realize we all struggle as spirits to advance, succeed and achieve.

THE MAGIC MIRROR OF REFLECTION

When the Long Bone lands in the outer realm of the Magic Mirror of Reflection one is called to consider what one has inherited from the ancestors, both in a personal fashion and in a more general societal fashion and also, and perhaps more importantly, what one may do to use the gifts and blessings one has received, or the inherited guidance and wisdom or even the troubles and challenges that have been left to one to solve, and make the world a better place for you, your kindred and the world at large.

If you had asked a question about love, romance, relationship, marriage, friendship or your social life, this response of the oracle says that one should reflect upon one's relationships and on one's effect upon others, throughout one's lifetime. What is the history of your relationships? How have you faired in relationships in the past? What is the history of your current relationships? And most importantly, what can you do better? Are you simply stuck in a cycle where you repeat the same things again and again? Always choosing the same sort of people to be involved with? And how is that working for you?

When you had an inquiry about business, finances, or job or career success or possibly your future prospects for prosperity overall, or even about a particular business venture or deal you have going, the position of the Long Bone reminds you that everyone has a history. What has come before this deal? How have the people you are involved with treated others in the past? Are they honest? Sly? Just plain crooked? Have they been successful in the past? And you? What is your track record for successful financial dealings? The past, in this case, has great bearing on the possibilities of fulfillment to this question and it is likely that history will be repeating itself.

If you had a question that has to do with health and healing, this placement of the Long Bone brings the weight of your ancestors' wishes for you to succeed into focus. It is true that there may be issues from the past that you have inherited that need your healing energy, but that is the point. You are meant to do better, live longer, be healthier and go farther than your ancestors did. Make them proud. Put forth your healing energy and make the future better than the past. Your ancestors support you.

If your inquiry involved your spiritual life and magical path, this placement of the Long Bone has you examining your spiritual history and the ones who have tread this path before you. It also indicates that there is definitely something to learn from the past. Look to those who have written about this path in the past. There are hints there that contain magical secrets that will prove enlightening and that you may use to further yours'elf in the world. Consider those who have stood out upon your path in the past, those who have borne it along and carried it further. But also consider all those who have tread this path and whose efforts have been forgotten, although they may affect you still. Remember the spirit of those who have been forgotten and honor their contribution to your path.

THE SACK OF GIVING

The Long Bone in the outer circle of the Sack of Giving indicates gifts that have come to you from your ancestors that will affect this situation. Because it is the outer region, it could be that these gifts are material in nature, which is to say they could be in the form of money, or heirlooms or some other thing that you have inherited, although it could also be a talent, ability, or even reputation or 'good name' that you have inherited. The point here, however, with the Sack of Giving is how you will use this gift. How you will pass it on so that it continues to influence the world in a positive way, and mostly how it will help and affect your own descendants and kindred. There is a duty of sharing and continuation here borne down through the ages.

If you had an inquiry that involved a question relative to love, romance, relationship, friendship, marriage or your social life, this placement of the Long Bone indicates connections that have past life energy to them. This is not necessarily karma in a bad sense, but rather the working out of your soulful link to someone else through the lifetimes. There is not necessarily a debt that must be paid, and yet when you feel that connection to someone, perhaps someone you just met that you've never known before and yet recognized immediately, give them a gift of magic. Perhaps, it has to do with something that has been in your magic or your aura for a long time. This is a thread of your destiny. Weave it into your life and your vision of the future.

If you were wondering about business, finances, job or career success and you get the Long Bone in this position, there is a strong possibility of getting some sort of inheritance, or that your actions from the past will have bearing on your current financial interests, or that your past business dealings will finally pay off. The important thing, however, is to use this money well. To make sure it helps others, insures your future, or goes to a good cause even if that cause is increasing your financial wellbeing and particularly the wellbeing of your family.

As to questions about health and healing, this placement often indicates that one needs to deal with issues from the past. Either a tendency to certain diseases because of one's genetic heritage or perhaps the granting of great health, great teeth or something else that one inherited that is on the positive side and to one's favor. Whichever is the case, do your healing magic and make the situation better. The same is true if you are helping others to heal. Take the situation as is, as it has come down to you, for we all have history, and move on from there toward greater health and healing ability.

And if you were making an inquiry about your magical and spiritual life and path, this fall of the Long Bone indicates a great heritage of magic and spirit behind and supporting you. In this case, because it has to do with spirit, it doesn't necessarily mean a genetic heritage, although it surely could be so, rather it is an inheritance of spirit and magic. There is a long tradition behind your practice, if you tune into it you will find increased power. If you accord those who have inspired and helped you on the path the recognition and honor they deserve, you will receive your own due in the course of time.

Be sure to give credit where credit is due. Don't grasp for credit for yours'elf, let it come to you.

THE PHILTRE OF TRUE LOVE

Having the Long Bone descend into the outer dimension of the Philtre of True Love is a very positive energy for making anything last a long time, for love enduring or for encountering someone or something that you will love nearly or perhaps forever and that will affect your life for lifetimes to come. This is magic manifesting but especially magic that awakens and speaks to our hearts and our imaginations. This is a place of inspiration and revelation. This is where soulmates meet and star mates gather.

If you asked about love, romance, relationship, marriage, friendship and social activity, this position of the Long Bone brings the blessings of your ancestors upon you in the form of love appearing in your life. This is either the renewal of an old love returned again in this life or a love from previous lives coming back into your life. More than likely, even if you have never seen this person before in this lifetime, you will recognize them immediately. You may not be able to place them in your memories, but you will know that you know them instinctively. However, will they recognize you? Approach carefully and with a bit of finesse. We are elfae, after all. Feel the situation out. Charm and enchantment are suggested here. Although for we elfin, charm and enchantment are advised nearly everywhere, in every situation and all the time. It's what we do.

Inquiries that have to do with business, finances, job success or career advancement, will find that one may very well discover what one really loves to do and also encounter some opening of the way in terms of doing it and making money by doing so. It is quite possible as well that something that you always wanted and desired in a material way, will finally come into your life. It appears as though by magic, and well, it is. You set a desire, a thought-form into the Universe some time ago and now that energy will return to you in manifest form. Even though you wished for this and put energy toward it at some time in the distant past, its appearance may still come as a surprise.

Questions that involve health and healing will find that this placement of the Long Bone promotes healing, but mostly of the things of the past. Something that you loved that seemed lost to you may return in a new guise. An old one who seemed to be flagging may very well hold on a bit longer due to the love you have for them and they for you. There is a revitalization of personal energy, but due to love. Love makes one feel young again. And this love, the love of the ancient, is no exception. Old things, old fashions, antiques and other things of the past bring joy into one's life and this is healing. Think of those ancients that lore and legend say could heal with a word or with touch.

One's spiritual and magical life find a union between the ancient and the new very productive. Reimagine the path. Honor what has come before. Send it your love, but make this path your own. Follow the joy it gives you. Bring joy to other people's lives as best you can. If the path is mere drudgery, a series of empty and boring rituals that are essentially meaningless to you and unfulfilling, if the path is merely an idea to you, a doctrine that has been pressed upon you or you have accepted, but which brings you no joy, it is the wrong path. Follow the way of your heart, the path of your imagination. The true elven path leads to love, light and tremendous celebration. This is the true ancient way, the way of the ancestors.

THE PHIAL OF EVERLASTING YOUTH

The Long Bone in the outer region of the Phial of Everlasting Youth generally indicates some great genetic heritage. Although, if you have health difficulties or body issues stemming from your past, your family or your upbringing, this position is very good for improving that situation and being better, stronger and more resilient than your antecedents were. But here also, we are speaking of the influence of the revival of the past. Quite possibly past fashions will come into style again, or simply history will be repeating itself in a slightly new way. Keep an eye out and you will see the trend as it is just beginning to start and perhaps take advantage of it and profit thereby.

If you asked a question that involved love, romance, relationship, marriage or friendship, this placement of the Long Bone signifies a revival of energy in relationships but especially those that have a familial connection. It is great for continuing relationships, reviving relationships, renewing your vows, so to speak, but not as strong for starting totally new relationships, unless there is a family connection involved. On the other hand, it is very good for starting relationships that will endure and will turn into long term affairs and certainly this is true if these relationships produce children.

When you are making an inquiry about business, finances, or your job or career success and future prosperity, this position is great for a revival of financial activity, especially of those things that have been going on a long time but didn't seem to be going anywhere for nearly forever. Then, things change and the whole situation alters. Your instincts prove to be correct and you realize that while it took a while to come together, your original impulses were on the right track. Therefore, enjoy the new energy while it lasts and do what you can to make it endure. Also, think of your family and those who will come after you. Have you made a will? Some day you will be the ancestor and with reincarnation you may very well be your own ancestor. Think of your future lifetimes.

Health and healing are most favored in this position. It is great for healing and for revival of one's health. One can feel the love of one's ancestors pouring into one's soul and reinvigorating one's spirit and increasing one's ability to interact in the world in a positive way. It is much harder to deal with the outer world when one feels sick, depressed or in pain. This placement will help relieve any suffering and make interacting with others a much greater pleasure.

One's spiritual life and magical path are also favored here, but mostly in terms of a stronger and an increasing connection to the Shining Ones and one's direct ancestors upon the path. Magic that was done ages ago is coming into effect now in order to move you along and ease your way in the direction you are meant to go. Follow this open path while you can. A clear path will not last forever but if you are determined you can advance quickly, at least for now, and that is all to your advantage.

Chapter 10:

The Short Bone

The Short or Small Bone refers to your personal past in this life but also, particularly, your past lives and how they influence the outcome of your inquiry.

The Inner Circle: The Torch of the Eternal Silver Flame of Elfin

If the Short Bone settles primarily upon or touches the torch at the center, it signifies that you are near to fulfilling your life mission. It doesn't mean your life is over, although it could be, but it does mean you will be moving on to a new quest and a new assignment. Really, you are moving up in the world of spirits and gaining a certain amount of recognition in the esoteric realms.

If instead, the Short Bone landed within the Inner Circle upon a Sacred Magical Treasure other than the Torch in the center, then please read the corresponding treasure below:

THE ORB OF HEALING

When the Short Bone falls into the inner circle of the Orb of Healing one has an opportunity to heal one's spirit and soul, to clear away one's karma, and to let go of the traumas of the past and to go forth into the future with a renewed and reinvigorated spirit and a vibrant soulfulness and by doing so step into a new realm of being and manifestation, on a higher level of magical power. One ascends upward toward the realms of the Shining Ones and while one may still have things to do and accomplish in this world, one has greater freedom in the realms of spirit and increased ability to function effectively there.

If you asked a question that involved love, romance, relationship, marriage, partnership or your social life, this position of the Short Bone brings a revival of your sense of faith, hope and vision about relationship. You may increasingly see the purposefulness of the ones you meet and to see as well the long-term interconnections of your life encounters. These are not isolated events in your life but are part of the flow of the Universe and there is history and a pattern behind all things going back to your earliest days in this and in previous lives that affect this situation. Ponder on that.

When you had an inquiry that was focused on business, financial concerns, job or career development and success, this placement of the Short Bone emphasizes your power to make the situation better through healing magic. Interference with others is to be avoided. One can promote one's own goals and desires but not at the expense of others. It is important to see the key to financial success in mutually beneficial agreements. Use the positive and the lure of success to move things and people in the direction you wish them to go. Remember, in this way your success benefits all others and all people, deep in their hearts, will support you because you are the pathway to their success.

When your question has to do with health and healing, you are blest to receive this response, for it is excellent for healing all things and making them better. Reach back to the purity of your childhood, your earliest and most innocent of stages and express that natural state of being into the world casting a spell of beneficent healing for everyone. If the issue is a specific one, relative to you or some other, remember this is the inner realm and the emphasis is more of shamanic healing through the planes of spirit than by utilizing medicines, herbal treatments or material cures. Chant your healing spells and let the magic do the rest. You will be guided as to what else to do. Pay attention to your dreams in this regard.

If you presented a question that featured your magical and spiritual path and life, you may feel certain that things are looking up for you. Whatever your past has been, this is the chance for a new beginning, or for a step upward to a new

272

level of magical potency and activity. Most of all, do your magic. Do your magic. Do your magic. Still, you may discover new spells or intuit improved methods for connecting with the Shining Ones. This is all to the good. Don't doubt, wave your wand about.

THE WAND OF WISHING

As the Short Bone descends to the inner dimension of the Wand of Wishing, some long held dream begins to come true. It is possible you have forgotten this wish since you made it so long ago when you were very young as a spirit, but the Universe and the Shining Ones have not forgotten and now the time has come when it will finally filter down into the mundane plane from the realms of the spirit and the imagination. Make another wish while the time is right. It may not come true for years, but it will not be forgotten.

If you posited a question about love, romance, friendship, marriage, partnership, or your social life, this fall of the Short Bone gives you a chance to affect the situation using your will, your intention and your magical powers. For elves, who are enchanters by nature, this means using the power of the personality, which is also to say one's charms to move things in the direction one desires. Cast your spells, chant your incantations, mix the herbs of relationship, make offerings to the spirits of love and bide your time. Fulfillment comes bringing flowers and chocolates.

When you have an inquiry about business, finances, or job advancement and career success this placement of the Short Bone brings luck from the past and a bonus in terms of your ability to do magic, right now, or in the near future, that will positively influence your material wellbeing. However, also consider your lives to come. Make magic for the future, not merely the immediate future, but position yours'elf for future lifetimes of abundance and success. Think in the long, long term and set forces in motion that may not come to fruition for ages to come.

When you present a question about health and healing to the oracle and get this response, there is immense energy for doing healing work. You have accumulated power, so use it now and spread the healing into your life. Also, healing energy from the past that you or someone else set in motion will be coming into your life and making this situation better all around. Reach out your arms as you would to the sun on the dawn of a bright and shiny day and draw in the healing vibrations. They are out there, sent by those that care, you just need to absorb them and then send them forth again, made stronger through your will.

If your query had to do with your spiritual life and magical progress, then you are surely blest by this movement of the magic. Life moves and develops in cycles. Magic and the moon do as well. Take advantage of the time and let your wishes be known to the Universe. Do whatever you do better. Strive to excel in your magic and in your spiritual life, be a better person and this will return to you as advancement upon the path and you will find that you are closer to Elfin and Faerie and the Shining Ones by doing so.

THE COIN OF THE REALM

When the Short Bone lands in the inner section of the Coin of the Realm, one is blest with the influence of the magic and the spirit realms due mostly to accumulated good karma, as well as the manifestation of one's own past spells and incantations, which appear in one's life as prosperity and abundance. This is not necessarily the realization of material things and benefits, but rather the manifestation of the energy that enables one to achieve what one wants and desires in the world. What is your vision for your material life? It is time to put as much energy as you can toward its achievement while the opportunity lasts.

If you were asking about love, romance, relationship, marriage and friendship, this position of the Short Bone is good for increased activity in your social life, but mostly with those that you already know, and especially with those from your past or your early life. It is not as powerful for starting new relationships; however, if there is someone that you are interested in, a series of preliminary gifts would be in order.

On the other hand, if you are inquiring about business, finances, job or career success, you are in luck. This is a great place for money in particular, but mostly for magic money, for found money, for money coming to you unexpectedly, from some unforeseen source, or as an inheritance. The energy is also very positive for doing magic for money, for prosperity and abundance, this will come to you in the future when this cycle comes around again. Place coins here and there where you wish to have prosperity come to you. Or create prosperity power and dust it around. In or near your mailbox, next to your phone, somewhere at your work. Draw abundance to you and let the spirits do the rest.

If you had a question about health or healing, then this is a good place for spending money on things that are healing for you or others. It is also favorable for people giving you gifts for having helped them to heal. If you were thinking about purchasing certain herbs or elixirs or potions, this is the time to do it. Spend money on your health and wellbeing and you will find that it is a very good investment.

When you were asking about your magical and spiritual path and development, then you will surely find that potent energy is coming your way. There is a bonus of magic for you to use and invest in your path. Do the magic that will further you and your kindred and you will discover that wondrous things will occur because of it. You must have done something right for this is a boon and a blessing for your life. Quite possibly, some secrets will be revealed to you that will give you greater understanding of your life, your purpose and the direction for your future and lead you to even greater developments.

THE FEATHER OF TRUTH TELLING

If the Short Bone descends to the inner circle of the Feather of Truth Telling, you may find it profitable to examine your earliest life, your upbringing and particularly those who had a strong influence on your early life. Just be honest with yours'elf about your life, the way you think, the attitudes you hold and how you came to hold them in the first place. Especially, look at your attitudes toward religion, spirit, magic and metaphysical subjects. How did you come to have these beliefs you currently embrace and how did your life lead you to them?

When you are asking about love, romance, relationship, marriage, family or friendship and you get this placement of the Short Bone, it is important to be honest with yours'elf and with others with whom you are closely connected about who you truly are and how it is you came to be that way. Don't pretend to be other than you are, they will sense you are different anyway. You could change yours'elf, but only if it is for the better, making you a superior personality. If they don't love the truth, you are better off without them. Let your elf light shine and you will attract those that are truly meant for you. If they can't accept your elfae nature, they and you are destined to go in different directions each finding their own path. For you that is a good thing, for them, who knows.

If you had an inquiry about business, finances, or your job

or career success and future prosperity, this position of the Short Bone suggests that you go back to what you wanted to be and do when you were very young and innocent and see how that evolved in your life and whether it still lives within you, even in a transformed state. The inner realm is a place of spirit, so this reply has more to do with magic, with your deep inner feelings, your dreams, primal aspirations and visions than with direct material manifestation. Seek to understand why you desire what you want and feel it deeply and in doing so draw it closer to you.

Questions that involve health and healing find favor in examining the roots and source of any malady. Not in the sense of how you contracted certain germs or viruses, but in the sense of the inner aspects of your soul, your thoughts and the openings in the seals of your magic circle that allowed them into your life. Reinforce your wards on the astral planes, imagine your complete and total health and wellbeing and your power to heal, but also seek out the worries and stresses that pound like demons upon the lines and sigils of protection and see how they first came to you and how they first got their hooks into you, and how, most importantly, you can master them and set them to healing.

This being the place of spirit greatly favors spiritual reflection and magical activity, so examine your path, from your earliest memories unto the present and see the future thereby, for history does repeat itself as the Earth spins around the Sun, the Sun around the Galaxy and we around upon the Earth. We just need to repeat ours'elves better, on a higher level of manifestation for this is how we learn, by repetition, improvement and, in time, innovation. Don't abandon the past, make it better by doing it better this time.

THE MAGIC MIRROR OF REFLECTION

If the Short Bone lands in the inner realm of the Magic Mirror of Reflection, one is called to examine ones'elf, one's early life in particular, and one's evolution as a spiritual and magical being. How did you come to be who you are today? How did you come by the beliefs that you currently hold? How did your spiritual viewpoint and evolution come about? What people or events did you experience and encounter that have shaped your life? In these reflections, you will find a light shining upon the path into the future.

If you posed a question regarding love, romance, relationship, friendship, marriage or partnership, this fall of the Short Bone suggests that you consider your relationships carefully. Be honest about yours'elf and about the effect you have on others, but also the effect these relationships have on you. Is this person "good company"? Do they inspire you toward the good? Do they lead you on or tempt you down the wrong path? Are they a guilty pleasure? If you are truly considering your spiritual evolution, is this the right relationship for you or are you just recycling bad habits?

When your question involves business, finances, job success, career advancement or other monetary concerns, this position for the Short Bone points you toward the past, especially your past, your motivations concerning money and the earliest impressions you have about yours'elf and your ability to succeed and make money in the world. Examine these memories closely. Being the inner realm, this is not so much about material fulfillment but what success means to you as a spiritual being. Success can sometimes lead people astray. If you were wealthy, would you truly do good with it, or would you waste it and yours'elf pursuing idle pleasures? Or cling to it desperately? How do you harmonize material success and spiritual development? Knowing this is the key to the future for you.

If you wanted to know about health and healing, the influence of this fall of the Short Bone promotes healing through truth and honesty. Be true to yours'elf. Be true to others and all things will move toward healing. Additionally, if you are genuinely and realistically clear about who you are as a spirit and your current level of development, then the truth about others will be obvious to you as well, and while you will surely wish to promote their wellbeing and to empower their quest for realization, you will not be able to be deceived no matter how bright their aura appears to be on the surface or how beautiful their material form.

Finally, this is the place of clarity and truth, thus if you are asking about your magical path and spiritual evolution, you need only ask the spirits. The Shining Ones will send you a sign soon to guide you upon your next turn upon the way. The way to Faerie is sometimes straight, sometimes narrow, sometimes anfractuous and sinuous like a snake that is giving birth to its own tail. There are many crossroads, but if you keep Elfin in your heart, it doesn't matter which one you take in the short run for in the long run you will end up at home with us in the radiant light of Elfin and the only difference in this path or that is the time it will take you to get there. Be honest with yours'elf and the swiftest path will be revealed to you.

THE SACK OF GIVING

When the Short Bone is found in the inner circle of the Sack of Giving, one is called to give generously of ones'elf, of one's energy, one's time and attention. This is a good time to make offerings to the spirit world but not in terms of material goods, not incense, per se, or fruit or other material objects, but of the time and energy one is spending upon one's magic and one's connection to spirit. Meditation is certainly recommended here, but also drumming, chanting and doing one's magic are highly favored.

If you presented an inquiry about love, romance, relationship, marriage, friendship or your social life and activity, this fall of the Short Bone indicates spending time in relationship to the spirits and to the astral forms and light bodies of those whom you wish to influence. If you wish to affect someone, then astral or imaginal travel, to visit them. Day Dream about your relationship and imagine it going well or in the direction your wish it to go. Don't, however, violate their magical circle, which is to say don't fantasize about doing things with them that they are not ready or willing to do. Shift the energy slowly, a step at a time and then things will move in the direction you desire. And give gifts and blessings of magic to them on the imaginal planes. Be expansive and generous. Remember, this more about them than you.

When your question involves business, money, work or career, this placement of the Short Bone denotes a time when making bargains with the spirits, especially the spirits and demi-gods that rule business and financial dealings, is very beneficial. Give to the spirits of prosperity and in doing so increase your wellbeing on the material plane through magic on the spirit planes. Everything is connected. Make prosperity powder and spread it around, blow it upon the wind, place it where you wish prosperity to come. Do magic; take action.

Questions regarding health and healing will find that giving to the spirits of healing is helpful. But more than that, do healing on the astral planes of being. This is where the true disorder and disease is originating in this case and by putting a lot of healing energy there, you will be curing the ailment at its source. Having done that, the body will respond favorably and health and healing will return.

It should be clear that giving to the spirit realms is what

this position of the Short Bone is about. Do you wish to advance in the realms of magic, to become a better person/spirit, to become more potent and powerful as a magic wielder, to progress spiritually, to become ever more enlightened? Simply continue to put the energy out there. If you are reading this, you have already obtained an advanced level of development. Now you just have to continue on, doing what you do, but ever striving to do it better.

THE PHILTRE OF TRUE LOVE

With the fall of the Short Bone in the inner region of the Philtre of True Love, you find that the love you have always sought comes to you. However, this may not necessarily be a manifestation in the material world. Being the inner realm, this may very well be a sense of being loved, or a sense of finally accepting and loving ones'elf. It could manifest as a connection between one's spirit and the Divine Magic. One finally understands in a very deep and personal way that one is truly special as an individual but that all others are unique in their own way as well and all are beloved of the Divine.

If you offered a question relative to love, romance, relationship, friendship, marriage and your social life, this position of the Short Bone is both harmonious and beneficial for relationships and connections to others, especially for relationships that you have inwardly hungered for and sought most of your life. This is the fulfillment of a dream, in a sense, but its manifestation is in terms of inner understanding more than anything. At last, you see the truth, the way, and in doing so the means by which you may obtain all that you desire in terms of relationship in this and other worlds and dimensions.

When your inquiry centered on business, financial concerns, job or career development, then this placement of the Short Bone gives you an edge in terms of making positive connections to others relative to money and business, but it also highlights business relationships that are long standing or which have some connection to your youth. Thus, it favors those who went to school together, or who share some outside interest. Use this connection to make your business relationship stronger and more secure.

As to questions that have to do with health or healing, this placement of the Short Bone emphasizes the healing power of old friends, long term connections, including and perhaps particularly spirits that one was involved with in one's younger days. You may have given up the religion of your upbringing, but it is possible that the chief spirit/god of that religion may still aid you in your healing work. We are not talking about the doctrines, or beliefs or dogmas of the religion but the spirit it is centered upon. Remember, the way people often portray a particular spirit as a god-form is most often based upon their own prejudices and preconceptions and frequently has little to do with the actual spirit or even the teachings and heart of that religion. But go deeper. Go to the very source of your earliest memories.

If you had a question about your spiritual life and magical path and evolution upon the planes of spirit, this fall of the Short Bone brings you in closer contact with the spirit world in a more intimate way. This is to say that you should be able to increasingly experience ecstasy and ecstatic revelation through this contact. The obligations of ritual and ceremony give way to the absolute joy of connection. You don't perform your spiritual practices because you think you have to do so, but because you love doing so. Let your magic and your path be easy and filled with delight. Do it because it calls you to it and because it awakens your imagination and allows your spirit to soar.

THE PHIAL OF EVERLASTING YOUTH

When the Short Bone appears in the inner realm of the Phial of Everlasting Youth, one begins to get a sense of the immortality of one's soulful spirit, one's connection to the Shining Ones (whose bodies of light are more resilient and enduring than our material bodies) and to the Universe and its evolution as a whole. Our bodies are not eternal as a form but the energy that composes them goes on forever. Our minds and feelings shift near constantly, but our consciousness endures even when we sleep, which is to say also when our bodies give up their integral structure. We are eternal spirits. Does this answer the question you posed to the oracle?

If you presented a question about love, romance, relationship, marriage, friendship and your social life, this fall of the Short Bone denotes the rejuvenating energy of love and friendship, its power to make life better and to set things going in the right direction. Be friends with everyone that will be friendly to you as best you may. That is the response of this placement. Make friends. That is a great and powerful magic and while it is true that some people will not accept your friendship, that some people are incapable of friendship, act as a true friend as best you are able and good things will come from this.

If you had an inquiry about business or money concerns, about job situations or career success this position for the Short Bone indicates that prosperity comes from keeping abreast of what is new in your field, always updating yours'elf and your information and evolving your abilities by ever striving to do what you do a little better each time. This will increase your knowledge, your skills and your ability to succeed in the world. But remember, this is the inner realms of spirit and the greatest knowledge you will gain will be through revelation and insight. Hone your business instincts

283

and intuition. Learn to draw money to you. Attract prosperity through right thinking.

When you had a question relative to health and healing, this landing for the Short Bone brings healing into your life through your youthful spirit and your connection to the Shining Ones. Draw down the eternally youthful energy of Elfin and let it fill your body and project it toward the bodies of those you are endeavoring to help heal. This will be good for them and you and produce positive benefits for the world as well.

And if you had a query about your magical path and spiritual life, this response of the oracle denotes a flow of vital energy into your life. The Force is with you, although being elfae it is more like the magic and the wonder are with you. We are enchanters, we don't force things, we allow them to flow creating channels of healing and fulfillment through which they may progress toward a better future for all. Sparkle, beloved kindred. Shine your elfae light unto the world. You are an eternal being temporarily passing through a transitory body.

The Outer Circle:
The Elf Horn of Calling

When the Short Bone goes beyond the circle of the oracle, it means that you have strayed from the path and need to take a moment to reorient yours'elf and reconnect with your quest. Most likely, the world has simply become too much for you and has overwhelmed you. That can happen sometimes. Hang on, hang tight and keep the light of Elfin in your heart and mind and you will find your way back again and those who have been obstructing your life in the background, those sneaky hidden forces seeking to undermine your efforts, will go away and good riddance.

If instead, the Short Bone landed within the Outer Circle, then please read the corresponding treasure below:

THE ORB OF HEALING

If the Short Bone comes up in the outer dimension of the Orb of Healing, there is a bit of personal healing coming your way, an easing of the path, and a renewal of energy with a rush of memories from your past reminding you of who you are, who you are meant to be and the true direction you are going. Have you forgotten yours'elf? Have you lost yours'elf in the world? Given up your dreams and visions? Stopped believing in yours'elf and the possibility that everything will eventually work out for the best? Have you become jaded and cynical? Start afresh. Now is the time.

When you had a question about love, romance, relationship, marriage or friendship and you draw this response, it indicates that relationships will heal if you actively seek to heal them. In fact, activity is called for here. Contact your old friends. Go out with those with whom you are currently involved. Do things together. Create memories and this will bring wonderful magic into your life and blessings in your future.

If you had an inquiry that focused upon business, financial concerns, job or career success and development, this position of the Short Bone is very favorable for an upswing in the financial cycle. This won't last, of course, the tide will go out again, so take advantage of this opportunity while you have the chance to do so. This is especially true for any business that is personal in nature, which is to say business that isn't just about making money but which also fulfills your dreams for making money and your creative spirit. Put energy toward doing what you truly wish to do as a life artist.

You have a chance here, take it.

If your question was directly about health and healing, you are blest with this response. This is especially true for personal healing and for increasing your powers and skills as a healer. But as the old admonition says: Healer, heal thys'elf, and from that healing energy will radiate from you that will spread into the world to help others to heal.

And if you were inquiring about your magical path and spiritual development, this position of the Short Bone is great for working on yours'elf, on increasing your powers in a positive way and particularly doing what you can to make your life and environment better for you and all who are connected to you. Make progress. The way is opening for you and you can advance at a quicker speed than the day to day acts of ritual and perseverance that are usually required. Step up to the next level and then take time to settle into the new situation. You will certainly need to go back to the day-to-day enactment of the way, but none-the-less, you will be a more powerful magic wielder than you were previously.

THE WAND OF WISHING

If the Short Bone lands in the outer circle of the Wand of Wishing, there is powerful energy for the fulfillment of your long-time dreams by doing your magic now. Cast spells. Chant your incantations. Weave your enchantments. Use your sorcery to look into the past that is the source of the present but know that your wishes are in motion and are coming true. Wish again for the future but mostly use what you have received well, investing its energy into things that will blossom again later on. In other words, enjoy the fruit of your magic but don't forget to plant the seeds for lifetimes that are to come.

If your inquiry was about love, romance, relationship,

marriage, friendship or your social life, this position of the Short Bone speaks favorably of obtaining your desires concerning relationship. But be clear about what you truly wish, what will genuinely fulfill you as an individual. Not merely who you wish to be involved with but what that relationship will be like. Sometimes, we fantasize about those who could never bring our true desires into realization. We have merely projected our fantasies upon them without contemplating their true natures. Think about what it is you wish in relationship and find someone who can satisfy those needs. Don't compromise your vision just to be with a particular person. This will just wind up making you miserable.

If you were asking about business, finances, job success or the future for your career, the Short Bone brings success if you really have your whole heart and soul into what you wish and desire. Are you involved in what you are doing for money? By that we mean, are you invested in it within yours'elf? Is your heart into it? This position rewards those things that we truly desire in a feeling way. Thus, again, we ask, is your heart really into it?

When your query has to do with health and healing, this placement for the Short Bone brings healing and health if you are happy with your life. Health here is a result of happiness and satisfaction. If you are not pleased with what you are doing, this will adversely affect your health and thus your healing ability. Find what enthuses you and take time to discover what truly brings you joy. This is the way to better health.

And if you were wondering about your spiritual life and magical path and evolution upon the path, this fall of the Short Bone is great for doing magic, now, about everything and fulfilling yours'elf as a person. It is not wrong to want things for yours'elf. But you do need to attain what you desire without harming others. And it helps greatly if all that you achieve also enables others to advance as well, then your success becomes their success and nearly everyone seeks to further you, for by doing so they are helping their own s'elves. A certain amount of ego strength is a good thing.

THE COIN OF THE REALM

If the Short Bone lands in the outer dimension of the Coin of the Realm, you shall be blest with material benefits coming into your life most likely from things or magic you have done in the past. It may come from your family or friends but it is not due to them but to your own actions/magic and karma that has brought you luck and a period of success and prosperity. Take a moment to enjoy it. You clearly have done something right.

If you were asking about love, romance, relationship, friendship, marriage or your social life and you get this response then it is most likely that the prosperity magic that is in motion in your life will come through relationship. If you share the wealth, so to speak, it will help secure your friendships, for people will know that your prosperity is theirs as well and they will seek your success in all that they do.

When you have asked a question that involves business, monetary concerns, job success or progress in your career, this fall of the Short Bone is a blessing for financial dealings of all sorts. Now is the time to invest, ask for a raise, change jobs or shift your career. The energy is positive for material blessings descending into your life, perhaps arising in your life from the pool of magic and wishes you have already made and the actions you have already taken. No cycle lasts forever, so make the most of it while it does.

If you posed an inquiry that had to do with health and healing, this response clearly favors you investing in your health, your diet and everything that will promote healing in your life. Those things you need to make a better life will be coming to you. Start today and begin to create the changes that will improve your life and your health as well as make you a more healing individual and personality. The result of this will be greater benefits yet and you will find that magic is swirling around you.

And if it so happens that you had a query about your magical path and spiritual development, this reply of the oracle brings you what you need to further your magic and your path. Do you need money to go to a gathering? To take a course in magic? To learn Qigong, Reiki or some other spiritual healing modality? To get those books that you think will help enlighten you and from which you can learn greater magic still? The money should be coming to you. And if the magic doesn't come in the form of money it may just appear in some other fashion, such as someone giving you the book you want. The point is the way is opening and you may advance as you will.

THE FEATHER OF TRUTH TELLING

With the Short Bone falling into the outer reaches of the Feather of Truth Telling, one is called to speak the truth, particularly about ones'elf and one's life and one's upbringing and one's personal history. It is time for a bit of revelation and it is likely that if you do this truly and sincerely others will reveal thems'elves as well. If they don't do so directly they will surely do so by their reactions to your revelations. Study them carefully but silently and subtly so they do not even notice that you are noticing.

When you asked a question about love, romance, relationship, marriage, friendship or partnership of any kind, this reply from the oracle denotes that the truth is going to

289

come out, whatever it is. However, the depth of this truth depends upon your own ability to be truthful with yours'elf but also with others. Are you being honest about your feelings? Are you looking at others honestly? Don't lie to yours'elf and you will know when others are being truthful. This is to say, the answer you seek will soon be revealed. Just, be open to whatever it is. The truth is out there.

If you were making an inquiry about business, finances, job or career success and development, this fall of the Short Bone gives you the opportunity to use the truth to your advantage. However, you should ask yours'elf, are you honest in your business dealings? Have you always been honest? Know that the truth is coming out and the past will emerge in some form or other, either as a revelation or as the movement of karma. Still, this is not necessarily bad for you, you can take this opportunity to set yours'elf on a true course toward real success based upon the integrity of your being.

When you had a question about health or healing and the Short Bone lands here, one needs to look at one's life, one's health throughout one's life, and one's diet, exercise regimen and other factors that affect one's health throughout one's life. Health is accumulative. We must be honest with ours'elves about our health habits, and be clear about the habits of those whom we are trying to help heal, and establish rituals of healing that will set us toward longevity and toward increasing our health and our energy. That is the answer to your question. Do what is healing for yours'elf and others and keep doing it.

Regarding questions about your magical and spiritual life and path, this placement of the Short Bone brings you luck if you are realistic and honest to yours'elf about your magic and your powers and your personal history. It is also very important that you give credit where credit is due. If you act like you are totally s'elf created and don't honor those who have helped you and inspired you on the way, you are not only cheating them but depriving yours'elf of the power of your own lineage. Honor those who have enlightened and empowered your magic and your path, and greater truths will be revealed to you.

THE MAGIC MIRROR OF REFLECTION

When the Short Bone lands in the outer dimension of the Magic Mirror of Reflection, one is called to examine one's past in this life, especially the first twenty-nine years of one's life, for those years recapitulate in an encapsulated form all of one's previous incarnations in a humanoid body. Most pre-humanoid and very early humanoid forms were experienced in the womb. What were you like as a child? What were your interests? What did you experience? What scars do you bear from that period? All of these will tell you much about yours'elf and your development both as a spirit and a soulful being, but also in this outer realm it will tell you about the development of you as an individual spirit and your material life and thus the challenges you have faced through the ages.

If you had an inquiry that involved love, romance, marriage, relationship, friendship or your social prospects, this fall of the Short Bone calls you to contemplate, quite honestly, your earliest life and the relationships you had then, which have formulated the way you interact in relationships now. Also, examine the early lives of those you are interested in or involved with in order to understand their own approach to relationship. Know also, however, that the sharing of personal history is surely the abridged and usually the officially approved version. Use your intuition to look deeper and find true understanding.

When you present a question about business, finances or job success or progress in your career to the oracle, this placement of the Short Bone suggests that you look to your own work habits and skills that you developed in your early life, and thus to previous lifetimes and see what you can do to enhance and improve them. Remember that one's failings and weaknesses can also sometimes be turned to one's advantage and certainly they can be overcome with effort. Further, consider your earliest experience in the material world. What were your parents' attitude about money? Were you rich or poor in your early life? And how did that affect the way you view money, success and its acquisition today.

If you had a question that had to do with health and healing, think back about your early life and your health. Were you strong? You can be so again. Were you sickly all the time? How did that affect your view of your ability to heal and to help others heal? Remember the shaman is sometimes called the 'wounded healer'. Often the shaman is the one who experienced some terrible disease, accident or other challenge to their health and overcame it. Not only that, the animal or being (virus) that attacked you, so to speak, may now be the spirit you can summon as an ally. After all, you mastered it; you are its master. What does your early life tell you about your ability to heal? That should tell you something of significance.

And if you are asking about your spiritual path and magical life, this position of the Small Bone denotes that you have been on the path a long time, both in this life and in previous lives, as evidenced by your early life. It may not have been entirely conscious but if you will look back you will see the signs that helped guide you and which even now may reveal to you the information that you seek. The path is contained in the beginning, like a seed, and all that comes after is hidden within.

THE SACK OF GIVING

When the Short Bone lands in the outer circle of the Sack of Giving, one is called to give generously, particularly to give gifts that are personally meaningful to the individuals one is giving them to but also meaningful to yours'elf as the one who is offering the gifts. This energy is made more powerful if the items have been with you for a while, absorbing your energy and thus passing your magic out into the world through gifting. This generosity will return to you manifold and will be increased in their return. So be as generous as you can, but most of all give something useful that also touches the heart and the soul of the other.

If you presented a question about love, romance, relationship, marriage or friendship to this oracle, this response indicates that giving tokens of appreciation will go a long way to easing the way in relationship. But remember, this is only part of the story. If you are giving in order to get, then the other will subconsciously, if not consciously, know that this is the case and be reserved and suspicious, even if they accept the gift. Give out of affection. Give because you really feel something for the individual and then all will move in the direction you desire. If they give you something in return, that is a good sign, if not, be patient, the magic will return to you in one form or another.

If you had an inquiry regarding business, finances, or your job advancement and career success, this is surely a good sign, although it does indicate that one needs to bring the personal touch into one's business life. Also, while giving is surely good with this position, it doesn't have to be in terms of out and out gifts, rather good deals are much appreciated. Don't just think of your own profit, give those you are involved with in business the best deal you can. And if this month and its bills requires a little more from you than usual, just think of it as a loan given to the Universe. It will pay you back with interest in time.

Give of yours'elf, if you have asked about healing energy. Give gifts that will make people feel better, become enlivened and have their spirit rejoice, but most of all give of yours'elf, your healing energy, your vibration, your enthusiasm and anything that you can think of that has helped you heal in the past that may help yours'elf or others to heal now. Do you have a lucky healing object? Share its energy with others and let the healing spread into the world.

And when your question involved your spiritual path and the development of your magic, which for elves often means the evolution of our powers of enchantment that flow from our personality, this placement of the Short Bone is highly favorable for sharing. Do magic to help others, to make the world a better place, to increase what is good in the world, to enable others to have more prosperous and abundant lives, but most of all do magic with others. Find others that excite and elicit your enchanting energy and go forth and enchant together. You will find that two or more elfae enchanting together are far more powerful than one alone.

THE PHILTRE OF TRUE LOVE

With the descent of the Short Bone into the outer demesne of the Philtre of True Love, one becomes aware of the fact that those that have always been meant for one as an individual soulful spirit begin appearing in one's life more frequently and more profoundly. This may indicate the appearance of true love, of one's soul mate, star mate and the entry into your life of those who prove to be your true best friends forever or, surely, for years to come. There is a purpose behind these encounters. There is fate and destiny at work, but this manifestation is also very much a fulfillment of inner needs and desires and is not simply about the spiritual realms but of real material satisfaction as well. More than likely, when this one or ones arrive you will feel like you always knew they were coming.

When the question you asked involved love, romance, relationship, marriage, partnership or friendship, this reply indicates that the relationships you have or desire will flourish, if these relationships align with your true inner needs and the magic you did as a child or young person when you first reached out toward the moon and stars hungering for connection, friendship and love. Otherwise, if they are not right for you they will fade away to make room for those who are truly intended for you and with whom you can create wondrous things, not the least of which are delightful memories of your time together.

If you had an inquiry about business, finances or job and career success and advancement, this position of the Short Bone is not strong for these issues, however, it does tend to attract to you those who may have a long-term influence upon your life and your career by giving you help, information that is useful or just setting an example of what may be done to succeed. It is good for making lasting connections and friendships, or alternately meeting someone that you will become personally involved with through work. It is very favorable for work related romance.

As to questions that are focused on health and healing, this is a favorable response in as much as meeting those that are meant for you and who bring meaning and purpose into your life, is a healing event in and of itself, but otherwise this position is not directly about healing unless you are a practicing healer and do regular healings. Then, it is quite possible that you will encounter someone who helps you up your game or will become a partner in your healing work.

And if you presented a question to the oracle about your spiritual and magical life and evolution, this position is all about the entry into your life of those who will be meaningful for you in the present and will most likely have an effect upon you for lifetimes to come. It is more than probable that you have worked together before and will do so again. There is surely a long-term bond here whose meaning can be found in the stars.

THE PHIAL OF EVERLASTING YOUTH

If the Short Bone falls in the outer dimension of the Phial of Everlasting Youth, one is filled with energy, with youthful vigor and determination and with a sense that there is within ones'elf something that is truly immortal. One realizes that the energy that composes one's being can neither be created nor destroyed, it can only transform and that while one's body is a wonderful vehicle for manifestation, and best when well maintained, one is not one's body but the spirit that inhabits that body and that spirit, here in the outer world, is being uplifted by the body with a sense of aliveness.

When you have made an inquiry about love, romance, relationship, friendship, partnership, marriage or your social life and you get the Short Bone here, your personal life quest comes to the fore. The reason you are here becomes evident in those that you are currently involved with or who now come into your life. Synchronistic, coincidental or accidental meetings and encounters are likely. These highlight the fact that you have a mission to fulfill. The Shining Ones are sending you a messenger, or perhaps an assistant, a fellow traveler, or someone who can guide you on the way. If you understand this, you will know what the answer to your question is. Relationships have meaning and purpose.

If you had a question that involved business, finances, or job or career success, this placement of the Short Bone gives you a fresh start, an opportunity to begin again or to start a new project or business venture. However, be wise. Remember, the energy behind this is youthful magic. It is potent but not necessarily experienced. Seek wise counsel before you leap into anything and, alas, due to the influence of this energy, the tendency to be rash and to jump before looking is, unfortunately, all too likely. Still, if you hesitate for too long, you may miss out.

Questions about health and healing are highly benefited by this youthful and thus healing power. You have the energy, now you just need to use it as wisely as you can. Spread the healing energy as far as is possible, as often as you are able and make the most of the time. Because of the influence of this placement, you should be able to do quite a bit of healing work for a long time. And instead of feeling drained after doing a healing, you should feel revitalized again very quickly. It is true that at some point you may just crash for a while, but upon awaking you will be back at it again and raring to go.

Inquiries that have to do with one's spiritual life and magical path will find that the time has come when one can make progress in one's spiritual development and evolution by acting in and through the world. Do your rituals, your magic, your ceremonies with enthusiasm. Suspend your doubt, have the faith of a child and let your magic flow into the world. You are shaping your life in all that you do and affecting the lives of others by doing so, as well. This is a good thing. If there is some magical object or tool that you have long thought about making or acquiring, this is certainly the time.

About the Authors

The Silver Elves, Zardoa and Silver Flame, are a family of elves who have been living and sharing the Elven Way since 1975. They are the authors of 45 books on magic and enchantment, including:

The Book of Elven Runes: A Passage Into Faerie;

The Magical Elven Love Letters, volume 1, 2, and 3;

An Elfin Book of Spirits: Evoking the Beneficent Powers of Faerie;

Caressed by an Elfin Breeze: The Poems of Zardoa Silverstar;

Eldafaryn: True Tales of Magic from the Lives of the Silver Elves;

Arvyndase (Silverspeech): A Short Course in the Magical Language of the Silver Elves;

The Elven Book of Dreams: A Magical Oracle of Faerie;

The Book of Elven Magick: The Philosophy and Enchantments of the Seelie Elves, Volume 1 & 2;

What An Elf Would Do: A Magical Guide to the Manners and Etiquette of the Faerie Folk;

The Elven Tree of Life Eternal: A Magical Quest for One's True S'Elf;

Magic Talks: On Being a Correspondence Between the Silver Elves and the Elf Queen's Daughters;

Sorcerers' Dialogues: A Further Correspondence Between the Silver Elves and the Founders of the Elf Queen's Daughters;

Discourses on High Sorcery: More Correspondence Between the Silver Elves and the Founders of the Elf Queen's Daughters;

Ruminations on Necromancy: Continuing Correspondence Between the Silver Elves and the Founders of the Elf Queen's Daughter;

The Elven Way: The Magical Path of the Shining Ones;

The Book of Elf Names: 5,600 Elven Names to Use for Magic, Game Playing, Inspiration, Naming One's Self and One's Child, and as Words in the Elven Language of the Silver Elves;

Elven Silver: The Irreverent Faery Tales of Zardoa Silverstar;

An Elven Book of Rhymes: Book Two of the Magical Poems of Zardoa Silverstar;

The Voice of Faerie: Making Any Tarot Deck Into an Elven Oracle;

Liber Aelph: Words of Guidance from the Silver Elves to our Magical Children;

The Shining Ones: The Elfin Spirits That Guide You According to Your Birth Date and the Evolutionary Lessons They Offer;

Living the Personal Myth: Making the Magic of Faerie Real in One's Own Personal Life;

Elf Magic Mail, The Original Letters of the Elf Queen's Daughters with Commentary by the Silver Elves, Book 1 and 2;

The Elves of Lyndarys: A Magical Tale of Modern Faerie Folk;

The Elf Folk's Book of Cookery: Recipes For a Delighted Tongue, a Healthy Body and a Magical Life;

Faerie Unfolding: The Cosmic Expression of the Divine Magic;

The Elements of Elven Magic: A New View of Calling the Elementals Based Upon the Periodic Table of Elements and

The Keys to Elfin Enchantment: Mastery of the Faerie Light Through the Portals of Manifestation.

Elf Quotes: A Collection of Over 1000 Ancient Elven Sayings and Wise Elfin Koans by The Silver Elves About Magic and The Elven Way;

The United States of Elfin Imagining A More Elven Style of Government;

Elven Geomancy: An Ancient Oracle of the Elfin Peoples for Divination and Spell Casting;

Creating Miracles In the Modern World: The Way Of the Elfin Thaumaturge;

The Magical Realms of Elfin: Answers to Questions About Being an Elf and Following the Elven Path;

Elven Psychology: Understanding the Elfin Psyche and the Evolutionary and Esoteric Purpose of Mental Disorders;

The Elves Say: A Collection of Over 1000 Ancient Elven Sayings and Wise Elfin Koans by The Silver Elves About Magic and The Elven Way, Volume 2; and

The Complete Dictionary of Arvyndase: The Elven Language of The Silver Elves.

The Silver Elves have had various articles published in *Circle Network News Magazine* and have given out over 6,000 elven names to interested individuals in the Arvyndase language, with each elf name having a unique meaning specifically for that person. They are also mentioned numerous times in *Not In Kansas Anymore* by Christine Wicker (Harper San Francisco, 2005), and *A Field Guide to Otherkin* by Lupa (Megalithica Books, 2007)), and are discussed in Nikolay Lyapanenko's book *The Elves From Ancient Times To Our Days: The Magical Heritage of "Starry People" and their Continuation Into the Modern World* (2017) that gives a detailed account of their involvement in the Elven Movement since 1975. An interview with the Silver Elves is also included in Emily Carding's recent book *Faery Craft Craft* (Llewellyn Publications, 2012*)*.

The Silver Elves understand the world as a magical or miraculous phenomena, and that all beings, by pursuing their own true path, will become whomever they truly desire to be. You are welcome to visit their website at http://silverelves@live.com and to join them on Facebook with names "Michael J. Love (Zardoa of The SilverElves)" and "Martha Char Love (SilverFlame of The SilverElves)."

You are invited to join their Elven and Otherkin groups on Facebook including:

The Magical Books of the Silver Elves where there are discussions about The Silver Elves books as well as about Elven and Otherkin philosophy and lifestyle.

Elf Witches of the Mystic Moon

Elven Life and Magic

Elvish Magical Chat

The Faerie Circle

The Elven Way and Friends

United Otherkin Alliance where faeries, dragons, kitsune, gnomes, hobbits, merkin, pixies, brownies, nymphs, driads, niaids, valkyrie, vampires, devas, and all manner of Faerie Folk gather!

Also you may enjoy reading The Silver Elves blog sites with over 40 articles posted: 1). *The Silver Elves Blog on Magic and Enchantment and The Elven* Way at https://silverelves.wordpress.com; and 2). *The Silver Elves* on the philosophy, magic and lifestyle of being elven at https://thesilverelves.blogspot.com.

Printed in Great Britain
by Amazon

80258041R00173